The Miracle of Forgiveness

SPENCER W. KIMBALL

BOOKCRAFT INC.
SALT LAKE CITY, UTAH
1969

LITHOGRAPHED IN U.S.A. BY
PUBLISHERS PRESS
SALT LAKE CITY, UTAH

To Camilla

Contents

Preface

And God wrought special miracles . . . (Acts 19:11.)

Our Lord, Jesus Christ, is that God of miracles. On one occasion, he said to the Jewish believers: "And ye shall know the truth, and the truth shall make you free." (John 8:32.)

Can any miracle compare with that one which is provided by Jesus? ". . . to loose the bands of wickedness, to undo the heavy burdens, and to let the oppressed go free . . ." (Isa. 58:6.) He healed the sick, cast out devils, calmed the storm and even raised the dead. But can any miracle be equal to that one which frees men from the fetters of ignorance, superstition, and transgression? The Prophet Joseph Smith said: "It is better to save a man than raise one from the dead."

Paul said: "O death, where is thy sting? O grave, where is thy victory? The sting of death is sin . . ." (1 Cor. 15:55-56.) And this prompts the statement, "There is no tragedy except in sin."

This book is not presented to entertain, but rather it has the serious purpose of presenting scriptures, experiences and exhortations with the hope that thereby many will be enticed to repent of their sins and indiscretions and set out to purify and perfect their lives.

This design arose from my years of ministry as a stake president and as an apostle, during which time I have had many experiences in dealing with transgressors, especially those involved in sexual sins, both inside and outside of marriage. The scriptures being the firm basis of law and happiness, I have constantly felt the need of a selection of them which I could recommend to the offenders. My jottings of references grew into a collection from which this book has evolved.

Because men and women are human and normally carnally minded, and because to do evil is usually easier than to do right, and because "all have sinned and come short of the glory of God," perhaps I have quoted far more scriptures on this subject of sexual sin than on any other.

To cure spiritual diseases which throttle us and plague our lives, the Lord has given us a sure cure—repentance.

I had made up my mind that I would never write a book and was even more determined when I read Job's warning: "Oh . . . that mine adversary had written a book." (Job 31:35.) Three main reasons changed my mind.

First, the need. When I come in contact almost daily with broken homes, delinquent children, corrupt governments, and apostate groups, and realize that all these problems are the result of sin, I want to shout with Alma: "O . . . that I might go forth . . . with a voice to shake the earth, and cry repentance unto every people." (Al. 29:1.)

Hence this book indicates the seriousness of breaking God's commandments; shows that sin can bring only sorrow, remorse, disappointment, and anguish; and warns that the small indiscretions evolve into larger ones and finally into major transgressions which bring heavy penalties. Because of the prevalence and gravity of sexual and other major sins, these receive particular emphasis. Warning signals and guidelines are given to reduce the danger of one's being blindly enticed into forbidden paths.

Having come to recognize their deep sin, many have tended to surrender hope, not having a clear knowledge of the scriptures and of the redeeming power of Christ.

Second, then, I write to make the joyous affirmation that man can be literally transformed by his own repentance and by God's gift of forgiveness which follows for all except unpardonable sins. It is far better not to have committed the sin; the way of the transgressor is hard; but recovery is possible.

Third, those of us whom the Lord has called to leadership have an inescapable responsibility, like that of Jacob and Joseph, to

. . . . [take] upon us the responsibility, answering the sins of the people upon our own heads if we did not teach them the word of God with all diligence; wherefore, by laboring with our might their blood might not come upon our garments. . . . (Jac. 1:19.)

Isaiah warns: "Cry aloud, spare not, lift up thy voice like a trumpet, and shew my people their transgression, and the house of Jacob their sins." (Isa. 58:1.) Ezekiel sounds the warning to leaders: " . . . Should not the shepherds feed the flocks?" (Ezek. 34:2.) And then: ". . . If [the watchman] blow the trumpet, and warn the people . . . whosoever . . . taketh not warning . . . his blood shall be upon his own head." (Ezek. 33:3-4.)

The trumpet is to sound " . . . nothing but repentance unto this generation." (D&C 6:9.) Thus the message is to all the world, not only to members of the true Church of Jesus Christ of Latter-day Saints.

These reasons, and the predominance given to the subject in the appeals of every prophet and spiritual leader from Adam onwards, seem to me to justify a book dealing exclusively with sin, repentance and forgiveness. This is so despite the fact that many Church writers have included the subject as part of a more comprehensive work.

In writing this book, I make no claim to originality or to literary genius. There may be nothing new or arresting here. On the other hand, I have deliberately repeated some scriptures to support varying facets of the subject or to insure a proper emphasis in the hope that those frustrated and in sin may wash "their robes in the blood of the Lamb," so that peace may settle down on them as the dews of heaven.

Likewise, in writing about sin and repentance, no intent is implied that either the writer or any of those quoted, except the Lord himself, is without fault. But we would not have much motivation to righteousness if all speakers and writers postponed discussing and warning until they themselves were perfected!

In Jacob's words: " . . . I know that the words of truth are hard against all uncleanness; but the righteous fear them not, for they love the truth and are not shaken." (2 Ne. 9:40.)

Perhaps some of the same feelings come to us all as came to Peter as he approached the end of his life:

> Yea, I think it meet, as long as I am in this tabernacle, to stir you up by putting you in remembrance;
>
> Knowing that shortly I must put off this my tabernacle, even as our Lord Jesus Christ hath shewed me.
>
> Moreover I will endeavour that ye may be able after my decease to have these things always in remembrance. (2 Pet. 1:13-15.)

I accept full responsibility for the contents of this book. Specifically, the Church and its leaders are totally absolved from the responsibility for any error which it may be found to contain.

It is impossible for me or any other mortal to save another's soul, but it is my humble hope that through this book some who are suffering the baleful effects of sin may be helped to find the way from darkness to light, from suffering to peace, from misery to hope, and from spiritual death to eternal life. If to any degree the book achieves this, and helps to confirm others in a life of righteous endeavor, my efforts in its production will have been justified.

Spencer W. Kimball

Chapter One

This Life Is the Time

. . . For all contracts that are not made unto this end have an end when men are dead.

—Doctrine & Covenants 132:7

For behold, this life is the time for men to prepare to meet God . . .

—Alma 34:32

IT IS THE DESTINY OF THE SPIRITS OF MEN TO COME TO this earth and travel a journey of indeterminate length. They travel sometimes dangerously, sometimes safely, sometimes sadly, sometimes happily. Always the road is marked by divine purpose.

The journey leads through infancy with its carefree activities but rapid learning; through childhood with its little disappointments and stubbed toes, its injured feelings, its keen excitements; through youth with its exuberance, its likes and dislikes, its fears and hopes and intensities; through the young married period with its responsibilities, its competitions, its ambitions, its family-rearing, its accumulating; and through older age with its achievements, culminations, goal-reaching, relaxation and retirement.

Throughout the entire journey there is opportunity for learning and growth and development toward the final goal. We see some people who merely travel, having no aim, direction, destination or purpose. Without road maps to guide them, they just travel along the way and in varying degrees pick up such things as will please the eye, tickle the vanities, satisfy hungers, quench thirsts, satisfy passions. And when the end of life draws nigh they have traveled but are little if any closer to their proper destination than when they started. Regrettably, some have totally lost their way.

Life's Divine Purpose

On the other hand, there are some who chart their courses, make wise, right decisions, and in large measure achieve their goals and reach their happy destinations. In doing this they are cooperating with the Creator in his stated purpose of life: "For behold, this is my work and my glory — to bring to pass the immortality and eternal life of man." (Moses 1:39.)

Since immortality and eternal life constitute the sole purpose of life, all other interests and activities are but incidental thereto. And since those objectives are the work and glory of God, they are the proper work of man also and are the major reason for his coming to earth. Of the two elements, the one great blessing — immortality — comes to man without his effort, as a gift from the Almighty. The other — eternal life — is a cooperative program to be developed by the Lord and his offspring on earth. It thus becomes the overall responsibility of man to cooperate fully with the Eternal God in accomplishing this objective. To this end God created man to live in mortality and endowed him with the potential to perpetuate the race, to subdue the earth, to perfect himself and to become as God, omniscient and omnipotent.

Our Father then sent to the earth a line of prophets to keep man in remembrance of his duties and his destiny, to warn him of dangers, and to point the way to his total victory. It appears that the spiritual perceptions of many peoples have been inadequate to a full understanding of God's purposes, and he has accordingly had them taught at lower levels. This is apparently what Alma meant when he said:

> For behold, the Lord doth grant unto all nations, of their own nation and tongue, to teach his word, yea, in wisdom, all that he seeth fit that they should have . . . (Al. 29:8.)

Unfortunately, God's people have too often rejected his way, to their own destruction. But the Lord has never permitted such people to be destroyed, nor permitted them to fail to reach their goal, without having taught them and warned them. For example, of the Jews it is recorded: " . . . and never hath any of them been destroyed save it were foretold them by the prophets of the Lord." (2 Ne. 25:9.)

The scriptures point clearly to the high purpose of man's existence. Abraham and Moses particularly were explicit on this matter, as is revealed by records made available to us through the modern Prophet Joseph Smith. That Prophet, having learned the drama and purpose of it all from the ancient records as well as from heavenly visitations, continued to receive through direct revelation further light and truth respecting man's great potential. Through him God has abundantly confirmed that man is the supreme creation, made in the image and similitude of God and his Son, Jesus Christ; that man is the offspring of God; that for man, and man alone, was the earth created, organized, planted and made ready for human habitation; and that, having within him the seeds of godhood and thus being a god in embryo, man has unlimited potential for progress and attainment.

Significance of Belief in God

This book presupposes a belief in God and in life's high purpose. Without God, repentance would have little meaning, and forgiveness would be both unnecessary and unreal. If there were no God, life would indeed be meaningless; and as with the antediluvians, the Babylonians, the Israelites and numerous other peoples and civilizations, we might find justification in an urge to live only for today, to "eat, drink and be merry," to dissipate, to satisfy every worldly desire. If there were no God there would be no redemption, no resurrection, no eternities to anticipate, and consequently no hope.

But there *is* a God, and he is loving, kind, just and merciful. There *is* a never-ending existence. Man will suffer or enjoy his future according to his life's works in mortality. Consequently, since mortal life is but a speck compared to the infinite duration of eternity, man should take great care that his present insures him joy and development and happiness for his eternal future.

Our Pre-mortal Understanding

In the record of an outstanding vision, Abraham amplified for us the purposes of God in creating the world and placing us upon it.

> Now the Lord had shown unto me, Abraham, the intelligences that were organized before the world was; and among all these there were many of the noble and great ones. (Abraham 3:22.)

In the council in heaven, the Lord clearly outlined the plan and its conditions and benefits. The earth was to be not only a place of residence for man but also a school and a testing-ground, an opportunity for man to prove himself. Agency would be given man so that he could make his own choices.

Life was to be in three segments or estates: pre-mortal, mortal, and immortal. The third stage would incorporate exaltation — eternal life with godhood — for those who would fully magnify their mortal lives. Performance in one estate would vitally affect the succeeding estate or estates. If a person kept his first estate, he would be permitted the second or the mortal life as a further period of trial and experience. If he magnified his second estate, his earth experience, eternal life would await him. To that end men go through the numerous experiences of earth life — "to see if they will do all things whatsoever the Lord their God shall command them." (Abraham 3:25.)

We mortals who now live upon this earth are in our *second estate*. Our very presence here in mortal bodies attests the fact that we "kept" our first estate. Our spirit matter was eternal and co-existent with God, but it was organized into spirit bodies by our Heavenly Father. Our spirit bodies went through a long period of growth and development and training and, having passed the test successfully, were finally admitted to this earth and to mortality.

One definite purpose of our spirits coming to this earth and assuming the mortal state was to obtain a physical body. This body was to be subject to all the weaknesses, temptations, frailties and limitations of mortality, and was to face the challenge to overcome self.

While we lack recollection of our pre-mortal life, before coming to this earth all of us understood definitely the purpose of our being here. We would be expected to gain knowledge, educate ourselves, train ourselves. We were to control our urges and desires, master and control our passions, and overcome our weaknesses, small and large. We were to eliminate sins of omission and of commission, and to follow the laws and commandments given us by our Father. That the effort involved dignifies and ennobles man has been recognized by the world's great thinkers. Dante, for example, put it this way: "Consider your origin; you were not formed to live like brutes, but to follow virtue and knowledge."[1]

We understood also that after a period varying from seconds to decades of mortal life we would die, our bodies would go back to Mother Earth from which they had been created, and our spirits would go to the spirit world, where we would further train for our eternal destiny. After a period, there would be a resurrection or a reunion of the body and the spirit, which would render us immortal and make possible our further climb toward perfection and godhood. This resurrection has been made available to us through

---

[1]Dante, *Divine Comedy*.

the sacrifice of the Lord Jesus Christ, the Creator of this earth, who performed this incomparable service for us — a miracle we could not perform for ourselves. Thus the way was opened for our immortality and — if we prove worthy — eventual exaltation in God's kingdom.

The Gospel Our Map

To pinpoint a destination not previously visited we usually consult a map. As a second great boon to us the Lord Jesus Christ, our Redeemer and Savior, has given us our map — a code of laws and commandments whereby we might attain perfection and, eventually, godhood. This set of laws and ordinances is known as the gospel of Jesus Christ, and it is the *only* plan which will exalt mankind. The Church of Jesus Christ of Latter-day Saints is the sole repository of this priceless program in its fulness, which is made available to those who accept it.

In order to reach the goal of eternal life and exaltation and godhood, one must be initiated into the kingdom by baptism, properly performed; one must receive the Holy Ghost by the laying on of authoritative hands; a man must be ordained to the priesthood by authorized priesthood holders; one must be endowed and sealed in the house of God by the prophet who holds the keys or by one of those to whom the keys have been delegated; and one must live a life of righteousness, cleanliness, purity and service. None can enter into eternal life other than by the correct door — Jesus Christ and his commandments.

Jesus made this very clear in these words:

> Verily, verily, I say unto you, He that entereth not by the door into the sheepfold, but climbeth up some other way, the same is a thief and a robber. (John 10:1.)

> I am the door: by me if any man enter in, he shall be saved, and shall go in and out, and find pasture. (John 10:9.)

And Jacob, the prophet theologian, warned:

> O then, my beloved brethren, come unto the Lord, the Holy One. Remember that his paths are righteous. Behold, the way

for man is narrow, but it lieth in a straight course before him, and the keeper of the gate is the Holy One of Israel; and he employeth no servant there; and there is none other way save it be by the gate; for he cannot be deceived, for the Lord God is his name. (2 Ne. 9:41.)

The Straight Way

We must not be surprised that God's requirements for eternal rewards are precise and invariable, since even man's society and government operates on such a basis. For instance, returning from abroad to the land of our nativity we must meet certain requirements and have evidence thereof in the form of passports, visas, doctors' certificates as to health and vaccinations, birth certificates and other documents. One cannot receive salary without having met satisfactorily the conditions of his employment. One cannot ride the bus, train, or plane without having paid his fare, and at the station or airport he must show evidence of it. One cannot become a citizen of any country without having met the requirements laid down by the laws of that nation. One cannot expect a degree from any college without having paid his tuition and fees, done his residence work, and shown proof of his having met the requirements. God's eternal rewards will similarly be dependent upon man's compliance with the required conditions.

Prevalence of Procrastination

One of the most serious human defects in all ages is procrastination, an unwillingness to accept personal responsibilities *now*. Men came to earth consciously to obtain their schooling, their training and development, and to perfect themselves, but many have allowed themselves to be diverted and have become merely "hewers of wood and drawers of water," addicts to mental and spiritual indolence and to the pursuit of worldly pleasure.

There are even many members of the Church who are lax and careless and who continually procrastinate. They live the gospel casually but not devoutly. They have complied with some requirements but are not valiant. They do no major crime but merely fail to do the things required — things like paying tithing, living the Word of Wisdom, having family prayers, fasting, attending meetings, serving. Perhaps they do not consider such omissions to be sins, yet these were the kinds of things of which the five foolish virgins of Jesus' parable were probably guilty. The ten virgins belonged to the kingdom and had every right to the blessings — except that five were not valiant and were not ready when the great day came. They were unprepared through not living all the commandments. They were bitterly disappointed at being shut out from the marriage — as likewise their modern counterparts will be.

One Church member of my acquaintance said, as she drank her coffee: "The Lord knows my heart is right and that I have good intentions, and that I will someday get the strength to quit." But will one receive eternal life on the basis of his good intentions? Can one enter a country, receive a scholastic degree, and so on, on the strength of good intent unsupported by appropriate action? Samuel Johnson remarked that "hell is paved with good intentions." The Lord will not translate one's good hopes and desires and intentions into works. Each of us must do that for himself.

Only the Valiant Exalted

One may be saved in any one of three kingdoms of glory — the telestial, the terrestrial, or the celestial — but one can reach exaltation only in the highest of the three heavens or degrees in the celestial glory. Paul told the Corinthians that:

> There are also celestial bodies, and bodies terrestrial: but the glory of the celestial is one, and the glory of the terrestrial is another.
>
> There is one glory of the sun, and another glory of the moon, and another glory of the stars: for one star differeth from another star in glory.
>
> So also is the resurrection of the dead. . . (1 Cor. 15:40-42.)

And through the Prophet Joseph Smith came amplification of Paul's statement:

> In the celestial glory there are three heavens or degrees; And in order to obtain the highest, a man must enter into this order of the priesthood [meaning the new and everlasting covenant of marriage];
>
> And if he does not, he cannot obtain it.
>
> He may enter into the other, but that is the end of his kingdom; he cannot have an increase. (D&C 131:1-4.)

Only the valiant will be exalted and receive the highest degree of glory, hence "many are called, but few are chosen." (D&C 121:40.) As the Savior put it, ". . . strait is the gate, and narrow the way, which leadeth unto life, and few there be that find it." And conversely, " . . . wide is the gate, and broad is the way, that leadeth to destruction, and many there be which go in thereat." (Matt. 7:13, 14.)

It is true that many Latter-day Saints, having been baptized and confirmed members of the Church, and some even having received their endowments and having been married and sealed in the holy temple, have felt that they were thus guaranteed the blessings of exaltation and eternal life. But this is not so. There are two basic requirements every soul must fulfill or he cannot attain to the great blessings offered. He *must* receive the ordinances and he *must* be faithful, overcoming his weaknesses. Hence, not all who claim to be Latter-day Saints will be exalted.

But for those Latter-day Saints who are valiant, who fulfill the requirements faithfully and fully, the promises are glorious beyond description:

> Then shall they be gods, because they have no end; therefore shall they be from everlasting to everlasting, because they continue; then shall they be above all, because all things are subject unto them. Then shall they be gods, because they have all power, and the angels are subject unto them. (D&C 132:20.)

Dangers of Delay

Because men are prone to postpone action and ignore directions, the Lord has repeatedly given strict injunctions and issued solemn warnings. Again and again in different phraseology and throughout the centuries the Lord has reminded man so that he could never have excuse. And the burden of the prophetic warning has been that *the time to act is now, in this mortal life.* One cannot with impunity delay his compliance with God's commandments.

Note Amulek's words, especially those forceful statements involving timing, which are in italics:

> Yea, I would that ye would come forth and harden not your hearts any longer; for behold, *now is the time and the day of your salvation;* and therefore, if ye will repent and harden not your hearts, immediately shall the great plan of redemption be brought about unto you.
>
> For behold, *this life is the time for men to prepare to meet God;* yea, behold *the day of this life is the day for men to perform their labors.*
>
> And now, as I said unto you before, as ye have had so many witnesses, therefore, I beseech of you that ye do not procrastinate the day of your repentance until the end; *for after this day of life, which is given us to prepare for eternity,* behold, if we do not improve our time *while in this life,* then cometh *the night of darkness wherein there can be no labor performed.*
>
> *Ye cannot say, when ye are brought to that awful crisis, that I will repent, that I will return to my God.* Nay, ye cannot say this; *for that same spirit which doth possess your bodies at the time that ye go out of this life, that same spirit will have power to possess your body in that eternal world.* (Al. 34:21-34. Italics added.)

Even if we leave aside the many scriptures which bear similar testimony, reading and prayerfully meditating upon this one brings an awe-inspiring conviction of the need to repent — *now!*

From the modern apostle Melvin J. Ballard we obtain an emphasis of Amulek's expression in these terms:

> . . . But this life is the time in which men are to repent. Do not let any of us imagine that we can go down to the grave not having overcome the corruptions of the flesh and then lose in the grave all our sins and evil tendencies. They will be with us. They will be with the spirit when separated from the body.

It is my judgment that any man or woman can do more to conform to the laws of God in one year in this life than they could do in ten years when they are dead. The spirit only can repent and change, and then the battle has to go forward with the flesh afterwards. It is much easier to overcome and serve the Lord when both flesh and spirit are combined as one. This is the time when men are more pliable and susceptible. We will find when we are dead every desire, every feeling will be greatly intensified. When clay is pliable it is much easier to change than when it gets hard and sets.

This life is the time to repent. That is why I presume it will take a thousand years after the first resurrection until the last group will be prepared to come forth. It will take them a thousand years to do what it would have taken but three-score and ten to accomplish in this life.[2]

President Joseph F. Smith's revelation of 1918 contains these words: ". . . the dead had looked upon the long absence of their spirits from their bodies as a bondage."[3] Another quotation from Elder Ballard amplifies President Smith's thought:

. . . When we go out of this life, leave this body, we will desire to do many things that we cannot do at all without the body. We will be seriously handicapped, and we will long for the body; we will pray for that early reunion with our bodies. We will know then what advantage it is to have a body.

Then, every man and woman who is putting off until the next life the task of correcting and overcoming the weakness of the flesh are sentencing themselves to years of bondage, for no man or woman will come forth in the resurrection until they have completed their work, until they have overcome, until they have done as much as they can do.[4]

Eternal Marriage Now for Latter-day Saints

Nowhere is the time element more fully stressed than in the matter of eternal marriage. It is true that a merciful Father makes special post-mortal provision for those who do not hear the gospel in this life, but for Latter-day Saints

---

[2]Melvin J. Ballard, "Three Degrees of Glory."

[3]Joseph F. Smith, *Gospel Doctrine* (Salt Lake City: Deseret Book Co., 1966), p. 475.

[4]Melvin J. Ballard, "Three Degrees of Glory."

the time is *now*. Read the word of the Lord respecting the marriage covenant:

> . . . I reveal unto you a new and an everlasting covenant; and if ye abide not that covenant, then are ye damned; for no one can reject this covenant and be permitted to enter into my glory. (D&C 132:4.)

That covenant is celestial marriage.

Relative to this subject, in our own dispensation the Lord enlarges somewhat on a statement he made to the people in Palestine:

> For strait is the gate, and narrow the way that leadeth unto the exaltation and continuation of the lives, and few there be that find it, because you receive me not *in the world* neither do ye know me.
>
> But if ye receive me *in the world,* then shall ye know me, and shall receive your exaltation; that where I am ye shall be also.
>
> This is eternal lives — to know the only wise and true God, and Jesus Christ, whom he hath sent. I am he. Receive ye, therefore, my law.
>
> Broad is the gate, and wide the way that leadeth to the deaths; and many there are that go in thereat, because they receive me not, neither do they abide in my law. (D&C 132:22-25. Italics added.)

How impressive the Lord makes the time element! Why should he so emphasize it over and over if there were no significance to it? Would these phrases *in the world* and *out of the world* mean that one could go haphazardly through the years of mortality "eating, drinking, and being merry," ignoring all the commandments and failing to keep his life clean, and still receive the blessings?

Judgment According to Knowledge

Knowledge of the gospel has come to many men and women in this life together with adequate opportunity to live it. Such will be judged by the gospel law. Should one not have had opportunities to hear and understand the gospel in this mortal life, that privilege will be given him hereafter. Judgment is according to knowledge and compliance.

Latter-day Saints are in the first category. Having been blessed with the gospel privileges they are and will be judged on gospel criteria. Where the law is, it is a serious error not to comply with it, as the following scriptures emphasize:

> Jesus said unto them, If ye were blind, ye should have no sin: but now ye say, We see; therefore your sin remaineth. (John 9:41.)

> If I had not come and spoken unto them, they had not had sin: but now they have no cloke for their sin. (John 15:22.)

> And that servant, which knew his Lord's will, and prepared not himself, neither did according to his will, shall be beaten with many stripes.

> But he that knew not, and did commit things worthy of stripes, shall be beaten with few stripes. For unto whomsoever much is given, of him shall be much required. . . .(Luke 12:47-48.)

Jacob's words to his people might have been spoken directly to us:

> But wo unto him that has the law given, yea, that has all the commandments of God, like unto us, and that transgresseth them, and that wasteth the days of his probation, for awful is his state! (2 Ne. 9:27.)

Some Opportunities End at Death

Thus for us who know but do not comply, the opportunities for certain limitless blessings have an end when death closes our eyes.

> And after that you have received this, if you keep not my commandments you cannot be saved in the kingdom of my Father. (D&C 18:46.)

King Benjamin's graphic statement is indeed a sobering thought:

> Therefore if that man repenteth not, and remaineth and dieth an enemy to God, the demands of divine justice do awaken his immortal soul to a lively sense of his own guilt, which doth cause him to shrink from the presence of the Lord, and doth fill his breast with guilt, and pain, and anguish, which is like an un-

quenchable fire, whose flame ascendeth up forever and ever. Mos. 2:38.)

This is the state of those who knowingly fail to live the commandments in this life. They will bring upon themselves their own hell.

Blessings of Repentance and Forgiveness

Our loving Father has given us the blessed principle of repentance as the gateway to forgiveness. All sins but those excepted by the Lord — basically, the sin against the Holy Ghost, and murder — will be forgiven to those who totally, consistently, and continuously repent in a genuine and comprehensive transformation of life. There is forgiveness for even the sinner who commits serious transgressions, for the Church will forgive and the Lord will forgive such things when repentance has reached fruition.

Repentance and forgiveness are part of the glorious climb toward godhood. In God's plan, man must voluntarily make this climb, for the element of free agency is basic. Man chooses for himself, but he cannot control the penalties. They are immutable. Little children and mental incompetents are not held responsible, but all others will receive either blessings, advancements, and rewards, or penalties and deprivation, according to their reaction to God's plan when it is presented to them and to their faithfulness to that plan. The Lord wisely provided for this situation and made it possible that there might be good and evil, comfort and pain. The alternatives give us a choice and thereby growth and development.

Help from the Holy Ghost

In the life of everyone there comes the conflict between good and evil, between Satan and the Lord. Every person who has reached or passed the age of accountability of eight years, and who with a totally repentant heart is baptized properly, positively will receive the Holy Ghost. If heeded, this member of the Godhead will guide, inspire, and warn, and will neutralize the promptings of the evil one. The Lord made this very clear:

> Therefore, as I said unto mine apostles I say unto you again, that every soul who believeth on your words, and is baptized by water for the remission of sins, shall receive the Holy Ghost. (D&C 84:64.)

On this we have also the classic words of Moroni:

> And by the power of the Holy Ghost ye may know the truth of all things. (Moro. 10:5.)

Take the Uncrowded Path

In summary, the way to eternal life is clear. It is well marked. It is difficult. Evil and good influences will be ever present. One must choose. Generally the evil way is the easier, and since man is carnal that way will triumph unless there be a conscious and a consistently vigorous effort to reject the evil and follow the good.

> But remember that he that persists in his own carnal nature, and goes on in the ways of sin and rebellion against God, remaineth in his fallen state and the devil hath all power over him. (Mos. 16:5.)

This earth life is the time to repent. We cannot afford to take any chances of dying an enemy to God.

Accordingly it is important that all the sons and daughters of God upon this earth may "see with their eyes and hear with their ears and understand with their hearts" the purpose of life and their responsibilities to themselves and their posterity, and that they may determine to walk the uncrowded path which is *strait* and which is *narrow*. The time to quit evil ways is before they start. The secret of the good life is in protection and prevention. Those who yield to evil are usually those who have placed themselves in a vulnerable position.

Blessed and fortunate indeed are those who can resist evil and live all the days of their lives without yielding to temptation. But for those who have fallen, repentance is the way back. Repentance is always in order, even in the eleventh hour, for even that delayed action is better than none at all. The thief on the cross who said, "Lord, remember me when thou comest into thy kingdom" was far better off than the one who threw into the Lord's teeth, "If thou be the Christ, save thyself and us." (Luke 23: 39, 42.)

As we have seen, one can wait too long to repent. Many of the Nephites did. Of these, Samuel the Lamanite said:

> But behold, your days of probation are past; ye have pro- crastinated the day of your salvation until it is *everlastingly too late,* and *your destruction is made sure*; yea, for ye have sought all the days of your lives for that which ye could not obtain; and ye have sought for happiness in doing iniquity, which thing is con- trary to the nature of that righteousness which is in our great and Eternal Head. (Hel. 13:38. Italics added.)

Again, observe the emphasis in the words italicized. And let us not suppose that in calling people to repentance the prophets are concerned only with the more grievous sins such as murder, adultery, stealing, and so on, nor only with those persons who have not accepted the gospel ordi- nances. All transgressions must be cleansed, all weaknesses must be overcome, before a person can attain perfection and godhood. Accordingly the intent of this book is to stress the vital importance of each of us transforming his life through repentance and forgiveness. Future chapters will deal with the various aspects of this subject in greater detail.

Oliver Wendell Holmes said: "Many people die with their music still in them. Why is this so? Too often it is because they are always getting ready to live. Before they know it, time runs out." Tagore expressed a similar thought in these words: "I have spent my days stringing and un- stringing my instrument, while the song I came to sing remains unsung."

My plea therefore is this: Let us get our instruments tightly strung and our melodies sweetly sung. Let us not die with our music still in us. Let us rather use this precious mortal probation to move confidently and gloriously upward toward the eternal life which God our Father gives to those who keep his commandments.

Chapter Two

No Unclean Thing
Can Enter

> *. . . All men, everywhere, must repent, or they can in nowise inherit the kingdom of God, for no unclean thing can dwell there, or dwell in his presence . . .*
>
> —Moses 6:57

As we discussed in Chapter 1, the road of life is plainly marked according to the divine purpose, the map of the gospel of Jesus Christ is made available to the travelers, the destination of eternal life is clearly established. At that destination our Father waits hopefully, anxious to greet his returning children. Unfortunately, many will not arrive.

The reason is forthrightly stated by Nephi — ". . . There cannot any unclean thing enter into the kingdom of God . . ." (1 Ne. 15:34.) And again, ". . . no unclean thing can dwell with God . . ." (1 Ne. 10:21.) To the prophets the term *unclean* in this context means what it means to God. To man the word may be relative in meaning — one minute speck of dirt does not make a white shirt or dress unclean, for example. But to God who is perfection, cleanliness means moral and personal cleanliness. Less than that is, in one degree or another, uncleanliness and hence cannot dwell with God.

Were it not for the blessed gifts of repentance and forgiveness this would be a hopeless situation for man, since no one except the Master has ever lived sinless on the earth. Naturally, there are all degrees of sin. At worst, the deep sinner is in the thrall of Satan. As Jesus put it, his "whole body [is] full of darkness." The Savior went on to express the impossibility of serving God, of being close to him, under these circumstances:

> No man can serve two masters: for either he will hate the one, and love the other; or else he will hold to the one, and despise the other. Ye cannot serve God and mammon. (Matt. 6:24.)

We Belong Where We Serve

Sin, then, is service to Satan. It is a truism that men are "his whom they list to obey." Many scriptures affirm this statement. Jesus pointed to this truth when he said to the Jews, "Whosoever committeth sin is the servant of sin." (John 8:34.) Paul, writing to the Romans, said:

> Neither yield ye your members as instruments of unrighteousness unto sin: but yield yourselves unto God, as those that are alive from the dead, and your members as instruments of righteousness unto God.
>
> For sin shall not have dominion over you. . .
>
> Know ye not, that to whom ye yield yourselves servants to obey, his servants ye are to whom ye obey; whether of sin unto death, or of obedience unto righteousness? (Rom. 6:13, 15-16.)

Peter too emphasizes this bondage:

> For when they speak great swelling words of vanity, they allure through the lusts of the flesh, through much wantonness, those that were clean escaped from them who live in error.
>
> While they promise them liberty, they themselves are the servants of corruption: for of whom a man is overcome, of the same is he brought in bondage. (2 Pet. 2:18-19.)

It might be observed that the term *lust* is not necessarily limited in its connotation to sexual desire. It can imply any fleshly or worldly appetite or urge carried to excess. Satan will eagerly use other urges which suit his purpose, as well as sexual ones, in an effort to enslave men until, as Mormon put it:

> . . . They are led about by Satan, even as chaff is driven before the wind, or as a vessel is tossed about upon the waves, without sail or anchor, or without anything wherewith to steer her; and even as she is, so are they. (Morm. 5:18.)

Reality of Satan

In these days of sophistication and error men depersonalize not only God but the devil. Under this concept Satan is a myth, useful for keeping people straight in less enlightened days but outmoded in our educated age. Nothing is further from reality. Satan is very much a personal, individual spirit being, but without a mortal body. His desires to seal each of us his are no less ardent in wickedness than our Father's are in righteousness to attract us to his own eternal kingdom. A glimpse of Satan's tactics, as well as a terrifyingly accurate character sketch, is given us by Nephi in this prophecy respecting our own day:

> For behold, at that day shall he rage in the hearts of the children of men, and stir them up to anger against that which is good.
>
> And others will he pacify, and lull them away into carnal security, that they will say: All is well in Zion; yea, Zion prospereth, all is well—and thus the devil cheateth their souls, and leadeth them away carefully down to hell.
>
> And behold, others he flattereth away, and telleth them there is no hell; and he saith unto them: I am no devil, for there is none—and thus he whispereth in their ears, until he grasps them with his awful chains, from whence there is no deliverance.
>
> Yea, they are grasped with death, and hell; and death, and hell, and the devil, and all that have been seized therewith must stand before the throne of God, and be judged according to their works, from whence they must go into the place prepared for them. . . (2 Ne. 28:20-23.)

Yes, the devil is decidedly a person. He is also clever and trained. With thousands of years of experience behind him he has become superbly efficient and increasingly determined. Young people often feel and say, when governing hands are outstretched to them, "I can take care of myself." In fact even more experienced adults cannot afford to be sure of their resistance to Satan. Teenage girls or boys certainly need to be properly fortified and protected if they are to cope with the efficient, highly-trained, superior powers which are ever alert to opportunities for temptation.

It is a smart person, young or old, who will accept advice and counsel from experienced people who know the pitfalls, the crumbling walls, and the cracking dams which bring on destruction.

Old Sins, New Names

Sins may be classified in many categories. They range from the simple improprieties and indiscretions to the shedding of innocent blood and the sin against the Holy Ghost. There are sins against ourselves, sins against our loved ones, sins against our fellowmen, sins against our communities, sins against the Church, sins against humanity. There are sins which are known to the world and others which are so carefully hidden that the sinner is the only mortal being who knows of the error.

Sometimes a new generation gives old sins new names — often designations which remove any implication of sin — and as one reads the long scriptural list of transgressions he does not recognize them by their modern names. But they are all there in the scriptures, and are all here and practiced in our own day.

Sometimes a person, not discovering in the scriptures the modern name for the particular sin or perversion of which he is guilty, eases his conscience by trying to convince himself that, after all, it is not too bad because it is not specifically prohibited. For instance, the word *petting* may never be found in the scriptures but the act of petting is repeatedly condemned. Likewise other sins and perversions may not be named in the scriptures by their modern appellations, but a careful scrutiny of the scriptures will reveal that all these things were done to their shame by the

Romans and the Corinthians and the Ephesians and the children of Israel and other peoples throughout the ages.

Then again, in interviewing young people and sometimes older ones, I find that many do not know the meaning of the names of the sins in the old scriptures. One young man said, "I know what adultery is, but what is this fornication and is it wrong?" A prominent social worker said that there were many young people who had grown to maturity physically yet had never been told in plain terms that sexual relations outside of marriage were deep sins. Accordingly, though it is an unpleasant discussion, this book will discuss such subjects in subsequent chapters.

Scriptural List of Sins

Since the scriptural catalog is so complete, particularly in the writings of the early-day apostles, let us list the sins the scriptures describe. For example, Paul's prophecy to Timothy about the conditions of our own day has been fulfilled with depressing precision.

> This know also, that in the last days perilous times shall come.

> For men shall be lovers of their own selves, covetous, boasters, proud, blasphemers, disobedient to parents, unthankful, unholy,

> Without natural affection, trucebreakers, false accusers, incontinent, fierce, despisers of those that are good,

> Traitors, heady, highminded, lovers of pleasures more than lovers of God;

> Having a form of godliness, but denying the power thereof: from such turn away.

> For of this sort are they which creep into houses, and lead captive silly women laden with sins, led away with divers lusts. . . (2 Tim. 3:1-6.)

Paul warned the Romans of similar sins:

> . . . Uncleanness through the lusts of their own hearts, to dishonour their own bodies between themselves:

> Who . . . worshipped and served the creature more than the Creator. . .

. . . God gave them up unto vile affections: for even their women did change the natural use into that which is against nature:

And likewise also the men, leaving the natural use of the woman, burned in their lust one toward another; men with men working that which is unseemly. . .

Backbiters, haters of God, despiteful, proud, boasters, inventors of evil things, disobedient to parents.

. . . Covenantbreakers, without natural affection, implacable, unmerciful:

Who knowing the judgment of God, that they which commit such things are worthy of death, not only do the same, but have pleasure in them that do them. (Rom. 1:24-27, 30-32.)

A few more types of sin are mentioned in Paul's words to the Corinthians:

. . . Neither fornicators, nor idolaters, nor adulterers, nor effeminate, nor abusers of themselves with mankind,

Nor thieves, nor covetous, nor drunkards, nor revilers, nor extortioners, shall inherit the kingdom of God. (1 Cor. 6:9-10.)

John the Revelator catalogues the transgressions which will merit the second death:

But the fearful, and unbelieving, and the abominable, and murderers, and whoremongers, and sorcerers, and idolaters, and all liars, shall have their part in the lake which burneth with fire and brimstone: which is the second death. (Rev. 21:8.)

Sexual sin receives repeated condemnation in the scriptures. To get our definitions clear, let us realize that heterosexual intercourse is the sin of fornication when committed by the unmarried and is adultery when indulged in by married people outside of their marriage covenants. Both are grievous sins in God's sight. Wrote Paul:

Know ye not that your bodies are the members of Christ? shall I then take the members of Christ, and make them members of an harlot? God forbid.

What? know ye not that he which is joined to an harlot is one body? for two, saith he, shall be one flesh.

Flee fornication. . . (1 Cor. 6:15-16, 18.)

In other epistles Paul makes additional emphasis and lists further sins. (See Rom. 1:24-32; 1 Cor. 3:16-17;

6:9-10; 10:8; Eph. 5:3-7; Gal. 5:19-21; Col. 3:5, 7-8; 1 Thess. 4:3-5.)

As we read the scriptures quoted or referred to above, we observe that they list virtually all the modern transgressions, though sometimes under ancient names. Let us review the lengthy list:

Murder, adultery, theft, cursing, unholiness in masters, disobedience in servants, unfaithfulness, improvidence, hatred of God, disobedience to husbands, lack of natural affection, high-mindedness, flattery, lustfulness, infidelity, indiscretion, backbiting, whispering, lack of truth, striking, brawling, quarrelsomeness, unthankfulness, inhospitality, deceitfulness, irreverence, boasting, arrogance, pride, double-tongued talk, profanity, slander, corruptness, thievery, embezzlement, despoiling, covenantbreaking, incontinence, filthiness, ignobleness, filthy communications, impurity, foolishness, slothfulness, impatience, lack of understanding, unmercifulness, idolatry, blasphemy, denial of the Holy Ghost, Sabbath breaking, envy, jealousy, malice, maligning, vengefulness, implacability, bitterness, clamor, spite, defiling, reviling, evil speaking, provoking, greediness for filthy lucre, disobedience to parents, anger, hate, covetousness, bearing false witness, inventing evil things, fleshliness, heresy, presumptuousness, abomination, insatiable appetite, instability, ignorance, self-will, speaking evil of dignitaries, becoming a stumbling block; and in our modern language, masturbation, petting, fornication, adultery, homosexuality, and every sex perversion, every hidden and secret sin and all unholy and impure practices.

These are transgressions the Lord has condemned through his servants. Let no one rationalize his sins on the excuse that a particular sin of his is not mentioned nor forbidden in scripture.

Purity Essential to Eternal Life

Whoever else suffers, every sin is against God, for it tends to frustrate the program and purposes of the Almighty.

Likewise, every sin is committed against the sinner, for it limits his progress and curtails his development.

In our journey toward eternal life, purity must be our constant aim. To walk and talk with God, to serve with God, to follow his example and become as a god, we must attain perfection. In his presence there can be no guile, no wickedness, no transgression. In numerous scriptures he has made it clear that all worldliness, evil and weakness must be dropped before we can ascend unto "the hill of the Lord." The Psalmist asked:

> Who shall ascend into the hill of the Lord? or who shall stand in his holy place?

And he answered the question:

> He that hath clean hands, and a pure heart; who hath not lifted up his soul unto vanity, nor sworn deceitfully. (Ps. 24:3-4.)

Writing of his vision of the celestial city, John said:

> And there shall in no wise enter into it any thing that defileth, neither whatsoever worketh abomination, or maketh a lie: but they which are written in the Lamb's book of life. (Rev. 21:27.)

After enumerating many sins, Paul told the Galatians:

> . . . As I have also told you in time past, that they which do such things shall not inherit the kingdom of God. (Gal. 5:21.)

From the beginning God has left no doubt in the minds of his people that only the clean and pure will inherit his kingdom. To Adam he gave the commandment:

> Wherefore teach it unto your children, that all men, everywhere, must repent, or they can in nowise inherit the kingdom of God, for no unclean thing can dwell there, or dwell in his presence . . . (Moses 6:57.)

Numerous scriptures attest to the same principle — that only the pure can dwell with God. (For example, see Mos. 2:37; Al. 11:37; Titus 1:15-16.) It can be no other way, for ". . . to be carnally-minded is death, and to be spiritually-minded is life eternal." (2 Ne. 9:39.) Jesus himself expressed the thought superbly in the Beatitudes — "Blessed are the pure in heart: for they shall see

God." (Matt. 5:8.) Purity of heart means perfection; and the perfect will not only see God but will have friendship with him.

This concept that sin estranges one from God, and if not repented of will keep us from his presence, is not confined to the ancient prophets. The modern Prophet Joseph Smith similarly saw sin as a major obstacle to salvation and godhood. He said on one occasion:

> . . . If you wish to go where God is, you must be like God, or possess the principles which God possesses, for if we are not drawing towards God in principle, we are going from him and drawing towards the devil. Yes, I am standing in the midst of all kinds of people.
>
> Search your hearts, and see if you are like God. I have searched mine, and feel to repent of all my sins.
>
> We have thieves among us, adulterers, liars, hypocrites. If God should speak from heaven, he would command you not to steal, not to commit adultery, not to covet, nor deceive, but be faithful over a few things. As far as we degenerate from God, we descend to the devil and lose knowledge, and without knowledge we cannot be saved, and while our hearts are filled with evil, and we are studying evil, there is no room in our hearts for good, or studying good . . . [1]

Need Is Discipline

When I was a young boy I took care of a Jersey bull which became vicious and charged me several times. All I needed to do to halt his attack was to jerk the chain attached to the ring in his nose and he became docile and manageable. As he became less tractable, I added a long bamboo pole fastened to the ring in his nose. I now had him totally under subjection, for I could hold him back or lead him forward. He was under my control.

So does sin, as a ring in the nose, have the sinner under subjection. So is sin like handcuffs on the wrists, a ring in the nose, and slave bands around the neck.

_____

[1] Joseph Smith, *Teachings of the Prophet Joseph Smith,* selected and arranged by Joseph Fielding Smith (Salt Lake City: Deseret Book Co., 1938), pp. 216-217.

But to carry the analogy further, my bull, had he been human, might have disciplined himself. Then with no ring in the nose he would have controlled his own actions. So it is with human sin — self-control, self-mastery, can be substituted for the dominion of sin, and the sinner can move by his own agency toward God rather than under the control of sin toward Satan.

The term may not be popular in this age of license and lack of restraint, but what is needed is self-discipline. Can we imagine the angels or the gods not being in control of themselves in any particular? The question is of course ludicrous. Equally ridiculous is the idea that any of us can rise to the eternal heights without disciplining ourselves and being disciplined by the circumstances of life. The purity and perfection we seek is unattainable without this subjection of unworthy, ungodlike urges and the corresponding encouragement of their opposites. We certainly cannot expect the rules to be easier for us than for the Son of God, of whom it is recorded:

> Though he were a Son, yet learned he obedience by the things which he suffered;
>
> And being made perfect, he became the author of eternal salvation unto all them that obey him. (Heb. 5:8-9.)

"Unto all them that obey him" — these are the operative words for us. And obedience always involves self-discipline. So does repentance, which is the way to annul the effects of a previous lack of obedience in one's life. The dividends from both obedience and repentance amply repay the effort.

Repentance the Only Way

Repentance is ever the key to a better, happier life. All of us need it, whether our sins are the grievous ones or the more commonplace. Through repentance we perceive more clearly the contrasts of Paul's statement: "For the wages of sin is death; but the gift of God is eternal life

through Jesus Christ our Lord." (Rom. 6:23.) Through
repentance we may "be sanctified from all sin, and enjoy
the words of eternal life in this world, and eternal life in
the world to come, even immortal glory." (Moses 6:59.)

And there is no other way.

Chapter Three

...*None Righteous,*
No, Not One

The greatest of all faults is to be conscious of none.

—Carlyle

WHEN WE HEAR SERMONS DECRYING TRANSGRESSION and urging the need for repentance, most of us are peculiarly apt at applying the point exclusively to others. Someone said that we spend too much time confessing other people's sins. Apparently it is much easier to see those sins than our own, and to walk complacently through life without acknowledging our own need to mend our ways.

All Are Sinners

Yet everyone sins in some degree, and hence no one may properly call others to repentance without including himself. Thus we read in John's writings:

> If we say that we have no sin, we deceive ourselves, and the truth is not in us.

> If we say that we have not sinned, we make him a liar, and his word is not in us. (1 John 1:8, 10.)

Likewise the Psalmist sang:

> The fool hath said in his heart, There is no God. They are corrupt, they have done abominable works, there is none that doeth good.

> The Lord looked down from heaven upon the children of men, to see if there were any that did understand and seek God.

> They are all gone aside . . . there is none that doeth good, no, not one. (Ps. 14:1-3.)

Other scriptures have a similar emphasis:

> For there is not a just man upon the earth, that doeth good, and sinneth not. (Eccles. 7:20.)

> Who can say, I have made my heart clean, I am pure from sin? (Prov. 20:9.)

> Wherefore, as by one man sin entered into the world, and death by sin; and so death passed upon all men, for that all have sinned. (Rom. 5:12.)

The Prophet Joseph Smith in his prayer of dedication of the Kirtland Temple implored: "O Jehovah, have mercy upon this people, and as all men sin forgive the transgressions of thy people, and let them be blotted out forever." (D&C 109:34.)

It was because of the universality of sin, the seriousness of sin, and the nearness of the end of the world, that the Lord revealed to his latter-day Prophet, Joseph Smith, the instruction, "Say nothing but repentance unto this generation." (D&C 6:9.)

One of the oft-told stories about the late President J. Golden Kimball concerns his witticism to the effect that "the Brethren cannot cut me off the Church — I repent too often." Here is a great lesson, if it is correctly interpreted. There is never a day in any man's life when repentance is not essential to his well-being and eternal progress.

But when most of us think of repentance we tend to narrow our vision and view it as good only for our husbands, our wives, our parents, our children, our neighbors, our friends, the world — anyone and everyone except ourselves. Similarly there is a prevalent, perhaps subconscious, feeling that the Lord designed repentance only for those who commit murder or adultery or theft or other heinous crimes. This is of course not so. If we are humble and desirous of living the gospel we will come to think of repentance as applying to everything we do in life, whether it be spiritual or temporal in nature. Repentance is for every soul who has not yet reached perfection.

Church Members Need Repentance

Another misconception some Latter-day Saints have is that repentance is only for the person who does not belong to the Church of Jesus Christ. This notion ignores not only gospel doctrine and common sense, but also specific revelations to the Prophet Joseph Smith in which the Lord took more than one occasion to chastise the saints and call them to repentance for their wrong-doings. In Kirtland, for example, he spoke out against offenders within the Church and told them pointedly:

> Behold, I, the Lord, am not well pleased with many who are in the Church at Kirtland;
>
> For they do not forsake their sins, and their wicked ways, the pride of their hearts, and their covetousness, and all their detestable things, and observe the words of wisdom and eternal life which I have given unto them.
>
> Verily I say unto you, that I, the Lord, will chasten them and will do whatsoever I list, if they do not repent and observe all things whatsoever I have said unto them. (D&C 98:19-21.)

A few months later the Lord mentioned specific sins of which the Missouri saints had been guilty:

> Behold, I say unto you, there were jarrings, and contentions, and envyings, and strifes, and lustful and covetous desires among them; therefore by these things they polluted their inheritances. (D&C 101:6.)

Even those in the school of the prophets needed chastisement and repentance:

> Nevertheless . . . contentions arose in the school of the prophets; which was very grievous unto me, saith your Lord; therefore I sent them forth to be chastened. (D&C 95:10.)

And Emma, the Prophet's wife, by revelation was called to repentance:

And again, verily I say, let mine handmaid forgive my servant Joseph his trespasses; and then shall she be forgiven her trespasses . . . (D&C 132:56.)

Even Prophets Not Perfect

Even the Prophet Joseph Smith, great as he was, was not perfect and the Lord had to call him to repentance: "And now I command you, my servant Joseph, to repent and walk more uprightly before me, and to yield to the persuasions of men no more." (D&C 5:21.)

The young Prophet needed repentance as all men do. He was honest in his confessions of weakness. In his teens when he had been lonely in the intense persecution following his glorious vision, he was left to all kinds of temptations. He says:

> . . . I frequently fell into many foolish errors, and displayed the weakness of youth, and the foibles of human nature; which, I am sorry to say, led me into divers temptations, offensive in the sight of God. . . (Joseph Smith 2:28.)

While Joseph was human and therefore fallible, he was free from major sins, and he hastens to make clear:

> . . . In making this confession, no one need suppose me guilty of any great or malignant sins. A disposition to commit such was never in my nature. But I was guilty of levity, and sometimes associated with jovial company, etc., not consistent with that character which ought to be maintained by one who was called of God as I had been. . . (Joseph Smith 2:28.)

There are enemies to God's cause who have tried to make much of this statement, but good men recognize it as a simple and honest confession which is consistent with the character of a great though still imperfect man.

Important to our consideration is the Prophet's acknowledgement of his errors, and his repentance and his prayers for forgiveness: "In consequence of these things," he wrote, "I often felt condemned for my weakness and imperfections . . ." And on that special night, as probably numerous times before, he knelt at his bed. As he described it: ". . . I betook myself to prayer and supplication to Almighty

God for forgiveness of all my sins and follies, and also for a manifestation to me, that I might know of my state and standing before him . . ." (Joseph Smith 2:29.)

Every person is subject to error if he is not always watchful, for victory over Satan is attained only by constant vigilance. In the Doctrine and Covenants the Lord makes clear that no man is immune from temptations, and not even a prophet may trifle with sacred things. He warns:

> For although a man may have many revelations, and have power to do many mighty works, yet if he boasts in his own strength, and sets at naught the counsels of God, and follows after the dictates of his own will and carnal desires, he must fall and incur the vengeance of a just God upon him. (D&C 3:4.)

The reprimand continues:

> Behold, thou art Joseph, and thou wast chosen to do the work of the Lord, but because of transgression, if thou art not aware thou wilt fall. (D&C 3:9.)

Remember that the transgression of which the young Prophet was guilty was not murder, nor sexual sins, nor cursing, nor any of the acts usually called sins. He had but yielded to the powerful persuasion of his friend and benefactor, Martin Harris, to trust in the hands of that man the English translation of the sacred Book of Mormon writings, which became lost through this error.

> But remember, God is merciful; therefore, repent of that which thou hast done which is contrary to the commandment which I gave you, and thou art still chosen, and art again called to the work;

> Except thou do this, thou shalt be delivered up and become as other men, and have no more gift. (D&C 3:10-11.)

The Lord's chastisement of Joseph Smith recalls that administered to another prophet, the great Moses. Because of a momentary sin, committed under stress (see Numbers 20:9-12), Moses was deprived of the great opportunity and blessing of leading the children of Israel into the promised land after their forty years of wandering in the wilderness.

If even the Lord's chosen prophets are not immune from the need to repent, what of the rest of us? Clearly, repentance is for all — Latter-day Saints as well as others.

Sins Among the Saints

It is my pleasure to go often into the homes of the leaders in the missions, wards, and stakes of Zion. I am deeply appreciative of the fact that most of our people are trying to live the commandments of the Lord.

But I also find parents who have lost the natural affection for their children. I find children who disown their parents and evade responsibility for them in their parents' old age. I find husbands who desert their wives and their children, and who use almost every pretext to justify such action. I find wives who are demanding, unworthy, quarrelsome, uncooperative, and worldly, and who thereby provoke their husbands to similar responses. I find husbands and wives, living under the same roof, who are selfish, unbending, and unforgiving, and who with their misunderstandings have hardened their hearts and poisoned their minds and the minds of their children.

I find those who gossip and bear false witness against their neighbors. I find brethren who hale each other into the courts on trivial matters which could have been settled by themselves outside of legal channels. I find blood brothers and sisters who fight over inheritances and bring each other into the courts of the land, dragging before the public the most intimate and personal family secrets, leaving nothing sacred, showing little regard for each other but only for what financial gain they might acquire by such selfish action.

In an eastern city I saw one family split wide apart — half of the brothers and sisters on one side, and half on the other — in a most disgraceful feud. At the funeral services half of them sat on one side of the aisle and half on the other. They would not speak to each other. The property involved was worth only a few thousand dollars, and yet because of it blood brothers and sisters became avowed enemies.

I have seen people in wards and branches who impugn the motives of the authorities and of each other and make them an "offender for a word," for things which have been said or thought or were imagined to have been. I have seen branches broken wide apart by people who say unkind things about each other, who brought into their meetings the spirit of Lucifer instead of the Spirit of Christ.

There are those who accept no responsibility and give no time to Church service, but who are constant critics of those who do. There are some who are guilty, and worldly, and give lip service only. There are those who hypocritically make pretensions and fail to live up to them, those who are intolerant and prejudiced, those who are unkind to their families.

For these and other unmentioned eccentricities, sins and transgressions, all stand in need of repentance. Following chapters will say more about the sins which threaten us as individuals, as a church, and as a society. After that we will consider the means of repentance and the miracle of forgiveness which God performs on those who truly repent.

Chapter Four

These Things Doth the Lord Hate

> These six things doth the Lord
> hate: yea, seven are an abomina-
> tion unto him:
>
> A proud look, a lying tongue,
> and hands that shed innocent
> blood,
>
> An heart that deviseth wicked
> imaginations, feet that be swift in
> running to mischief,
>
> A false witness that speaketh
> lies, and he that soweth discord
> among brethren.
>
> —Proverbs 6:16-19

THE CURSE OF THE EARTH IS SIN. IT COVERS EVERY AREA. It takes on numerous forms and dresses itself in many kinds of apparel, depending on factors such as the stratum of society in which it is operating. But whether man calls it convention or business, or uses any other euphemism, if it offends God's law it is sin.

Some would categorize as minor the sins discussed in this chapter, but when not repented of they will still keep us from eternal life. Perhaps most of us have our share of them. Here they are treated only briefly and with no thought that the list is exhaustive.

Idolatry

From Mount Sinai came God's unalterable command:

> Thou shalt have *no other* Gods before me.

> Thou shalt not make unto thee *any graven image,* or *any likeness of any thing* that is in heaven above, or that is in the earth beneath, or that is in the water under the earth:

> Thou shalt *not bow down* thyself to them, *nor serve them* . . . (Ex. 20:3-5. Italics added.)

This proscription embraces not only images in the form of God or of man, but the likeness of anything which is earthly in any form. It would include both tangible and less tangible things, and everything which entices a person away from duty, loyalty, and love for and service to God.

Idolatry is among the most serious of sins. There are unfortunately millions today who prostrate themselves before images of gold and silver and wood and stone and clay. But the idolatry we are most concerned with here is the conscious worshipping of still other gods. Some are of metal and plush and chrome, of wood and stone and fabrics. They are not in the image of God or of man, but are developed to give man comfort and enjoyment, to satisfy his wants, ambitions, passions and desires. Some are in no physical form at all, but are intangible.

Many seem to "worship" on an elemental basis — they live to eat and drink. They are like the children of Israel who, though offered the great freedoms associated with national development under God's personal guidance, could not lift their minds above the "flesh pots of Egypt." They cannot seem to rise above satisfying their bodily appetites. As Paul put it, their "God is their belly." (Phil. 3:19.)

Modern idols or false gods can take such forms as clothes, homes, businesses, machines, automobiles, pleasure boats, and numerous other material deflectors from the path to godhood. What difference does it make that the item concerned is not shaped like an idol? Brigham Young said: "I would as soon see a man worshipping a little god made of brass or of wood as to see him worshipping his property."[1]

Intangible things make just as ready gods. Degrees and letters and titles can become idols. Many young men decide to attend college when they should be on missions first. The degree, and the wealth and the security which come through it, appear so desirable that the mission takes second place. Some neglect Church service through their college years, feeling to give preference to the secular training and ignoring the spiritual covenants they have made.

Many people build and furnish a home and buy the automobile first — and then find they "cannot afford" to pay tithing. Whom do they worship? Certainly not the Lord of heaven and earth, for we serve whom we love and give first consideration to the object of our affection and desires. Young married couples who postpone parenthood until their degrees are attained might be shocked if their expressed preference were labeled idolatry. Their rationalization gives them degrees at the expense of children. Is it a justifiable exchange? Whom do they love and worship — themselves or God? Other couples, recognizing that life is not intended primarily for comforts, ease, and luxuries, complete their educations while they move forward with full lives, having their children and giving Church and community service.

Many worship the hunt, the fishing trip, the vacation, the weekend picnics and outings. Others have as their idols the games of sport, baseball, football, the bullfight, or golf. These pursuits more often than not interfere with the worship of the Lord and with giving service to the building up of the kingdom of God. To the participants this emphasis may not seem serious, yet it indicates where their allegiance and loyalty are.

Still another image men worship is that of power and prestige. Many will trample underfoot the spiritual and often the ethical values in their climb to success. These

[1]*Journal of Discourses*, 6:196.

gods of power, wealth, and influence are most demanding and are quite as real as the golden calves of the children of Israel in the wilderness.

Rebellion

A common sin is rebellion against God. This manifests itself in wilful refusal to obey God's commandments, in rejection of the counsel of his servants, in opposition to the work of the kingdom — that is, in the deliberate word or act of disobedience to God's will.

A classic example of rebellion against God is Judas Iscariot, who actually betrayed his Lord to murderers. Another example is King Saul. Strong and capable, originally filled with high potential, this chosen young man became proud and rebellious. We find the Prophet Samuel's rebuke to the self-centered, egotistical ruler:

> . . . When thou wast little in thine own sight, wast thou not made the head of the tribes of Israel, and the Lord anointed thee king over Israel?
>
> Wherefore then didst thou not obey the voice of the Lord?
>
> . . . Hath the Lord as great delight in burnt offerings and sacrifices, as in obeying the voice of the Lord? Behold, to obey is better than sacrifice, and to hearken than the fat of rams.
>
> For rebellion is as the sin of witchcraft, and stubbornness is as iniquity and idolatry. . . Thou hast rejected the word of the Lord. . . (1 Sam. 15:17, 19, 22-23.)

Of the Book of Mormon people, who were rapidly sinking in wickedness, it is recorded:

> Now they did not sin ignorantly, for they knew the will of God concerning them, for it had been taught unto them; therefore they did wilfully rebel against God. (3 Ne. 6:18.)

Latter-day Saints are similarly blessed with light and knowledge. They are equally condemned of the Lord if they rebel against the revealed truths of the gospel.

Among Church members rebellion frequently takes the form of criticism of authorities and leaders. They "speak evil of dignities" and "of the things that they understand

not," says Peter. (2 Pet. 2:10, 12.) They complain of the
programs, belittle the constituted authorities, and generally
set themselves up as judges. After a while they absent
themselves from Church meetings for imagined offenses,
and fail to pay their tithes and meet their other Church
obligations. In a word, they have the spirit of apostasy,
which is almost always the harvest of the seeds of criticism.
Unless they repent they shrivel in the destructive element
they have themselves prepared, poison themselves with mix-
tures of their own concocting; or as Peter puts it, they
"perish in their own corruption." Not only do *they* suffer
but their posterity also. In modern times the Lord has
described their fate in these words:

> Cursed are all those that shall lift up the heel against mine
> anointed, saith the Lord, and cry they have sinned when they
> have not sinned before me, saith the Lord. . .
>
> But those who cry transgression do it because they are the
> servants of sin, and are the children of disobedience themselves.
>
> And those who swear falsely against my servants. . .
>
> Their basket shall not be full, their houses and their barns
> shall perish, and they themselves shall be despised by those that
> flattered them.
>
> They shall not have right to the priesthood, nor their posterity
> after them from generation to generation. (D&C 121:16-18, 20-
> 21.)

Such people fail to bear testimony to their descendants,
destroy faith within their own homes, and actually deny the
"right to the priesthood" to succeeding generations who
might otherwise have been faithful in all things.

One is reminded of how the Lord showed his displeas-
ure at rebellion against his servant Moses when he up-
braided Aaron and Miriam and afflicted the latter with
leprosy. (See Num. 12:1-10.) Moses was the Lord's
anointed. To criticize and complain against the servant was
rebellion against the Master.

One would wish that the rebellious would stop and ask
themselves questions such as: "Do my philosophy and my

critical efforts bring me closer to Christ, to God, to virtue, to prayer, to exaltation?" "What have I gained by my criticism — peace, joy and growth, or merely satisfaction to my pride?" "What have I gained by my sin other than immediate carnal satisfaction?"

In cases where the rebellious exercise repentance, that repentance may be sparked in various ways. Some men come to recognize their sins from introspection while others must be brought to their knees by outside forces. Many, having realized their transgressions, begin their repentance in secrecy. Others must be apprehended and chastised and punished before they begin their transformation. Some even need to be disciplined by forced inactivity, disfellowshipping, or even excommunication before they realize their plight and the need to transform their lives. None of us should resent being reminded of our responsibilities and being called to repent of our sins. The Lord may choose to chasten us in this way or some other, but it is all for our own good.

> . . . My son, despise not thou the chastening of the Lord, nor faint when thou art rebuked of him:
>
> For whom the Lord loveth he chasteneth, and scourgeth every son whom he receiveth.
>
> If ye endure chastening, God dealeth with you as with sons; for what son is he whom the father chasteneth not? (Heb. 12:5-7.)

One of the Church authorities spoke to a certain stake conference kindly and plainly but in strong terms calling attention to some of the weaknesses common to the people of that community. Commenting on the talk someone made the remark: "I suppose he is the only one who will reach the heights. He will be mighty lonesome." The person could appropriately have said: "That was a just criticism and I will move forward to correct my ways." Instead he manifested the spirit of rebellion against legitimate correction. No doubt he is one of those who would say, if a scriptural rebuke were referred to: "But that was Christ or the old prophets; anyone would accept rebuke or criticism from them." This overlooks the Lord's statement that what is given the people ". . . whether by mine own voice or by the voice of my servants, it is the same." (D&C 1:38.)

A prevalent form of rebellion is the "higher criticism" which is the delight of those Church members who become proud of their intellectual powers. Reveling in their supposed superiority they argue back and forth, analyze with their unaided intellect what can only be discerned by the eye of faith, and challenge and debunk such Church doctrines and policies as do not pass their critical examination. In all this they undermine the faith of those less qualified in knowledge and logic, sometimes apparently gaining pleasure from this result. But the Lord's word to such people is still what it was two thousand years ago:

> . . . Except ye be converted, and become as little children, ye shall not enter into the kingdom of heaven.
>
> Woe unto the world because of offences! for it must needs be that offences come; but woe to that man by whom the offence cometh! (Matt. 18:3, 7.)

One punishment for the rebel against truth is that he loses the power to perceive the truth. Hear these words of Jacob:

> But behold, the Jews were a stiffnecked people; and they despised the words of plainness, and killed the prophets, and sought for things that they could not understand. Wherefore, because of their blindness, which blindness came by *looking beyond the mark,* they must needs fall. . . . (Jac. 4:14. Italics added.)

Traitors

What shall be said of those members who press so hard and publicize their criticisms of the Church that they give encouragement to its enemies and embarrass its leadership and the other faithful members? Being "false to an obligation or duty" is one definition of a traitor — and surely baptized members have an obligation to support the Church and further its ends.

What could be more despicable than a traitor to a friend, a church, a nation, or a cause? Paul thought this defection ugly enough that he included it in his prophecy of latter-day sins. (See 2 Tim. 3:4.) The traitor often works in the dark, deceitfully. The quislings, the Benedict Arnolds, the John C. Bennetts, the William Laws and the Francis and Chauncey Higbees — does anyone love or admire them? We are not without traitors in the Church today, those who would destroy that which is good to win their own selfish earthly rewards or to accomplish their base schemes.

Sabbath-Breaking

We have become a world of Sabbath breakers. On the Sabbath the lakes are full of boats, the beaches are crowded, the shows have their best attendance, the golf links are dotted with players. The Sabbath is the preferred day for rodeos, conventions, family picnics; and ball games are played on the sacred day. Even the "stranger that is within thy gates" is pressed into service. "Business as usual" is the slogan for many, and our holy day has become a holiday. And because so many people treat the day as a holiday numerous others cater to the wants of the fun-lovers and money-makers.

Sabbath-breakers too are those who buy commodities or entertainment on the Sabbath, thus encouraging pleasure palaces and business establishments to remain open — which they otherwise would not do. If we buy, sell, trade or support such on the Lord's day we are rebellious as the children of Israel, the dire consequences of whose transgressions against this and other commandments should be a permanent warning to us all.

Although Israel's swift and severe punishment for infractions is not exacted today, this does not lessen the seriousness of the offense to the Lord for violating his day. The importance of honoring the Sabbath was reiterated in our day to the Prophet Joseph Smith in revelation from the Lord:

> And that thou mayest more fully keep thyself unspotted from the world, thou shalt go to the house of prayer and offer up thy sacraments upon my holy day.

It should be noted that this is a "thou shalt" command.

> For verily this is a day appointed unto you to rest from your labors, and to pay thy devotions unto the Most High;

> Nevertheless thy vows shall be offered up in righteousness on all days and at all times;

> But remember that on this, the Lord's day, thou shalt offer thine oblations and thy sacraments unto the Most High, confessing thy sins unto thy brethren, and before the Lord.

> And on this day thou shalt do none other thing, only let thy food be prepared with singleness of heart that thy fasting may be perfect, or, in other words, that thy joy may be full. (D&C 59:9-13.)

Note here that while the Lord lays stress upon the importance of the Sabbath day and its proper observance, he requires of his people "righteousness on all days and at all times."

Lovers of Money

The possession of riches does not necessarily constitute sin. But sin may arise in the acquisition and use of wealth. Paul implied this distinction in his statement to Timothy:

> For the love of money is the root of all evil: which while some coveted after, they have erred from the faith, and pierced themselves through with many sorrows.

> But thou, O man of God, flee these things; and follow after righteousness, godliness, faith, love, patience, meekness. (1 Tim. 6:10-11.)

Book of Mormon history eloquently reveals the corrosive effect of the passion for wealth. Each time the people became righteous, they prospered. Then followed the transition from prosperity to wealth, wealth to the love of wealth, then to the love of ease and luxury. They moved then into spiritual inactivity, then to gross sin and wickedness, then on to near destruction by their enemies. This caused them to repent, which brought back righteousness, then prosperity, and the cycle had begun all over again.

Had the people used their wealth for good purposes they could have enjoyed a continuing prosperity. But they seemed unable for a sustained period to be simultaneously wealthy and righteous. For a limited time some people can "hold the line," but they deteriorate spiritually when money is abundant. The writer of Proverbs says:

> A faithful man shall abound with blessings: but he that maketh haste to be rich shall not be innocent. (Prov. 28:20.)

John warned against love for worldly things:

> Love not the world, neither the things that are in the world. If any man love the world, the love of the Father is not in him.
>
> For all that is in the world, the lust of the flesh, and the lust of the eyes, and the pride of life, is not of the Father, but is of the world.
>
> And the world passeth away, and the lust thereof: but he that doeth the will of God abideth for ever. (1 John 2:15-17.)

President Brigham Young expressed his fears that the riches of the world would canker the souls of his people in our own dispensation, when he said:

> Take courage, brethren . . . plow your land and sow wheat, plant your potatoes. . . It is our duty to preach the Gospel, gather Israel, pay our tithing and build temples. The worst fear I have about this people is that they will get rich in this country, forget God and His people, wax fat, and kick themselves out of the Church and go to hell. This people will stand mobbing, robbing, poverty, and all manner of persecution and be true. But my greatest fear is that they cannot stand wealth.

Brigham Young also warned that Latter-day Saints who turn their full attention to money-making soon become cold in their feelings toward the ordinances of the house of God. They neglect their prayers, become unwilling to pay any donations; the law of tithing becomes too great a test for them; and they finally forsake their God. They fall under Jacob's stricture:

> But wo unto the rich, who are rich as to the things of the world. For because they are rich they despise the poor, and they persecute the meek, and their hearts are upon their treasures; wherefore, their treasure is their God. And behold, their treasure shall perish with them also. (2 Ne. 9:30.)

The Lord required the rich young ruler to divest himself of his wealth. (Luke 18:22.) Undoubtedly he read the thoughts of the rich young man and was able to discern that his treasure was his god. The young man seemed willing to do almost anything for the opportunity to serve the Lord and to be exalted — except to give up his riches.

The gracious Creator assures us that the earth and all good things in it are for man.

> . . . The fulness of the earth is yours, the beasts of the field and the fowls of the air, and that which climbeth upon the trees and walketh upon the earth; yea, and the herb, and the good things which come of the earth. . . Yea, all things which come of the earth . . . are made for the benefit and the use of man . . .
>
> And it pleaseth God that he hath given all these things unto man; for unto this end were they made to be used, with judgment, not to excess, neither by extortion. (D&C 59:16-18, 20.)

How gracious and kind of our loving and provident Lord! Clearly he does not delight in poverty or suffering, in want or deprivation. He would want all men to enjoy everything created, if man could only do so without the loss of dependence and worthiness, if he could only prevent himself from straying from the Creator to the creature.

Stealing

The sin of stealing is very much with us in modern America. What an indictment of a people who generally live in plenty! The scripture reads:

> Men do not despise a thief, if he steal to satisfy his soul when he is hungry;
>
> But if he be found, he shall restore sevenfold; he shall give all the substance of his house. (Prov. 6:30-31.)

In some Eastern countries, where poverty is the rule and suffering and starvation a common spectre, some theft and dishonesty can be understood — though not reconciled or excused — but in the Western world where most people are getting the necessities of life and even some luxuries, there is no justification for stealing. Yet robberies are reported constantly in our large cities and thievery is common. Homes must be bolted, cars locked, bicycles chained to trees. Thieves resort to extortion, blackmail, and even kidnapping.

Can anyone truthfully claim that he did not know stealing was wrong? Possessiveness seems to be a basic impulse in humans, but while a child may want other children's toys, he soon comes to know that they are not his. Small thefts grow into larger ones unless the desire is curbed. Parents who "cover up" for their children, excuse them and pay for their misappropriations, miss an important opportunity to teach a lesson and thereby do untold damage to their offspring. If the child is required to return the coin or the pencil or the fruit with an appropriate apology, it is likely that his tendencies to steal will be curbed. But if he is lionized and made a little hero, if his misappropriation is made a joke, he is likely to continue in ever-increasing thefts. Most burglars and hold-up men would not have become so if they had been disciplined early.

The thief generally finds his loot not worth the cost when he is caught and suffers punishment. A man who defrauded his employer's firm of several thousands of dollars and fled, and was hunted almost all the way around the world, finally returned to his home and surrendered himself to the authorities. He was almost penniless. He could not account for his actions, other than that he was too weak to resist the temptation. "No amount of money is worth it, whether it be $10,000 or $10 million," he said. "Almost every hour of every day during the past months I have wanted to stop running," he told the authorities. "You cannot realize the agony of running and running and running and always knowing there is no stopping . . . The price I pay is heavy — all I got out of it wasn't worth the worry and fear, and the humiliation my family has suffered."

This urge to take another's property is exhibited in many forms — theft, bribery, driving hard bargains, evasion of income taxes, extortion, covetousness, greedy court actions, misrepresentations which seek to take something for nothing, and so on. Anyone who practices any such form of dishonesty needs to repent, develop a clear conscience, and be free from fetters, chains, worries, and fears.

Unholy Masters

Paul speaks of "unholy masters" and surely has reference to those who would defraud servants or employees and would not properly compensate for labors done or goods furnished. He likely has in mind men who are unkind, demanding and inconsiderate of their subordinates.

> And, ye masters, do the same things unto them, forbearing threatening: knowing that your Master also is in heaven; neither is there respect of persons with him. (Eph. 6:9.)

In short, the employer should treat his employees according to the golden rule, remembering that there is a Master in heaven who judges both employer and employee. Paul likewise enjoined a lofty standard upon employees:

> Servants, be obedient to them that are your masters according to the flesh . . . in singleness of your heart, as unto Christ;

> Not with eyeservice, as menpleasers; but as the servants of Christ,

> . . . With good will doing service, as to the Lord, and not to men. . . (Eph. 6:5-6.)

We may take this to mean, in modern terms, that the servant and employee should consistently give honest service, full and complete, and do for his employer what he would want an employee to do for him if he himself were the employer. Any other course calls for repentance.

Improvidence

In close relationship to the matters of employers and employees is the sin of being improvident. Man has the moral obligation and responsibility not only of providing for himself and being a profitable servant but also of caring and providing for his own family. "The sluggard will not plow," says Proverbs, "by reason of the cold; therefore shall he beg in harvest, and have nothing." (Prov. 20:4.) Likewise Paul: "But if any provide not for his own, and specially for those of his own house, he hath denied the faith, and is worse than an infidel." (1 Tim. 5:8.)

False Witness

The sin of false witness is committed in many ways. Guilty ones are gossipers and bearers of tales, whisperers, those destitute of truth, liars, quarrelers, deceitful persons. Sometimes these weaknesses are thought of as minor, yet they break hearts, destroy reputations and wreck lives. To such offenders, Paul said:

> Let all bitterness, and wrath, and anger, and clamour, and evil speaking, be put away from you, with all malice:

> And be ye kind one to another, tenderhearted, forgiving one another, even as God for Christ's sake hath forgiven you. (Eph. 4:31-32.)

Included in this group of sinners are those mentioned by Paul: flatterers, double-tongued, slanderers, filthy communicators, those who are envious, spiteful, jealous, bitter, biters and devourers of each other, defilers, revilers, evil speakers, provokers, haters, inventors of evil things, stumbling blocks.

Of course, no one sees himself in this category. It is always the other person who gossips, invents tales, slanders, and is double-tongued. But are not we all guilty to some degree and do not all of us need introspection, self-analysis and then repentance?

People often bear false witness with malicious intent. For instance, election candidates sometimes arrange for the "whisperer," the clever one who makes no formal accusation but by innuendos and half-truths and subtle suggestion quietly undermines an unsuspecting opponent. Often they come on the eve of the election, too late to be answered. Such so-called "mud-slinging" should be beneath the dignity of honorable men. Base emotions like jealousy, covetousness, envy, and vengefulness sometimes prompt the same kind of false accusations in everyday life, which are left to fester while the victim is ignorant of the attack.

Another aspect of false witness is the "debate" — not the formal debate in high school or college forensics but that of the egotist who feels compelled to debate and argue every situation. In politics or religion or any other field he will fight hard and long to gain a point regardless of where truth stands. There are those who argue even the wrong side in order to win the debate, or for a fee.

In the Church we have teachers who develop in a class an argument which they call discussion and, on pretense of getting participation, damage the faith of class members. I heard of one teacher who proposed to his class during a lesson on the divinity of Christ's mission that he, the teacher, would take the position that Christ was an impostor and his work a fake. The class was to defend Christ's divinity. Being so well prepared and with his class taken unawares, the teacher proved by logic that Christ was a fraud — or at least, when the class was dismissed some vital questions were unanswered and the issue was still undetermined. The man loved to debate, to argue. But his witness was false.

With the false witness can be classed the flatterer, the insincere, the liar, the gossip. Of such Isaiah wrote: "Wo unto them that call evil good, and good evil, that put darkness for light, and light for darkness, that put bitter for sweet, and sweet for bitter!" (2 Ne. 15:20.) Such things the Lord hates.

> These six things doth the Lord hate: yea, seven are an abomination unto him:
>
> A proud look, a lying tongue, and hands that shed innocent blood,
>
> An heart that deviseth wicked imaginations, feet that be swift in running to mischief,
>
> A false witness that speaketh lies, and he that soweth discord among brethren. (Prov. 6:16-19.)

One is reminded of what Diogenes said in answer to the question, "What animal has the most disastrous bite?" He replied: "Of tame animals, the flatterer, of wild ones, the slanderer."

Lies and gossip which harm reputations are scattered about by the four winds like the seeds of a ripe dandelion held aloft by a child. Neither the seeds nor the gossip can ever be gathered in. The degree and extent of the harm done by the gossip is inestimable.

Vulgarity

Paul called it filthy communication. In this category of sin could also be foolish talking, profanity, taking the name of the Lord in vain, lewd talking. Would this not also include pornography with its viciousness, its deliberate purpose of defiling youth?

As regards profanity or taking the name of the Lord in vain, the names of Deity should be used only in prayer or in dignified address or speech, and certainly never in needless or careless utterance. To use the usual swear words is bad enough — they brand one as crude and careless — but to use profanely any of the names of our Lord is absolutely inexcusable. Should one ever slip in this way he should repent in "sackcloth and ashes," the same as if he had committed any one of the other serious sins. Closely linked to this cursing is being ungodly, irreverent, profane, idolatrous or blasphemous, denying the Holy Ghost, "speaking evil of dignities."

In the category of taking the name of the Lord in vain, we might include the use by unauthorized persons of the name of Deity in performing ordinances. In modern scripture the Lord warned:

> Wherefore, let all men beware how they take my name in their lips—
>
> For behold, verily I say, that many there be who are under this condemnation, who use the name of the Lord, and use it in vain, having not authority. (D&C 63:61-62.)

Presumptuous and blasphemous are they who purport to baptize, bless, marry, or perform other sacraments in the name of the Lord while in fact lacking his specific authorization. And no one can obtain God's authority from reading the Bible or from just a desire to serve the Lord, no matter how pure his motives.

Word of Wisdom Violation

Drinking is a curse of our day as Paul's writings indicate it was in his day. To drink the forbidden alcoholic beverages is a sin for us who have made covenants with God and have been commanded to abstain. No one will ever become an alcoholic who never breaks the law of the Lord concerning drinking.

As in the days of Noah, we are "eating and drinking, marrying and giving in marriage." (Matt. 24:38.) Our numerous dinners and banquets are often spiced with liquor, on which fellowship and entertaining depend so completely in some circles. Liquor is common in train and plane. To many, the cocktail hour is indispensable. Service clubs, business organizations, and government budgets provide for it.

What an indictment when social life in courts and banquet halls and embassies is centered around alcohol, and when deals and even treaties are consummated over a liquor serving! How barren the host who can entertain only by serving liquor to guests, and how desolate the guest who cannot have a good time without liquor!

Drinking curses all whom it touches — the seller and the buyer and the consumer. It brings deprivation and sorrow to numerous innocent ones. It is associated with graft, immorality, gambling, fraud, gangsterism, and most other vices. In its wake come wasted money, deprived families, deteriorated bodies, reduced minds, numerous accidents. It has everything against it, nothing for it, yet states sell it and receive revenue from it, and it has become an accepted "normal" part of modern life.

Using this tool of Satan is especially a sin to all Latter-day Saints who know the law of the Word of Wisdom. Given as a Word of Wisdom and not by commandment in 1833, it was declared a commandment in 1851 by a prophet of God. It should be considered in that light and, if violated, repented of as with other sins of major seriousness. The poison, bad enough itself, is secondary to the disobedience of the commands of God. To know the law and not abide by it, is sin. The Redeemer warned:

> And take heed to yourselves, lest at any time your hearts be overcharged with surfeiting, and drunkenness, and cares of this life, and so that day come upon you unawares. (Luke 21:34.)

Relative to using tobacco, the Lord revealed in 1833:

> And again, tobacco is not for the body, neither for the belly, and is not good for man, but is an herb for bruises and all sick cattle... (D&C 89:8.)

This is categorical. In recent years science has established to the satisfaction of all reasonable men that tobacco is injurious to man's health. Common sense forbids its use. Much more important, the use of it by members of the Lord's Church is in violation of the commands of God and should be repented of as with other serious sins.

The use of tea and coffee also is forbidden by the Lord, and true followers of the Master will greatly desire to please him by living this and all his commandments. In addition to those items specifically covered in the Word of Wisdom, wise people will avoid other destructive substances. The world may say that smoking and social drinking and tea and coffee are normal, but thanks be to the Lord that in this case, as in many others, the Church of the Lord has different "norms."

Drug Habits

Often more injurious even than the costly, harmful and obnoxious practice of drinking is the drug habit. The stories of the "dope racket" found in our newspapers and magazines are shocking. One report showed that New York City had thousands of teen-age drug addicts. Despite local, national, and international efforts to curb the distribution of such narcotics, a U. S. Senate crime investigating committee found such drugs easy to get in most of the nation's cities.

One should shun this habit as he would any deadly plague. Young people as well as older ones should beware of tampering with such injurious habits as glue-sniffing, taking LSD, smoking marijuana cigarettes, and so on. These are not only sinful in and of themselves, but will lead to more serious drug habits and to the addict's spiritual, moral, and physical downfall. All such narcotic habits should be repented of and ever after shunned. Even sleeping pills, tranquilizers and such which were thought to be harmless have sometimes brought injury and death; these might well be limited or avoided and, if used at all, taken only under the strict supervision of a reputable physician.

Covenantbreakers

Akin to many of the other sins is that of the covenant-breaker. The person baptized promises to keep all the laws and commandments of God. He has partaken of the sacrament and re-pledged his allegiance and his fidelity, promising and covenanting that he will keep all God's laws. Numerous folks have gone to the temples and have re-covenanted that they would live all the commandments of God, keep their lives clean, devoted, worthy, and serviceable. Yet many there are who forget their covenants and break the commandments, sometimes deliberately tempting the faithful away with them.

Of those who break covenants and promises made in sacred places and in solemn manner, we can apply the Lord's words as follows:

> . . . a wicked man, who has set at naught the counsels of God, and has broken the most sacred promises which were made before God, and has depended upon his own judgment and boasted in his own wisdom. (D&C 3:12-13.)

Haters of God

Another of the sins named by Paul is committed by "haters of God." To hate God is the direct antithesis of the commandment, "Thou shalt have no others gods before me." Many men become haughty when they get a little smattering of knowledge and they rationalize themselves out of their belief in God. Since all that we have to enjoy and profit by comes from the true and living God, any who have become estranged from their Lord, even in the slightest, have a need for deep repentance to bring about a reconciliation with him.

Paul fiercely denounced those who "served the creature more than the Creator," the "haters of God." There were in those days, as today and among our own people, groups who deny "the Lord that bought them" with his own blood, and yet claim membership in his Church and in their hypocrisy and egotism pretend allegiance. There are those who receive the benefits of the Church while not only failing to make any contributions to it but actually being destructive of it and its standards. Those hypocritical unbelievers use their powers to destroy rather than to build up.

Ingratitude

Ingratitude is a distressing sin which kindles the Lord's anger. (See D&C 59:21.) It is often manifest in "disobedience to parents," which Paul condemns. Many young people demand and receive much from parents and then show little or no gratitude, as though the parents owed it to them without any consideration or appreciation on their part. There must have been children in Paul's day who thanklessly took for granted their many blessings and opportunities, for he continued to warn the saints at Rome and others against this weakness.

When the Savior healed the ten lepers and only one thanked him, he pointed out the nine ingrates as a lesson to all when he said, "Were there not ten cleansed?" (Luke 17:17.) Adults as well as the youth are often guilty, being disobedient and unthankful to their Heavenly Father who gives them all. Many fail to show their gratitude through service, through family prayers, through the payment of their tithes, and in numerous other ways God has a right to expect.

Unmercifulness

Lack of mercy also is a weakness of serious proportions. Paul linked it with many of the sins we generally regard as more serious. The Lord said, "Blessed are the merciful: for they shall obtain mercy." (Matt. 5:7.) He underlined the point with the parable of the unmerciful servant who, though forgiven ten thousand talents of debt, would not forgive his own debtor who owed him but a hundred pence. The penalty for his harshness was very severe. (Matt. 18:23-35.)

Anger

Paul warns against the wrathful — those who become angered when things go wrong. When they are released from Church positions, they sometimes become angry and will not return to other service but pout and complain and are fiercely critical of all that is done by those who have offended them. Sometimes their anger reaches implacable hatred and bitterness, and they and their loved ones suffer in faith and activity, and sometimes in membership and salvation. There are many who might today have been active and faithful in the Church but who are on the outside because some progenitor — a father, a grandfather or great-grandfather — became embittered and apostatized.

God Abhors Sin

"These six things doth the Lord hate." Yes, because they are sins he hates them. For the same reason he hates all the transgressions discussed in this chapter, and all others too. Athough he loves the sinner, he "cannot look upon sin with the least degree of allowance." (D&C 1:31.) As sinners we will better appreciate his love and kindness if similar abhorrence for sin impels us to transform our lives through repentance.

Chapter Five

The Sin Next to Murder

> *. . . These things are an abomination in the sight of the Lord; yea, most abominable above all sins save it be the shedding of innocent blood or denying the Holy Ghost.*
>
> —Alma 39:5

THERE ARE SINS WHICH ARE SO SERIOUS THAT WE know of no forgiveness for them. These we will discuss in greater detail in a later chapter. There are also sins which approach the unforgivable ones in seriousness but seem to come in the category of the forgivable. These are the diabolical crimes of sexual impurity. In varied form they run from aberrations involving self-abuse, sex stimulation, and self-pollution to abhorrent and unnatural practices involving others. Whether named or unnamed in scriptures or the spoken word, any sexual act or practice which is "unnatural" or unauthorized is a sin.

It is unfortunate that Church leaders must discuss these sins of corruption but they would be under condemnation if they failed to warn and forewarn and protect and fortify. To educate the people in moral matters certainly is the duty of the spiritual advisers even though it is often repugnant and unpleasant. As in previous ages, God's people must never be left with the excuse that they did not know.

Sexual Sin Defiles

Transgression and uncleanness and filth are found in all sexual sins. In clarifying a parable, the Savior said:

> . . . Out of the heart of men, proceed evil thoughts, adulteries, fornications, murders,
>
> Thefts, covetousness, wickedness, deceit, lasciviousness, an evil eye, blasphemy, pride, foolishness:
>
> All these evil things come from within, and defile the man. (Mark 7:21-23.)

It is not the soil of earth or the grease on a person's hands that defile him; nor is it the fingernails "edged in black," the accumulated perspiration from honest toil, or the body odor resulting from heavy work. One may bathe hourly, perfume oneself often, have hair shampooed frequently, have fingernails manicured daily, and be a master at soft-spoken utterances, and still be as filthy as hell's cesspools. What defiles is sin, and especially sexual sin.

Next to Murder in Seriousness

The enormity of this sin is underlined by numerous scriptures, and particularly by Alma's words to his immoral son:

> Know ye not, my son, that these things are an abomination in the sight of the Lord; yea, most abominable above all sins save it be the shedding of innocent blood or denying the Holy Ghost? (Al. 39:5.)

The Lord apparently rates adultery close to premeditated murder, for he said: "And again, I command thee that thou shalt not covet thy neighbor's wife; nor seek thy neighbor's life." (D&C 19:25.)

To a young man seeking help who had allowed himself to indulge heavily in fornication but was not quite yet repentant, I wrote:

> . . . Your sin is the most serious thing you could have done in your youth this side of murder. . . . Your last experience in immorality was far more obnoxious than the first. You had been to the temple and had made solemn vows of chastity before God and holy angels. You made covenant that you would never have such ungodly relations. You had already done it and then did it again with that solemn promise on your lips. . . .

The grievousness of the sin enhances the difficulty of repenting. Sometimes offenders reach the point of no return and cannot repent, for the Spirit of the Lord will not always strive with man. Esau sold his birthright for "one morsel of meat." Many young people sell their birthrights or put them in serious jeopardy for one hour in dark places, one unwarranted thrill, one exciting experience in a car or in a harlot's bed. One sad experience may not totally destroy, for repentance is in order, but one experience of fornication can break down the bars, blast and scar a life, and start a soul on a lifetime of regret and anguish.

Dangers to Youth

This area of conduct presents a tremendous temptation, especially to the youth of this age of loose talk and loose action on college campuses and elsewhere which favor pre-marital sex experience. How can one believe deeply in God and his scriptures and yield to unchastity? It is wholly wrong. President David O. McKay has pleaded:

> . . . Your virtue is worth more than your life. Please, young folk, preserve your virtue even if you lose your lives. Do not tamper with sin . . . do not permit yourselves to be led into temptation. Conduct yourselves seemly and with due regard, particularly you young boys, to the sanctity of womanhood. Do not pollute it.

Another modern prophet, President Heber J. Grant, has stressed the Word of Wisdom in this connection, not merely for its intrinsic importance but because of what it often leads to.

> Nearly always those who lose their chastity first partake of those things that excite passions within them or lower their resistance and becloud their minds. Partaking of tobacco and liquor is calculated to make them a prey to those things which, if indulged in, are worse than death itself. There is no true Latter-day Saint who would not rather bury a son or a daughter than to have him or her lose his or her chastity — realizing that chastity is of more value than anything else in all the world.[1]

---

[1] Heber J. Grant, *Gospel Standards,* compiled by G. Homer Durham (Improvement Era, 1941), p. 55.

The Apostle Paul taught continence for the unmarried. "For I would that all men were even as I myself . . . I say therefore to the unmarried and widows, It is good for them if they abide even as I." (1 Cor. 7:7-8.) Taking such statements in conjunction with others he made it is clear that he is not talking about celibacy, but is urging the normal and controlled sex living in marriage and total continence outside marriage. (There is no real evidence that Paul was never married, as some students claim, and there are in fact indications to the contrary.)

Premarital heterosexual intercourse is usually in the category of fornication — which is illicit sexual intercourse between the unmarried. Adultery is usually defined as this act when committed by married people other than with their respective marriage partners. The Bible seems often to use the terms *adultery* and *fornication* interchangeably.

The sin of fornication is well known, and the scriptures from beginning to end decry this act of defilement. Yet many modern writers, even those of prominence and including some ministers of religion, have stated that there could be no harm if two consenting parties engage in premarital sexual experience. Our civilization is certain to disintegrate, however, when a practice like this moves toward being universal. No nation can long continue to exist on such an irresponsible philosophy. Broken homes, illegitimacy, venereal diseases, and emotional disturbances connected with such developments are certainly not the exclusive concern of "two consenting adults." The Lord knew this and gave commandments accordingly, and all rationalizations contrary to these are sinfully wrong.

Yet we have too many young people in the Church who do not give God's law on physical intimacy its proper priority. One survey revealed that seven out of nine girls who lost their virtue suffered that loss in cars after dances and parties. In another survey, in which seminary teachers asked students to place certain commandments of the Lord in the order of their importance, the Word of Wisdom placed first and chastity fifth. Yet another survey showed that ten of twelve students had petted to the point that they considered their virtue lost. It is hoped that these surveys were not typical of all of our youth.

Many rationalize that this attraction of two unmarried people is love, and they seek thereby to justify their intimate relations. This is one of the most false of all of Satan's lies. It is lust, not love, which brings men and women to fornication and adultery. No person would injure one he truly loves, and sexual sin can only result in injury.

The importance of continence in the unmarried is underlined by the divine approval given it in the vision to John the Revelator, in which he saw the Lamb of God standing on Mount Sion and with him 144,000 having the Father's name written in their foreheads. Of these the voice from heaven said: "These are they which were not defiled with women; for they are virgins . . . and in their mouth was found no guile: for they are without fault before the throne of God." (Rev. 14:4-5.)

Steps to Fornication

Among the most common sexual sins our young people commit are necking and petting. Not only do these improper relations often lead to fornication, pregnancy, and abortions — all ugly sins — but in and of themselves they are pernicious evils, and it is often difficult for youth to distinguish where one ends and another begins. They awaken lust and stir evil thoughts and sex desires. They are but parts of the whole family of related sins and indiscretions. Paul wrote as if to modern young people who deceive themselves that their necking and petting are but expressions of love: "Wherefore God also gave them up to uncleanness through the lusts of their own hearts, to dishonour their own bodies between themselves." (Rom. 1:

24.) How could the evils of petting be more completely described?

Too often, young people dismiss their petting with a shrug of their shoulders as a *little* indiscretion, while admitting that fornication is a base transgression. Too many of them are shocked, or feign to be, when told that what they have done in the name of petting was in reality fornication. The dividing line is a thin, blurry one, and Paul probably referred to these sins ranging from petting to fornication when he said: "For it is a shame even to speak of those things which are done of them in secret." (Eph. 5:12.) And the Lord perhaps was referring to this evil when in our own time he was reiterating the Ten Commandments: ". . . Neither commit adultery, nor kill, nor do anything like unto it." (D&C 59:6.)

Our young people should know that their partners in sin will not love or respect them if they have freedom in fondling their bodies. Such a practice destroys respect, not only for the other person but for self. It destroys the ultimate respect for virtue. And it ignores the oft-repeated prophetic warning that one should give his or her life rather than to yield to loss of virtue.

Too many have lost themselves completely in sin through this doorway of necking and petting. The devil knows how to destroy our young girls and boys. He may not be able to tempt a person to murder or to commit adultery immediately, but he knows that if he can get a boy and a girl to sit in the car late enough after the dance, or to park long enough in the dark at the end of the lane, the best boy and the best girl will finally succumb and fall. He knows that all have a limit to their resistance.

Those who have received the Holy Ghost after baptism certainly know that all bodily contacts of this kind are pernicious and abominable. They recognize too that the God of yesterday, today, and tomorrow continues to demand continence and to require that people come to the marriage altar as virgins, clean and free from sex experience.

Almost like twins, "petting" — and especially "heavy petting" — and fornication are alike. Also like twins, the one precedes the other, but most of the same characteristics are there. The same passions are aroused and, with but slight difference, similar bodily contacts are made. And from it are likely to come the same frustrations, sorrows, anguish, and remorse.

All those who have slipped into the disgraceful and most reprehensible habit of transgressing through petting should immediately change their lives, their habits, and their thought patterns, repent sorely in "sackcloth and ashes," and by confession get so far as possible a clearance from the Lord and the leaders of his Church so that a measure of peace may accompany them through their lives. To those who have been properly taught and who have properly appraised the evils and have restrained and protected themselves from these foul acts, God bless them and help them to continue their virginity and cleanness, that they may never have the remorse and anguish which has or will come to their brothers and sisters who have indulged.

The Curse of Adultery

Through Moses came the solemn command, "Thou shalt not commit adultery." (Ex. 20:14.) This act between married people is a most heinous transgression, so serious that it has been the subject of sermons by prophets and leaders in all gospel dispensations. The death penalty was exacted for it in the days of Israel, as it was also for many of the sex sins so common in today's society. Perhaps in no other way could such sin be controlled. Generations of slavery had not helped Israel much in climbing toward exaltation. They were weak and needed to be disciplined. In all the lands into which they came they found the same cursed practices — idolatry and adultery, intermingled and closely related. "The adulterer and the adulteress shall surely be put to death." (Lev. 20:10.)

Apparently the death penalty was still on the law books in the days of Christ, for the scribes and Pharisees brought to the Lord the woman taken in adultery, seeking to trap him. They said Moses had commanded that such a person should be stoned to death, and asked him what he had to say of the matter. With his usual sublime understanding he put the tempters to rout and sent the woman to repent of her sin. (See John 8:1-11.)

James E. Talmage wrote:

> . . . The woman's accusers were "convicted by their own conscience"; shamed and in disgrace they slunk away. . . . They knew themselves to be unfit to appear either as accusers or judges. . . . "When Jesus had lifted up himself, and saw none but the woman, he said unto her, Woman, where are those thine accusers? hath no man condemned thee? She said, No man, Lord. And Jesus said unto her, Neither do I condemn thee: go, and sin no more."[2]

Note that the Lord did not forgive the woman of her serious sin. He commanded quietly, but forcefully, "Go, and sin no more." Even Christ cannot forgive one in sin. The woman had neither time nor opportunity to repent totally. When her preparation and repentance were complete she could hope for forgiveness, but not before then.

According to a celebrated statistic quoted in a magazine article, more than half the nation's married men and over a quarter of its married women are untrue to their marriage vows. They are guilty of the notorious sin of adultery, which is encouraged by the approval and the "fun" image given to it in movies and on television. The article spoke of fifteen million divorced persons living in the United States and said there are 400,000 new divorces annually, creating 800,000 more divorced persons. Of these millions of divorced persons, many are opportunists and are on the prowl. Millions of married people, many of them unhappy, are the victims. Since divorce is often hard, inconvenient, or slow to get, impatient ones commit adultery; thus more

---

[2]James E. Talmage, *Jesus the Christ* (Salt Lake City: Deseret Book Co., 1962), p. 406.

homes are broken, more unhappy families result, and the population of divorced men and women climbs constantly.

Some point to the 400,000 new divorces annually and see this as dramatic evidence of the sexual needs of the couples concerned. They note that many live the double life because they find that supporting a second family is intolerable, so the illegal romances go forward and the marriages stand as unhappy ones. But whatever the rationalizations and arguments, there are no circumstances which justify adultery. Regardless of what the world does, The Church of Jesus Christ of Latter-day Saints must continue to fortify its people against sin and to stand firm for total fidelity and solid home and family life.

Warning to Working Wives

A word of warning is in order about wives going out to work. They leave their husbands each day and work often in the presence of other men where they are exposed to flirtations, displays of interest and affection, and confidences — all in a situation freed from family concerns and thus inducing the relaxation in which romantic attractions can develop. This setup can be fraught with danger to the home.

Of course it is recognized that some widows and occasionally wives with families at home must work to support their families. But this ought not to be done where avoidable. Mothers of unmarried children should come home and, where necessary, let standards of living and luxury reduce to a point where the salary of the husband will suffice. The numerous luxuries are far too costly when a marriage and children's welfare are on the scales. The point is underlined in a sermon by Elder Boyd K. Packer:

> . . . I would go back to the home that has a mother there. . . . I ask you . . . what good is a big picture window and the lavish appointments and the priceless decor in a home if there is no mother there? The mother as a mother, not as a breadwinner, is an essential figure in this battle against immorality and wicked-

ness. I would also go back to the family where children were
accountable and where father was the head of the family.

Would you think me naive if I were to propose that this
battle ultimately will be won on such simple grounds as the children coming in after school to homemade bread and jam and
Mama there? Or on such grounds as Daddy and Mama taking
their youngsters to Sacrament meeting? Or that tender hug as
they are put to bed and Daddy and Mama saying, "We need
you in this family. You are a part of us, no matter what your
troubles are, you can come home."

Avoid Even the Thought

The final act of adultery is not the only sin. For any
man or woman to begin to share affection or romantic interest with any other than the spouse is an almost certain
approach to ultimate adultery. There must be no romantic
interest, attention, dating, or flirtation of any kind with
anyone so long as either of the participating people is still
legally married, regardless of the status of that marriage.
Indeed, even the thought of adultery is sinful, as Jesus
emphasized:

> Ye have heard that it was said by them of old time, Thou
> shalt not commit adultery:
>
> But I say unto you, That whosoever looketh on a woman
> to lust after her hath committed adultery with her already in
> his heart. (Matt. 5:27-28.)

And again, when Jesus amplified this thought to the
Nephites:

> Behold, I give unto you a commandment, that ye suffer none
> of these things to enter into your heart;
>
> For it is better that ye should deny yourselves of these things
> . . . than that ye should be cast into hell. (3 Ne. 12:29-30.)

The Adulteress

One of the most inspiring of the Old Testament stories
is the experience of our ancestor, Joseph — a youth who
set a great example to young and old. He stood tall and
stalwart as he resisted his evil temptress. Exerting the wiles

of a wicked, voluptuous woman, displaying all her advantages of high station, beauty, and political power, she did everything she could to attract the handsome young leader. When all else failed she attempted force and intimidation and blackmail. But Joseph stood his ground. He refused to yield to her pleadings. Her clothing, or lack of it, her perfumes, her sexy advances, her pleadings — all these bombarded a clean young man willing to suffer any penalty in order to keep his virtue. When all her womanly wiles failed, and he attempted to escape from her, she held to his clothes and tore them off his body. With lies of deceit she reported the incident, reversing the guilt to him. Joseph was thrown into prison to suffer unjustly for the very crime he had resisted to the end. (See Gen. 39.)

Long afterwards, the writer of the Proverbs, knowing that this type of woman exists in all generations of time, warned man against her.

> Lust not after her beauty in thine heart; neither let her take thee with her eyelids.
>
> For by means of a whorish woman a man is brought to a piece of bread: and the adulteress will hunt for the precious life.
>
> Can a man take fire in his bosom, and his clothes not be burned?
>
> Can one go upon hot coals, and his feet not be burned?
>
> So he that goeth in to his neighbour's wife; whosoever toucheth her shall not be innocent. (Prov. 6:25-29.)

And again the wise Solomon warned:

> And, behold, there met him a woman with the attire of an harlot, and subtil of heart.
>
> So she caught him, and kissed him, and with an impudent face said unto him,
>
> I have decked my bed with coverings of tapestry, with carved works, with fine linen of Egypt.
>
> I have perfumed my bed with myrrh, aloes, and cinnamon.
>
> Come, let us take our fill of love until the morning: let us solace ourselves with loves.
>
> For the goodman is not at home, he is gone a long journey:

With her much fair speech she caused him to yield, with the flattering of her lips she forced him.

He goeth after her straightway, as an ox goeth to the slaughter. . . .

. . . As a bird hasteth to the snare, and knoweth not that it is for his life.

. . . Many strong men have been slain by her.

Her house is the way to hell, going down to the chambers of death. (Prov. 7:10, 13, 16-19, 21-23, 26-27.)

How much double standard was tolerated in those days we do not know, but certainly today there is no such double standard in the eyes of God, and men are often the greater offenders. Every man who compromises with decency and commits the heinous crimes will be dealt with by the Lord as severely as will the woman. And be it remembered that even though the blow often seems to fall most heavily upon the woman, no man will escape the total penalties of suffering and torture and remorse and deprivations.

Excommunication the Penalty

For the benefit of Latter-day Saints the Lord has given us a direct and well-defined statement on adultery.

. . . If a man receiveth a wife in the new and everlasting covenant, and if she be with another man, and I have not appointed unto her by the holy anointing, she hath committed adultery and shall be destroyed.

If she be not in the new and everlasting covenant, and she be with another man, she has comitted adultery.

And if her husband be with another woman, and he was under a vow, he hath broken his vow and hath committed adultery. (D&C 132:41-43.)

The penalty in this life is similarly clearly defined:

Thou shalt not commit adultery; and he that committeth adultery, and repenteth not, shall be cast out. (D&C 42:24.)

To be "cast out" is to be excommunicated. Excommunication hangs over the head of the adulterer on a very

tiny thread, like Damocles' sword. The sin is forgivable
providing the repentance is sufficiently comprehensive.
"But if he doeth it again, he shall not be forgiven, but shall
be cast out." (D&C 42:26.)

Love in Marriage

No men or women will bring on themselves this blight
of adultery if they will strictly keep the law which follows:

> Thou shalt love thy wife [husband] with *all* thy heart, and
> shalt cleave unto her [him] and none else. (D&C 42:22. Italics
> added.)

There are many aspects to love in marriage, and sex
is an important one. Just as married partners are not for
others, they *are* for each other. Paul knew the approaches
to adultery and the ways to avoid them:

> . . . Let every man have his own wife, and let every woman
> have her own husband.
>
> Let the husband render unto the wife due benevolence: and
> likewise also the wife unto the husband.
>
> The wife hath not power of her own body, but the husband:
> and likewise also the husband hath not power of his own body,
> but the wife.
>
> Defraud ye not one the other, except it be with consent for a
> time, that ye may give yourselves to fasting and prayer; and come
> together again, that Satan tempt you not for your incontinency.
> (1 Cor. 7:2-5.)

Even though sex can be an important and satisfactory part of married life, we must remember that life
is not designed just for sex. Even marriage does not make
proper certain extremes in sexual indulgence. To the
Ephesian saints Paul begged for propriety in marriage: "So
ought men to love their wives as their own bodies. He that
loveth his wife loveth himself." (Eph. 5:28.) And perhaps
the Lord's condemnation included secret sexual sins in
marriage, when he said: ". . . And those who are not pure,
and have said they were pure, shall be destroyed, saith the
Lord God." (D&C 132:52.)

Speaking of normal and controlled sex life in marriage, President J. Reuben Clark said in his address to the MIA Conference in 1954:

> You newlyweds have gone into the House of the Lord, you have been sealed with the holy spirit of promise. You, groom, have the priesthood. Through that sealing your bride has the blessings of the priesthood, not the priesthood itself. By virtue of the fact that you have the priesthood, you become the head of the family. What kind of a head of a family are you going to be? If I might make a very trite statement, the bride has not become your chattel by marriage to you; she is a complement of you in the family. For that purpose, she was created, that the two of you might go forward in a life that shall answer to the commandment given to you when you were married, "Multiply and replenish the earth," one of the great commandments given to Adam in the beginning. . . .

> If you will observe, you grooms, that one principle, it will tend to bring into your home more of happiness and contentment and peace than any other one thing of which I can think. How are you going to be the head of the family? You should be the head of the family in patience, in forbearance, in forgiveness, in kindness, in courtesy, in consideration, in respect and in all the other Christian virtues. You should be the head of the family in devotion and loyalty. If you are that kind of a head of a family, there will be nothing but happiness even as they bring further responsibilities.

In this comment President Clark was emphasizing the position of the husband. It goes almost without saying that the wife has responsibilities of equal importance to be a kind, considerate helpmeet to her husband.

Choose Righteousness and Peace

It is well to remember that, awful, horrible and serious as adultery and other sexual sins are, the Lord has kindly provided forgiveness on condition of repentance commensurate with the sin. But where these sins are concerned, even more than with less grievous ones, prevention is so much better than cure. Being warned, let us keep well away from the first step — the romantic thought outside of our marriage relationship, the drink which dulls the judgment and releases the inhibitions, the boy-and-girl "talk" in the parked car after the dance, and so on.

Preventing sexual and other sins will put us ultimately in the blessed condition Alma described:

> And may the Lord bless you, and keep your garments spotless, that ye may at last be brought to sit down with Abraham, Isaac, and Jacob, and the holy prophets who have been ever since the world began, having your garments spotless even as their garments are spotless, in the kingdom of heaven to go no more out. (Al. 7:25.)

With this as the long-term goal, and with the assurance of peace of mind in this life, all the best motivations are on the side of righteousness.

Chapter Six

Crime Against Nature

> *. . . Their women did change the natural use into that which is against nature:*
>
> *And likewise also the men, leaving the natural use of the woman, burned in their lust one toward another; men with men working that which is unseemly. . .*
>
> —Romans 1:26-27

MOST YOUTH COME INTO CONTACT EARLY WITH MASTURBATION. Many would-be authorities declare that it is natural and acceptable, and frequently young men I interview cite these advocates to justify their practice of it. To this we must respond that the world's norms in many areas — drinking, smoking, and sex experience generally, to mention only a few — depart increasingly from God's law. The Church has a different, higher norm.

Thus prophets anciently and today condemn masturbation. It induces feelings of guilt and shame. It is detrimental to spirituality. It indicates slavery to the flesh, not that mastery of it and the growth toward godhood which is the object of our mortal life. Our modern prophet has indicated that no young man should be called on a mission who is not free from this practice.

While we should not regard this weakness as the heinous sin which some other sexual practices are, it is of itself bad enough to require sincere repentance. What is more, it too often leads to grievous sin, even to that sin against nature, homosexuality. For, done in private, it evolves often into mutual masturbation — practiced with another person of the same sex — and thence into total homosexuality.

Sin of the Ages

Homosexuality is an ugly sin, repugnant to those who find no temptation in it, as well as to many past offenders who are seeking a way out of its clutches. It is embarrassing and unpleasant as a subject for discussion but because of its prevalence, the need to warn the uninitiated, and the desire to help those who may already be involved with it, it is discussed in this chapter.

This perversion is defined as "sexual desire for those of the same sex or sexual relations between individuals of the same sex," whether men or women. It is a sin of the ages. It was present in Israel's wandering days as well as after and before. It was tolerated by the Greeks. It was prevalent in decaying Rome. The ancient cities of Sodom and Gomorrah are symbols of wretched wickedness more especially related to this perversion, as the incident of Lot's visitors indicates. (See Gen. 19:5.) So degenerate had Sodom become that not ten righteous people could be found (see Gen. 18:23-32), and the Lord had to destroy it. But the revolting practice has persisted. As far back as Henry the Eighth this vice was referred to as *the abominable and detestable crime against nature.* Some of our own statutes have followed that apt and descriptive wording.

Sin in sex practices tends to have a "snowballing" effect. As the restraints fall away, Satan incites the carnal man to ever-deepening degeneracy in his search for excitement until in many instances he is lost to any former considerations of decency. Thus it is that through the ages, perhaps as an extension of homosexual practices, men and women have sunk even to seeking sexual satisfactions with animals.

Unnatural and Wrong

All such deviations from normal, proper heterosexual relationships are not merely unnatural but wrong in the sight of God. Like adultery, incest, and bestiality they carried the death penalty under the Mosaic law.

> If a man also lie with mankind, as he lieth with a woman, both of them have committed an abomination: they shall surely be put to death. . . .
>
> And if a man lie with a beast, he shall surely be put to death: and ye shall slay the beast.
>
> And if a woman approach unto any beast, and lie down thereto, thou shalt kill the woman, and the beast: they shall surely be put to death. . . . (Lev. 20:13, 15-16.)

The law is less severe now, and so regrettably is the community's attitude to these grave sins — another evidence of the deterioration of society. In some countries the act *per se* is not even illegal. This "liberalizing" process is reflected in the United States by communities of homosexuals in our larger cities who demand acceptance of their deviate beliefs and practices as "normal," who sponsor demonstrations and draw up petitions to this end, who are formally organized, and who even print their own perverted journals. All this is done in the open, to the detriment alike of impressionable minds, susceptible urges, and our national decency.

But let us emphasize that right and wrong, righteousness and sin, are not dependent upon man's interpretations, conventions and attitudes. Social acceptance does not change the status of an act, making wrong into right. If all the people in the world were to accept homosexuality, as it seems to have been accepted in Sodom and Gomorrah, the practice would still be deep, dark sin.

Those who would claim that the homosexual is a third sex and that there is nothing wrong in such associations can hardly believe in God or in his scriptures. If God did not exist, such an unnatural and improper practice might be viewed differently, but one could never justify it while accepting the holy scriptures.

> That which breaketh a law, and abideth not by law, but seeketh to become a law unto itself, and willeth to abide in sin, and altogether abideth in sin, cannot be sanctified by law, neither by mercy, justice, nor judgment. Therefore, they must remain filthy still. (D&C 88:35.)

Paul pinpointed the problem relating to all sexual sins and perversions when he wrote:

> Know ye not that ye are the temple of God, and that the Spirit of God dwelleth in you.
>
> If any man defile the temple of God, him shall God destroy; for the temple of God is holy, which temple ye are. (1 Cor. 3:16-17.)

Threat to Family Life

Of the adverse social effects of homosexuality none is more significant than the effect on marriage and home. The normal, God-given sexual relationship is the procreative act between man and woman in honorable marriage. It was so expressed and commanded to the first man and woman on the earth:

> So God created man in his own image, in the image of God created he him; male and female created he them.
>
> And God blessed them, and God said unto them, Be fruitful, and multiply, and replenish the earth. . . . (Gen. 1:27-28.)
>
> Therefore shall a man leave his father and his mother, and shall cleave unto his wife; and they shall be one flesh. (Moses 3:24.)

Marriage is ordained of God to men, and Paul tells Timothy that those who forbid to marry have departed from the faith and have given heed to seducing spirits and doctrines of devils. (1 Tim. 4:1,3.) "Neither is the man without the woman, neither the woman without the man, in the Lord." (1 Cor. 11:11.) The concept has been reiterated in our own dispensation:

> And again, verily I say unto you, that whoso forbiddeth to marry is not ordained of God, for marriage is ordained of God unto man.

> Wherefore, it is lawful that he should have one wife, and they twain shall be one flesh, and all this that the earth might answer the end of its creation. (D&C 49:15-17.)

The institution of marriage is further elevated in the 132nd Section of the Doctrine and Covenants, wherein the Lord makes clear that only through the eternal union of man and woman can they achieve eternal life. As an example, he says that the wife is given to the man "to multiply and replenish the earth, according to my commandment, and to fulfil the promise which was given by my Father before the foundation of the world, and for their exaltation in the eternal worlds, that they may bear the souls of men; for herein is the work of my Father continued, that he may be glorified." (D&C 132:63.) Such references of course relate to celestial marriage.

In this context, where stands the perversion of homosexuality? Clearly it is hostile to God's purpose in that it negates his first and great commandment to "multiply and replenish the earth." If the abominable practice became universal it would depopulate the earth in a single generation. It would nullify God's great program for his spirit children in that it would leave countless unembodied spirits in the heavenly world without the chance for the opportunities of mortality and would deny to all the participants in the practice the eternal life God makes available to us all.

As Grievous as Adultery

Because of the seriousness of this sin it carries a heavy penalty for the unrepentant. The offender may realize that disfellowshipment or excommunication is the penalty for heavy petting, adultery, fornication and comparable sins if there is not adequate repentance, yet he often supposes that because his acts have not been committed with the opposite sex he is not in sin. Let it therefore be clearly stated that the seriousness of the sin of homosexuality is equal to or greater than that of fornication or adultery; and that *the Lord's Church will as readily take action to disfellowship or excommunicate the unrepentant practicing homosexual as it will the unrepentant fornicator or adulterer.*

Church Program for Assistance

Recognizing the seriousness of this problem in modern society and the need which offenders have to be assisted back to normal living, the Church has appointed two of its General Authorities to help on a Church level. Under the direction of the two Brethren many have been helped in faraway places, as well as in areas near the Church headquarters, through the bishops and stake presidents concerned. The success of this rehabilitation program has become known to the police, the courts and the judges, who refer many cases directly to the two Brethren, sometimes on a probation basis.

Curable and Forgivable — With Effort

After consideration of the evil aspects, the ugliness and prevalence of the evil of homosexuality, the glorious thing to remember is that it is curable and forgivable. The Lord has promised that all sins can be forgiven except certain ones enumerated, and this evil was not among those named. Thus it is forgivable if totally abandoned and if the repentance is sincere and absolute. Certainly it can be overcome, for there are numerous happy people who were once involved in its clutches and who have since completely transformed their lives. Therefore to those who say that this practice or any other evil is incurable, I respond: "How can you say the door cannot be opened until your knuckles are bloody, till your head is bruised, till your muscles are sore? It can be done."

Of course it is not to be had merely for the asking. It involves mastering self. Plato had a word to say on this: "The first and greatest victory is to conquer yourself; to be conquered by yourself is of all things most shameful and vile."

Our ills are usually of our own begetting. They must be corrected by ourselves. Man is the master of his destiny, be it good or bad. Man has the inherent capacity to heal himself physically. A doctor may cleanse a wound, sew it up, bandage it well, but the natural power of the body must do the healing. Likewise, a healing process in the spirit and mind must come from within — from self-will. Others may help to cauterize the wound, suture it, and provide a clean, proper environment for the healing, but the body, with the aid of the Spirit, must heal itself. Accordingly some totally conquer homosexuality in a few months, others linger on with less power and require more time to make the total comeback. The cure is as permanent as the individual makes it and, like the cure for alcoholism, is subject to continued vigilance.

Men have come to their Church leaders dejected, discouraged, embarrassed, terrified, and have gone out later full of confidence and faith in themselves, enjoying self-respect and the confidence of their families. In some cases, wives have come in to express tearful thanks for bringing their husbands back to them. They have not always known what the problem was, but they had sensed it and realized they had lost their husbands. Men have come first with downward glances and have left the final interview months later looking the interviewer straight in the eye. After the first interview, some have admitted: "I'm glad I was arrested. I have tried and tried to correct my error but knew I'd have to have help and had not the courage to ask for it."

Of all the numerous people who have come through this special Church program, very few have been excommunicated. (These few were belligerent and rebellious and unyielding, and practically demanded such action.) Our method is one we think would be approved by the Savior. We remind the person of his likeness to and affinity with God:

> And I, God, created man in mine own image, in the image of mine Only Begotten created I him; male and female created I them. (Moses 2:27.)

> The Lord said unto Enoch: Behold these thy brethren; they are the workmanship of mine own hands, and I gave unto them their knowledge, in the day I created them; and in the Garden of Eden, gave I unto man his agency. (Moses 7:32.)

This kind of approach of helpfulness, not condemnation; of understanding, not accusations; of sympathy, not threats — this has brought many men to their knees in surrender and gratitude and helped them back to normality. With this inspiration a person has new hope. If he is in the image of God he is impelled to reach upward, for he must now be like God whose son he is. He has new handholds. He is no longer low and degenerate. He must climb up.

Continued contact seems to be helpful. To have the man return to report success in his efforts or even to tell of partial failure is helpful, and to these continuing visits much credit is due for recoveries. An additional strength comes from the realization that they will be making reports, and people thus control themselves and their thoughts a day at a time, a week at a time; and soon the months have passed and their thoughts are under control and their actions are above reproach.

Thus our approach is a positive one, dwelling upon the glories of the gospel and all its blessings, the happiness of proper family life, the joy in individual cleanliness. Its success is reflected in the numerous lives blessed with complete recovery.

Acceptance of Personal Responsibility Vital

As with any other sin, forgiveness and recovery are dependent upon the offender's repentance, which begins with recognition of the sin and acceptance of personal responsibility for it. There are those who are deeply entrenched in the habit and have no apparent desire to cleanse themselves and build toward a moral life. They are belligerent and totally uncooperative.

One young man persistently lied. He kept insisting that he be told who had reported on him. It was made clear to him that the important thing was not who reported but how soon he placed himself in the way of spiritual medication. As he left the room, he was told kindly, "You apparently do not wish to discuss the problem tonight. You will before long, and you will find the door open and our hearts warm toward you." Several months passed and we heard nothing from him; then the phone rang one day, and there he was asking for an appointment. He came to see us and he unburdened his soul voluntarily, relief settled down upon him, and he began his comeback.

Next in seriousness to nonrecognition of the sin is the attempt to justify oneself in this perversion. Many have been misinformed that they are powerless in the matter, not responsible for the tendency, and that "God made them that way." This is as untrue as any other of the diabolical lies Satan has concocted. It is blasphemy. Man is made in the image of God. Does the pervert think God to be "that way"?

To those weaklings who argue this way, James answers:

Blessed is the man that endureth [i.e., resisteth] temptation: for when he is tried, he shall receive the crown of life, which the Lord hath promised to them that love him.

Let no man say when he is tempted, I am tempted of God: for God cannot be tempted with evil, neither tempteth he any man:

But every man is tempted, when he is drawn away of his own lust, and enticed.

Then when lust hath conceived, it bringeth forth sin: and sin, when it is finished, bringeth forth death.

Do not err, my beloved brethren. (Jas. 1:12-16.)

Sometimes not heavenly but earthly parents get the blame. Granted that certain conditions make it easier for one to become a pervert, the second Article of Faith teaches that a man will be punished for his own sins. He can, if normal, rise above the frustrations of childhood and stand on his own feet.

> The soul that sinneth, it shall die. The son shall not bear the iniquity of the father, neither shall the father bear the iniquity of the son. . . . (Ezek. 18:20.)

A man may rationalize and excuse himself till the groove is so deep he cannot get out without great difficulty. But temptations come to all people. The difference between the reprobate and the worthy person is generally that one yielded and the other resisted. And if the yielding person continues to give way he may finally reach the point of "no return." The Spirit will "not always strive with man." (D&C 1:33.)

Some say that marriage has failed. And while the number of divorces causes us to fear and admit it partly to be true, the principle of marriage is right. Some have changed their desires and yearnings and have convinced themselves that they are different and have no desire toward the opposite sex. This is quite understandable if the person has permitted himself to move in the other direction and has lavished his interests, desires, affections, and passions upon one of his own sex for long enough. It becomes ingrown. But let this individual repent of his perversion, force himself to return to normal pursuits and interests and actions and friendships with the opposite sex, and this normal pattern can become natural again.

No Turning Back

It is imperative that when one has once put his feet on the path to recovery and mastery there must be no turning back. "No man," said the Savior, "having put his hand to the plough, and looking back, is fit for the kingdom of God." (Luke 9:62.)

Yet Satan will not readily let go. Rather, he will probably send a host of new temptations to weaken the resolve of the repentant one. Luke is explicit as he draws the picture:

> When the unclean spirit is gone out of a man, he walketh through dry places, seeking rest; and finding none, he saith, I will return unto my house whence I came out.

And when he cometh, he findeth it swept and garnished.

Then goeth he, and taketh to him seven other spirits more wicked than himself; and they enter in, and dwell there: and the last state of that man is worse than the first. (Luke 11:24-26.)

The repenting one must avoid every person, place, thing or situation which could bring reminders of the sordid past. He must avoid pornography in any form — any stories or pictures or records which stimulate the passions. He should part company with ". . . the prince of this world" (the devil — John 14:30) and all such associates. He should make new friends, establish new locations and begin a totally new life. He must apply Paul's counsel:

Now we command you, brethren, in the name of our Lord Jesus Christ, that ye withdraw yourselves from every brother that walketh disorderly. . . . (2 Thess. 3:6.)

He should do whatever might be necessary to make the break — a clean-cut break — so he can start anew. To those who protest at the cost or inconvenience I quote:

For what is a man profited, if he shall gain the whole world, and lose his own soul? or what shall a man give in exchange for his soul? (Matt. 16:26.)

The Sweet Taste of Freedom

Many testimonial letters of gratitude have come to the Church offices expressing the joy of conquest and victory and the satisfactions from successful accomplishment. One from a young man is revealing. His deviation had come when he was only a ten-year-old boy and was the result of curiosity. But he could not wholly eradicate the memory of it. He wrote:

As I grew older I was too ashamed to tell anyone until I approached the missionary age. I knew it was not so serious as a childish act but nevertheless it was a burden through all the years and I had a guilty conscience. When I was interviewed for my mission, I received the blessed peace I should have had through all the years, for my kindly bishop cleared the slate and commended me for the many years of cleanliness. How grateful I was for the privilege of placing my burden on the bishop's shoulders. I felt well and clean.

Another young man who had waded in deep waters wrote:

> I am still laboring and adjusting to the new mental attitudes which have been formed during the past year. . . . I have been quite happy and content. There are still struggles, but through it all I can look back and see slow but sure improvement. . . . I can never fully express my gratitude for the help the Church has given me. At last, I am free from the fetters of such a damning slavery. Thanks sincerely.

Frequently, in their confessions, these men, relieved from some tension and happy in their prospects of a new life, are eager that their former tempters and associates also be helped. They have encouraged these people to seek help, and if they wish to receive help through the Church program it is gladly given. As has been said, the approach is kindly and not accusing. The person is permitted to tell his own story in his own way and then he is helped in a confidential way to transform himself.

God Loves the Sinner

In a nutshell, the Church program is like this:

1. *The Malady*: Mental and physical sin.

2. *The Vehicle*: The Church and its agencies and programs.

3. *The Medication*: The gospel of Jesus Christ with its purity, beauty, and rich promises.

4. *The Cure*: Proper attitudes and self-mastery through activity and good works.

Bishops and stake and mission presidents must be alert and watchful and treat with kindness but firmness all such offenders whose offenses come to their knowledge. In the careful and searching interviews the leaders give, these weaknesses are likely to be revealed. Many yielding to this ugly practice are basically good people who have become trapped in sin. They yield to a kind, helpful approach.

Those who do not must be disciplined when all other treatments fail.

Remember, the Lord loves the homosexual person as he does all of his other children. When that person repents and corrects his life, the Lord will smile and receive him.

Chapter Seven

Sins of Omission

> *A wrongdoer is often a man that has left something undone, not always he that has done something.*
>
> —Marcus Aurelius

T HUS FAR WE HAVE DISCUSSED PRINCIPALLY THE SINS of commission — wrong acts done, wrong thoughts entertained, and so on. This chapter is concerned with that other category of sin, sins of omission — failure to do what is right.

The effect of both types of sin can be serious, not only intrinsically but because each type leads naturally to and reinforces the other. For instance, the wrong act of fishing on Sundays involves omitting attendance at Sacrament meeting; conversely, simple non-attendance can, over a period, condition a person to spend Sunday in non-Sabbath pursuits like fishing. Either way Satan wins.

Action for Righteousness

People tend often to measure their righteousness by the absence of wrong acts in their lives, as if passivity were the end of being. But God has created "things to act and things to be acted upon" (2 Ne. 2:14), and man is in the former category. He does not fill the measure of his creation unless he *acts*, and that in righteousness. "Therefore to him that knoweth to do good and doeth it not," warns James, "to him it is sin." (Jas. 4:17.) And who "knoweth to do good" better than Latter-day Saints?

Reinforcing this concept is the Lord's word that the saints had "sinned . . . a very grievous sin" in not following through on the command to build the Kirtland Temple. (D&C 95:3.)

Evils of Spiritual Apathy

Jacob was thinking partly of sins of omission when he uttered the solemn words:

> But wo unto him that has the law given, yea, that has all the commandments of God, like unto us, and that transgresseth them, and that *wasteth the days of his probation,* for awful is his state! (2 Ne. 9:27. Italics added.)

Waste is unjustified, and especially the waste of time — limited as that commodity is in our days of probation. One must live, not only exist; he must do, not merely be; he must grow, not just vegetate. John the Revelator recorded for us significantly:

> Blessed are they that *do* his commandments, that they may have right to the tree of life, and may enter in through the gates into the [eternal] city. (Rev. 22:14. Italics added.)

Through that same apostle and prophet came the condemnatory words of the Lord to the Laodiceans, perhaps directed against the same kind of indifference, of apathy in spiritual matters, that we find among some Church members today:

> I know thy works, that thou art neither cold nor hot: I would thou wert cold or hot.
>
> So then because thou art lukewarm, and neither cold nor hot, I will spue thee out of my mouth. (Rev. 3:15-16.)

The symbolism of the barren fig tree (Matt. 21:19) is eloquent. The unproductive tree was cursed for its barrenness. What a loss to the individual and to humanity if the vine does not grow, the tree does not bear fruit, the soul does not expand through service!

In this connection, that father and mother may be in serious sin who make no effort to live the principles of the gospel, who fail to give service, who do not attend their meetings and carry out their other duties in the kingdom. They set an improper example for their children, who consequently will very often follow in the parental footsteps of neglect. It is frequently difficult for the parents to recognize the effects of their example until the damage is done, until the barrenness of their spiritual tree is plain for all to see. On such parents will be a dreadful responsibility.

To be passive is deadening; to stop doing is to die. Here then is a close parallel with physical life. If one fails to eat and drink, his body becomes emaciated and dies. Likewise if he fails to nourish his spirit and mind, his spirit shrivels and his mind darkens. Charles Steizle has pointed this out in graphic words:

What must I do to be damned? Nothing. That's all. You're damned — condemned — if you just sit still. That is the law of this physical world.

If you sit still long enough, you'll never get up again. If you never lift your arm, you'll soon be unable to raise it at all. If you remain in darkness and never use your eyes, you'll soon become blind.

It is the law in the mental world. If you never exercise your brain — never read, study, nor talk to anyone, never permit anyone to talk to you, your mind will became blank — maybe you'll become insane.

The most horrible punishment that could be inflicted upon you is not twenty years of hard labor, but twenty years of solitary confinement.

It's the law in the spiritual world. Simply shut your heart to all truth, and after a while you won't be able to believe anything — that is the severest penalty for not accepting truth.

The process of disintegration and death begins when a man shuts himself out from the forces that make for life.

The body and mind and spirit are kept alive through constant constructive use.[1]

---

[1]Charles Steizle, *Utah Labor News,* December 12, 1937.

Of the spiritual apathy which this condition represents, President David O. McKay has spoken as follows:

> The peril of this century is spiritual apathy. As the body requires the sunlight, good food, proper exercise, and rest, so the spirit of man requires the sunlight of the Holy Spirit; proper exercise of the spiritual functions; avoiding of evils that affect spiritual health, which are more ravaging in their effects than typhoid fever, pneumonia, or other diseases that attack the body.

As I have interviewed numerous young men for missions, I have asked them what grades they received in their college or in high school. Many times they have rather sheepishly admitted they could have done better. To be mediocre when only application and diligence would have netted superiority is an error akin to sin. It recalls the comment by Arnold Bennett:

> The real tragedy is the tragedy of the man who never in his life braces himself for his one supreme effort, who never stretches to his full capacity, never stands up to his full stature.

Parenthetically, it is pleasing to note that many of those same young men, stimulated in the mission field, fired with purpose, went back to the same college and received high grades.

We Covenant to Act

To be baptized is to enter into a covenant of commission. But to fail to be baptized when one is convinced the work is divine is a sin of omission, and penalties will be assessed for failure to meet this requirement. Tens of thousands of people having heard the gospel have failed to be baptized, giving trivial excuses. This is a most serious sin. The Lord told Nicodemus that he and others would not even see the kingdom of God if they rejected the required baptism.

The covenants we make with God involve promises to *do,* not merely to refrain from doing, to work righteousness as well as to avoid evil. The children of Israel made such covenants through Moses, saying, "All that the Lord hath spoken *we will do*" (Exodus 19:8, italics added), though hardly was Moses' back turned until they had broken their promise through wrongdoing. In the baptismal waters we give a similar undertaking and we repledge it in the ordinance of the sacrament. Not to honor these pledges, to refuse to serve or to accept responsibility and do less than one's best at it, is a sin of omission. Nor can we with impunity seek to cancel such obligations, as one misguided man supposed he could when he wrote to me as follows:

> I will appreciate it if you will remove my name from the roster of the Church. I find the restrictions and the requirements of the Church too great.

> I am unable to forego the four no's — tea, coffee, tobacco and liquor. To refuse those things I desire causes me more anxiety than I am able to cope with. And my personality requires acceptance from the crowd, and I feel unaccepted when unable to partake of the pleasures of my companions. Also, I find that I cannot give from three to five hours on Sunday and one-tenth of my earnings. This is against my basic nature — but some people overcome it.

Failure to act after one has made the covenant to do so, the shirking of responsibility in the kingdom, brings inevitable condemnation. This situation brings to mind the Savior's parable of the two sons.

> But what think ye? A certain man had two sons; and he came to the first, and said, Son, go work to day in my vineyard.
> He answered and said, I will not: but afterward he repented, and went.
> And he came to the second, and said likewise. And he answered and said, I go, sir: and went not.
> Whether of them twain did the will of his father? They say unto him, The first. Jesus saith unto them, Verily I say unto you, That the publicans and the harlots go into the kingdom of God before you. (Matt. 21:28-31.)

Declining to serve when called may constitute a sin of omission as well as one of commission. Certainly it is a sin of omission to accept responsibility, to covenant with the Lord, and then fail to do the work as well as possible. Such a person is not following the light he sees, a sin which the

Savior condemned in the Pharisees and by implication in all men who wilfully choose darkness or a lesser light:

> And Jesus said, For judgment I am come into this world, that they which see not might see; and that they which see might be made blind.
>
> And some of the Pharisees which were with him heard these words, and said unto him, Are we blind also?
>
> Jesus said unto them, If ye were blind, ye should have no sin: but now ye say, We see; therefore your sin remaineth. (John 9:39-41.)

Melchizedek Priesthood holders and those who have received their temple endowments have made further and specific pledges to *do,* to work righteousness. The Lord has expressed the mutual pledges between our Heavenly Father and the priesthood holders as an "oath and covenant," which is discussed in a later chapter. Suffice to say here that one breaks the priesthood covenant by transgressing commandments — but also by leaving undone his duties. Accordingly, *to break this covenant one needs only to do nothing.*

Many Opportunities for Omission

Clearly the potential for sins of omission is as broad as the converse opportunity for righteousness. Let us consider some examples.

The home teacher who is assigned the responsibility of teaching families must not fail to teach or to fulfill his assignment. The penalty is more severe than he thinks. He will be held accountable for difficult situations which arise in an assigned family and which with diligence he could have controlled.

Tithing is a law of God and is required of his followers. To fail to meet this obligation in full is to omit a weighty matter. It is a transgression, not an inconsequential oversight.

The Sabbath is a holy day in which to do worthy and holy things. Abstinence from work and recreation is important but insufficient. The Sabbath calls for constructive thoughts and acts, and if one merely lounges about doing nothing on the Sabbath, he is breaking it. To observe it, one will be on his knees in prayer, preparing lessons, studying the gospel, meditating, visiting the ill and distressed, sleeping, reading wholesome material, and attending all the meetings of that day to which he is expected. To fail to do these proper things is a trangression on the omission side.

Marriage is another example. The Lord has said that man is not without the woman, nor the woman without the man in the Lord. In other words, to marry is an obligation as well as an opportunity. Every normal person should find a proper mate and be sealed for eternity in the temple of the Lord. Failure to do so is disobedience and a sin of omission, unless every proper effort is made.

Once the marriage covenant is made, it is conceivable that a man might never be guilty of violence or of infidelity and yet could fail of the greatest blessings possible because of his failure in his covenant marriage. He should strive to be the perfect husband and the perfect father, and positively do all things to make his family relationships as the Lord would have them be. Similar requirements are made of the wife.

To carry the responsibility further, the command to multiply and replenish the earth and subdue it comes from the Lord also. To refuse to bear or refrain from the bearing of children is an error of omission. Of course, the mere bringing of children into the world does not fulfill the obligation. Nor have parents met all their responsibilities when they feed and clothe and give schooling and entertainment to their offspring. The great parental responsibility is not met unless fathers and mothers do all in their power to train their children to pray and walk uprightly before the Lord, giving proper example and positive verbal teaching. The daily family life, if well charted and regulated, supplemented by the twice-daily family kneeling prayer and the home teaching and home evening, is almost certain to bring up the children to become stalwart sons and daughters of

God and eligible for exaltation and eternal life. Any selfishness on the part of parents which would deprive the children of this training would be a sin of omission and answerable to the Great Judge when the time of judgment comes.

To proselyte and warn our neighbors of the divinity of the gospel is a command reiterated by the Lord: ". . . It becometh every man who hath been warned to warn his neighbor." (D&C 88:81.) More recently the living Prophet has emphasized "Every member a missionary." To sit passively by enjoying all the benefits of the gospel and the Church and not share them with others of God's children constitutes a serious sin of omission.

Likewise, failing to fast is a sin. In the 58th chapter of Isaiah, rich promises are made by the Lord to those who fast and assist the needy. Freedom from frustrations, freedom from thralldom, and the blessing of peace are promised. Inspiration and spiritual guidance will come with righteousness and closeness to our Heavenly Father. To omit to do this righteous act of fasting would deprive us of these blessings.

Consider the Ten Commandments. Some are negative, some are positive. This is significant. It is not sufficient to refrain from making other gods of stone or wood or gold, but one must actively love and serve the true and living God with total heart, might, mind and strength.

Inherent in the "thou shalt not" is the inference "thou shalt." It is not enough not to worship the man-made creations, but it is incumbent upon man to bow down in humility to our Father in heaven and serve him. It is not enough not to curse and blaspheme the name of Deity and think of him irreverently, but man must call upon his name frequently in personal, family and public prayers in reverence and adoration. We should speak often of him and his program. We should read of him and his works.

It is not sufficient that we do not kill or commit murder, but we should protect others from such crimes. Not only is suicide a crime, but one is obligated to protect and save and prolong his own life. Not only shall we not take life, but it is obligatory upon us to give life, both by bearing children into mortality and by leading people toward eternal life by teaching, proselyting and influencing them strongly toward that end.

It is not good enough merely to refrain from injuring parents; we must honor them. Nor is it sufficient to refrain from adultery. One must be positive and keep hands clean and heart pure and thoughts above reproach. Not only shall we not steal, but we shall protect others' possessions. We employ law enforcement officers, we cooperate with them and the judges; we help to develop a world where vice is unprofitable, uncomfortable and disappointing. Not only should we never bear false witness against neighbors, but the scriptures tell us we should love our fellowmen, serve them, speak well of them, build them up.

As to coveting, the Lord has made it clear that not only should we not lust for something belonging to another, but we should gladly share our own possessions. Our welfare work, our fast offerings, our tithing program, our missionary work — all these have in them this element of sharing the benefits with those less fortunate.

Excuses Irrelevant

Many and varied are the excuses for sins of omission, and they are all irrelevant. One is unwillingness to get involved. In a now-famous incident of a few years back, many people in New York City witnessed the fatal stabbing of a young woman who was screaming for help, but not one person made any effort to help her or even to alert the police. Similarly, many people will pass the scene of an accident without determining whether they can relieve the suffering of the injured or report to the patrolman.

In the parable of the Good Samaritan the priest and the Levite were base sinners. They found a person in dire distress, needing help they could have given him, but they crossed the street and avoided involvement. Had he died, some of the responsibility would have been theirs. His extra suffering due to their passing him by and leaving him without succor would also be laid to their charge.

Pilate attempted to wash from his hands the responsibility of defending the Christ or at least of insuring justice. He had said to the clamoring mob, "I find in him no fault at all." Yet he had the Master scourged and permitted the soldiers to injure the Lord with the crown of plaited thorns, ridicule him, place on him a purple robe, and strike him and taunt him. Of what avail was the water in the basin? How could Pilate cleanse himself of responsibility of the crucifixion by publicly washing his hands or by announcing: "I am innocent of the blood of this just person: see ye to it."? (Matt. 27:24.)

Likewise the Church member who has the attitude of leaving it to others will have much to answer for. There are many who say: "My wife does the Church work!" Others say: "I'm just not the religious kind," as though it does not take effort for most people to serve and do their duty. But God has endowed us with talents and time, with latent abilities and with opportunities to use and develop them in his service. He therefore expects much of us, his privileged children. The parable of the talents is a brilliant summary of the many scriptural passages outlining promises for the diligent and penalties for the slothful. (See Matt. 25:14-30.) From this we see that those who refuse to use their talents in God's cause can expect their potential to be removed and given to someone more worthy. Like the unproductive fig tree (see Matt. 21:18-20) their barren lives will be cursed. To them on judgment day will come the equivalent of these devastating words:

> . . . Thou wicked and slothful servant . . . Thou oughtest therefore to have put my money to the exchangers. . . . Take therefore the talent from him, and give it unto him which hath ten talents. . . . And cast ye the unprofitable servant into outer darkness: there shall be weeping and gnashing of teeth. (Matt. 25:26-29, 30.)

Repentance Relevant

Yes, sins of omission have much in common with those of commission. As we have seen, one common feature is their potential for damning the sinner. Equally true but more encouraging is that, like the positive wrongdoer, the slothful or inadequate servant can repent, exchange apathy for diligence, and receive God's forgiveness. And if he will do this without proscrastinating there awaits for him the Lord's great eternal reward:

> Well done, thou good and faithful servant: thou hast been faithful over a few things, I will make thee ruler over many things: enter thou into the joy of thy Lord. (Matt. 25:21.)

Chapter Eight

As a Man Thinketh

> . . . *Filthy dreamers defile the flesh* . . .
>
> —Jude 8

> *Thoughts are the seeds of acts.*

AKIN TO SINS OF OMISSION ARE "THOUGHT SINS." We learn from one of the proverbs: "For as he thinketh in his heart, so is he." (Prov. 23:7.)

Thoughts Shape Our Lives

A man is literally what he thinks, his character being the complete sum of all his thoughts. On this theme Henry Van Dyke gave us the following verse:

Thoughts Are Things

I hold it true that thoughts are things;
They're endowed with bodies and breath and wings;
And that we send them forth to fill
The world with good results, or ill.

That which we call our secret thought
Speeds forth to earth's remotest spot,
Leaving its blessings or its woes
Like tracks behind it as it goes.

We build our future, thought by thought,
For good or ill, yet know it not.
Yet, so the universe was wrought.
Thought is another name for fate;
Choose, then, thy destiny and wait.
For love brings love and hate brings hate.

Not only does a person become what he thinks, but often he comes to look like it. If he worships the God of War, hard lines tend to develop on his countenance. If he worships the God of Lust, dissipation will mark his features. If he worships the God of Peace and Truth, serenity will crown his visage. A thoughtful poet gave us this:

> A human face I love to view
> And trace the passions of the soul;
> On it the spirit writes anew
> Each thought and feeling on a scroll.
>
> There the mind its evil doings tells,
> And there its noblest deeds do speak;
> Just as the ringing of the bells
> Proclaims a knell or wedding feast.
>
> —Author unknown

Inescapably we reap what we sow. If a farmer wants to raise wheat he must sow wheat, if he wishes fruit he must plant fruit trees, and so with any other crop. The principle is equally binding in the mental and spiritual spheres, as James Allen has expressed it in his well-known book, *As a Man Thinketh*.

> As the plant springs from, and could not be without the seed, so every act of a man springs from the hidden seeds of thought, and could not have appeared without them. This applies equally to those acts called "spontaneous" and "unpremeditated" as to those which are deliberately executed. . . .
>
> . . . In the armory of thought [man] forges the weapons by which he destroys himself; he also fashions the tools with which he builds for himself heavenly mansions of joy and strength and peace. . . . Between these two extremes are all grades of character, and man is their maker and master. . . . Man is the master of thought, the moulder of character, and the maker and shaper of condition, environment and destiny.[1]

Cumulative Effect of Thoughts

This relationship of character to thought cannot be too strongly emphasized. How could a person possibly become what he is *not* thinking? Nor is any thought, when per-

---

[1]James Allen, *As a Man Thinketh*. The entire book is recommended to the thoughtful reader.

sistently entertained, too small to have its effect. The "divinity that shapes our ends" is indeed in ourselves. It is one's very self. In speaking of carving out a character, President David O. McKay has said:

> Your tools are your ideals. The thought in your mind at this moment is contributing, however infinitesimally, almost imperceptibly to the shaping of your soul, even to the lineaments of your countenance . . . even passing and idle thoughts leave their impression. Trees that can withstand the hurricane, sometimes yield to destroying pests that can scarcely be seen except with the aid of a microscope. Likewise, the greatest foes of the individual are not always the glaring evils of humanity but subtle influences of thought and of continual association with companions.

The cumulative effect of our thinking, and its power over life's circumstances, is strikingly expressed by James Allen:

> A man does not come to the almshouse or the jail by the tyranny of fate or circumstance, but by the pathway of grovelling thoughts and base desires. Nor does a pure-minded man fall suddenly into crime by stress of mere external force; the criminal thought had long been secretly fostered in the heart, and the hour of opportunity revealed its gathered power. Circumstance does not make the man; it reveals him to himself. No such conditions can exist as descending into vice and its attendant sufferings apart from vicious inclinations, or ascending into virtue and its pure happiness without the continued cultivation of virtuous aspirations, and man, therefore, as the lord and master of his thoughts is the maker of himself, the shaper and author of environment. . . .

> Let a man radically alter his thoughts and he will be astonished at the rapid transformation it will effect in the material conditions of his life. Men imagine that thought can be kept secret, but it cannot; it rapidly crystallizes into habit and habit solidifies into circumstance.[2]

This "solidifying into circumstance" is the key to most of the success stories we read. The successful man thinks he can. As someone expressed it briefly and pointedly, "Whether you think you can or you can't, you're right." Allen enlarges on this idea:

[2]*Ibid.*

He who cherishes a beautiful vision, a lofty ideal in his heart, will one day realize it. Columbus cherished a vision of another world, and he discovered it; Copernicus fostered the vision of a multiplicity of worlds and a wider universe, and he revealed it; Buddha beheld the vision of a spiritual world of stainless beauty and perfect peace, and he entered into it.[3]

Thoughts Govern Acts and Attitudes

The statement, "As a man thinketh, so is he," could equally well be rendered "As a man thinketh, so does he." If one thinks it long enough he is likely to do it. A minister acquaintance of mine, whom I knew rather well, was found by his wife hanging in the attic from the rafters. His thoughts had taken his life. He had become morose and despondent for two or more years. Certainly he had not come to suicide in a moment, for he had been a happy, pleasant person as I had known him. It must have been a long decline, ever steeper, controllable by him at first and perhaps out of hand as he neared the end of the trail. No one in his "right mind," and especially if he has an understanding of the gospel, will permit himself to arrive at this "point of no return."

Not only acts but attitudes rest on the thoughts we feed our minds. A young couple bickered and quarreled until their marriage was ended and divorce was final. They had been involved romantically with another erring couple. The man and the woman both wrote me, trying to smooth out the wrinkles and to make me feel justified and reconciled to their false conclusions. I acknowledged their letters in these terms:

Old man rationalization finally has convinced two basically good people that "evil is good, and good evil," and threads are now broken and solemn contracts are voided and solemn promises are abrogated when minds became incubators in which little thoughts grew to become vicious thoughts, and small acts of impropriety become near unforgivable acts affecting adversely the lives of four adults and many children. You have fallen in step

---

[3]*Ibid.*

with the world which seems intent on believing that *good is evil
and evil is good,* and that black is white and darkness is light.

Our Thoughts Influence Others

No one has a right arbitrarily to shape the thoughts of
others, but that is not to say that one's thoughts are entirely
his own affair. Each of us inevitably affects others by the
character his thoughts and actions have shaped. Each of
us is part of mankind and gives to others as well as receives
from them. One perceptive comment, whose authorship I
do not know, expressed it in this way:

> Into the hands of every individual is given a marvelous power
> for good or evil — the silent, unconscious, unseen influence of
> his life. This is simply the constant radiation of what man really
> is, not what he pretends to be. . . . Life is a state of constant
> radiation and absorption; to exist is to radiate; to exist is to be
> the recipient of radiation.
>
> Man cannot escape for one moment from this radiation of his
> character, this constant weakening or strengthening of others.
> He cannot evade the responsibility by saying it is an unconscious
> influence. He can select the qualities that he will permit to be
> radiated. He can select the calmness, trust, generosity, truth,
> justice, loyalty, nobility — make them vitally active in his char-
> acter — and by these qualities he will constantly affect the world.

Accountability for Our Thoughts

Thus far we have considered mainly the effect thoughts
have on our life here. But what of the hereafter?

When I was about fourteen years of age I read the
Bible through. It was a long, arduous task for me but I
finished it with a degree of pride. When I read that all
men would be judged according to their works, that seemed
plausible and I thought I must mind my actions and my
works. Then I read what the Savior said to the people of
Palestine.

> . . . Every idle word that men shall speak, they shall give
> account thereof in the day of judgment.
> For by thy words thou shalt be justified, and by thy words thou
> shalt be condemned. (Matt. 12:36-37.)

This seemed to me far-fetched, for when I "cussed" the cows which struck me in the eyes with their cockleburmatted tails or kicked over the milk bucket, I looked around and there was not a single soul in the corral to hear me; and though the cow could hear, perhaps she could not interpret. And when I quarreled with my brothers out in the field, I was sure there were no other ears within many blocks. How then could one be judged by his words?

That was bad enough but there was worse to follow, for I later read in the Book of Mormon the words of a prophet saying that even our thoughts will condemn us.

> . . . Our words will condemn us, yea, all our works will condemn us . . . and our thoughts will also condemn us; and in this awful state we shall not dare to look up to our God. . . . (Al. 12:14.)

It is well for all of us to realize that our thought sins as well as all other sins are recorded in heaven. Modern revelation gives us this:

> Nevertheless, ye are blessed, for the testimony which ye have borne is recorded in heaven for the angels to look upon; and they rejoice over you, and your sins are forgiven you. (D&C 62:3.)

And this:

> For verily the voice of the Lord is unto all men, and there is none to escape; and there is no eye that shall not see, neither ear that shall not hear, neither heart that shall not be penetrated. (D&C 1:2.)

If men's secret acts shall be revealed it is likely that their secret thoughts will also be revealed, for the iniquities of the rebellious shall be spoken from the housetops.

The one who harbors evil thoughts sometimes feels safe in the conviction that these thoughts are unknown to others and that they, like acts in the dark, are not discernible. The Revelator, John, seemed to clear this matter when he wrote:

> And I saw the dead, small and great, stand before God; and the books were opened: and another book was opened, which is the book of life: and the dead were judged out of those things

which were written in the books, according to their works. (Rev. 20:12.)

And in the last days an angel will "sound his trump, and reveal the secret acts of men, and the thoughts and intents of their hearts . . ." (D&C 88:109.)

Accordingly, men's deeds and thoughts must be recorded in heaven, and recording angels will not fail to make complete recordings of our thoughts and actions. We pay our tithing and the bishop records it in his book and gives us a receipt. But even if the entry fails to get in the ward record, we shall have full credit for the tithes we paid. There will be no omissions in the heavenly records, and they will all be available at the day of judgment. President John Taylor emphasized this:

> Man sleeps the sleep of death, but the spirit lives where the record of his deeds is kept.
>
> Man sleeps for a time in the grave, and by and by he rises again from the dead and goes to judgment; and then the secret thoughts of all men are revealed before him with whom we have to do; we cannot hide them; it would be in vain then for a man to say, "I did not do so and so"; the command would be, unravel and read the record which he has made of himself and let it testify in relation to these things, and all could gaze upon it.[4]

At that day we may be sure that we shall receive fair judgment. The judges will have the facts as they may be played back from our own records, and our voices and the pictures of our acts and the recordings of our thoughts will testify against and for us.

President J. Reuben Clark gave sober attention to this thought:

> But there is one whom you do not deceive, and that is Christ, our Lord. He knows all. Personally, I have felt that nobody need keep much of a record about me, except what I keep myself in my mind, which is a part of my spirit. I often question in my mind, whether it is going to require very many witnesses in addition to my own wrongdoing.

---

[4]*Journal of Discourses*, Vol. 11, pp. 78-79.

Perhaps sometime all of us have felt that we were misjudged and that our sincere and well-intentioned efforts were not understood. How comforting it is to know that on judgment day we shall be treated fairly and justly and in the light of the total, true picture and the discernment of the Judge!

Nothing Secret to God

There are no corners so dark, no deserts so uninhabited, no canyons so remote, no automobiles so hidden, no homes so tight and shut in but that the all-seeing One can penetrate and observe. The faithful have always known this. The doubters should take a sober look at the situation in the light of the electronic devices which have come into increasing use in the last few years and which are often delicate and tiny but so powerful as almost to annihilate man's personal privacy.

These devices can apparently be used to reveal actions and even to tap thoughts. The lie detector is almost commonplace. Dreams are analyzed. Wire tapping has come prominently into use. A certain paint has been used as a conductor of electricity. A tiny outlet can pick up anything said in a room. Transmitters are built into picture frames, door knobs, typewriters, clocks, and other things. A palm-size direction microphone with pocket receiver and "hearing aid" attachment is capable of picking up a whisper fifty feet away. An eight-year-old lad in an eastern city can pick up a conversation 100 feet away in other people's homes. A policeman aimed the device 150 feet and could understand much of what was being said. One specialist had his instrument in the olive in a nearby martini; another in the mouthpiece of a telephone; another in the glove compartment of the car dashboard, in the handle of his brief case, and even in the cavity of a tooth of an intimate associate.

In the light of these modern marvels can anyone doubt that God hears prayers and discerns secret thoughts? A printer's camera can make a negative three feet square.

What magnification! If human eyes and ears can so penetrate one's personal life, what may we expect from perfected men with perfected vision!

Every day, we record our voices on recording machines. Every day, pictures are taken and voices recorded and acts portrayed in live transmission over televison. The scriptures indicate the existence of records of our works and words. Surely it is not too great a stretch of the imagination in modern days to believe that our thoughts as well will be recorded by some means now known only to higher beings!

When I was a little boy, some imaginative story teller in offering his "greatest yarn" told of some woodsmen in the far north who sat around the campfire in the far-below zero weather, and all at once their voices failed to register sound. It was so cold that the sounds were frozen. Later, when the warm rays of the spring sun came, the frozen sounds of the cold winter began to thaw and there came back the total conversations of that cold night in camp.

Today, when sounds are picked out of the air from all around the world, this does not seem such a fanciful tale as it did to us long ago.

Discernment of God's Servants

God "knowest thy thoughts and the intents of thy heart." (D&C 6:16.) The Savior at Jacob's well, without ever having seen the adulterous Samaritan woman before, told her: ... "Thou hast had five husbands; and he whom thou now hast is not thy husband ..." (John 4:18.) The Lord knew of her adultery as he knew her whole life. Likewise the Lord looked into the dark recesses of the cold and corrupt hearts of the scribes and Pharisees who brought before him the woman taken in adultery. The Savior gave his classic answer, "He that is without sin among you, let him first cast a stone at her." (John 8:7.) Their thoughts condemned them, and they melted away like snow under a summer sun.

A similar power of discernment and perception comes to men as they become perfect and the impediments which obstruct spiritual vision are dissolved. For example, Ananias and Sapphira (see Acts 5:1-10) secretly conspired to lie to God, but Peter was inspired to read their thoughts. There are many examples of this power, both ancient and modern. A story came down to my family about my grandfather, Heber C. Kimball. I repeat it as it was told to me:

> Being in charge of the Endowment House, while the Temple was in the process of construction, Heber C. Kimball met with a group who were planning to enter the temple for ordinance work. He felt impressed that some were not worthy to go into the temple, and he suggested first that if any present were not worthy, they might retire. No one responding, he said that there were some present who should not proceed through the temple because of unworthiness and he wished they would leave so the company could proceed. It was quiet as death and no one moved nor responded. A third time he spoke, saying that there were two people present who were in adultery, and if they did not leave he would call out their names. Two people walked out and the company continued on through the temple.

Men of God are entitled to this discernment.

The Savior's Word on Thought Sins

Of vital interest to us is the interpretation of the Lord with regard to the sins of thought. His great sermons toward the beginning of his ministry revealed a new concept. He had been the author of the law under which the children of Israel had lived. He now seemed to hope that his people might begin to live the higher laws. At least, he felt to expound them and urged the people to observe them. He recalled the lower law and followed with the higher:

> Ye have heard that it was said by them of old time, Thou shalt not kill. . . .
>
> But I say unto you, that whosoever is angry with his brother without a cause shall be in danger of the judgment. . . . (Matt. 5:21-22.)

The killing is an act of aggression. But anger is a thought sin. It may be the forerunner of murder. But if one's thoughts do not get vicious nor violent he is unlikely to take life.

Again, Jesus spoke of the practice of "an eye for an eye and a tooth for a tooth," and came forward with the higher law:

". . . Whosoever shall smite thee on thy right cheek, turn to him the other also." (Matt. 5:39.)

This would be very difficult to do and it is the response of a man well on his way to perfection, but the rightness of it is apparent. To retaliate and fight back is human, but to accept indignities as did the Lord is divine. In advance, he was possibly anticipating the time when he himself would be tested; when he would permit himself to be kissed by a known traitor yet not resist; when he would be captured by a vicious mob yet not permit his loyal Apostle Peter to defend him, though Peter apparently was willing to die fighting for him.

A similar idea is involved in this contrast of the lower and higher laws:

Ye have heard that it hath been said, Thou shalt love thy neighbor, and hate thine enemy.

But I say unto you, Love your enemies, bless them that curse you, do good to them that hate you, and pray for them which despitefully use you, and persecute you. (Matt. 5:43-44.)

Then we have the moral laws. The Lord remembered the profligacy and wantonness and bestiality of the days of old against which such strict laws were enacted. Perhaps in that day, if one could refrain from actual physical adultery he had been accounted quite righteous, but now came the higher law:

Ye have heard that it was said by them of old time, Thou shalt not commit adultery:

But I say unto you, that whosoever looketh on a woman to lust after her hath committed adultery with her already in his heart. (Matt. 5:27-28.)

The thought that stirred the look that provoked the lust was evil in its beginning. To want, to desire, to crave — that is to lust. So when the thought is born which starts a chain reaction, a sin has already been committed. If the thought is sown, then develops into lust, it is almost certain to bring eventually the full harvest of the act of the heinous sin, adultery. Note that the term *lust* has other connotations in addition to the sexual one.

Murder is generally thought of as premeditated killing, and certainly no such act was ever completed unless the thought had preceded the action. No one ever robbed a bank until he had "cased" it, planned the robbery and considered the "getaway." Likewise adultery is not the result of a single thought. There first is a deterioration of thinking. Many sinful chain-thoughts have been coursing through the offender's mind before the physical sin is committed.

Yes, as a man thinketh, so *does* he. If he thinks it long enough he is likely to do it, whether it be theft, moral sin, or suicide. Thus the time to protect against the calamity is when the thought begins to shape itself. Destroy the seed and the plant will never grow.

Man alone, of all creatures of earth, can change his thought pattern and become the architect of his destiny.

Avoid the Initial Motivation

A graphic example of this came to my attention some years ago. In a community in the North, I visited a man occasionally who had above the desk in his printing establishment a huge picture of a nude woman. He laughed at the idea of its being destructive to his morals. But one day years later he came to me with a stained soul — he had committed adultery. His house had fallen in on him. Certainly the thoughts provoked by the things always before his eyes must have had a deteriorating effect on him. There may have been other factors, but surely this one played its part.

We would all be well advised to avoid the motivation to the evil thought. If persistently resisted it will "get the message" and stay away. When I was in business in Arizona, the calendar salesman came each year and we always bought calendars and gave them to customers as advertising. The first year the salesman spread out on the desk large, colored pictures of scantily clad girls, glamorous but shocking. We pushed them all aside and chose scenes, landscapes, and elevating pictures. In all the years following, that salesman never brought to me out of his car another suggestive picture.

Think Virtuous Thoughts

I came across the following sentence whose authorship I do not know:

> A famous artist said he would never allow himself to look at an inferior drawing or painting, to do anything low or demoralizing, lest familiarity with it should taint his own ideal and thus be communicated to his brush.

It would be well for each of us to observe the same principle, lest the tainting of his ideal be communicated to his eternal soul. Accordingly, let our thoughts rest upon sacred things.

> . . . *Let virtue garnish thy thoughts* unceasingly; then shall thy confidence wax strong in the presence of God; and the doctrine of the priesthood shall distil upon thy soul as the dews from heaven. (D&C 121:45. Italics added.)

President McKay likes to quote the following:

> Sow a thought, reap an act;
> Sow an act, reap a habit;
> Sow a habit, reap a character;
> Sow a character, reap an eternal destiny.

Such is the power — and the outcome — of our thoughts.

Chapter Nine

Point of No Return

> *But whoso breaketh this covenant*
> *after he hath received it, and al-*
> *together turneth therefrom, shall*
> *not have forgiveness of sins in this*
> *world nor in the world to come.*

—Doctrine & Covenants 84:41

IT IS TRUE THAT THE GREAT PRINCIPLE OF REPENTANCE is always available, but for the wicked and rebellious there are serious reservations to this statement. For instance, sin is intensely habit-forming and sometimes moves men to the tragic point of no return. Without repentance there can be no forgiveness, and without forgiveness all the blessings of eternity hang in jeopardy. As the transgressor moves deeper and deeper in his sin, and the error is entrenched more deeply and the will to change is weakened, it becomes increasingly near-hopeless, and he skids down and down until either he does not want to climb back or he has lost the power to do so.

Everlastingly Too Late

Perhaps the Book of Mormon contains the best examples and references on this. In the words of Amulek:

For behold, if ye have procrastinated the day of your repentance even until death, behold, ye have become subjected to the spirit of the devil, and he doth seal you his; therefore, the Spirit of the Lord hath withdrawn from you, and hath no place in you,

> and the devil hath all power over you; and this is the final state of the wicked. (Al. 34:35.)

There is a sad note of finality in that last statement. It matches the words of Samuel the Lamanite to those who would procrastinate the day of their salvation — "it is everlastingly too late, and your destruction is made sure" (Hel. 13:38); and it recalls those of Mormon relative to his wicked contemporaries — "the sorrowing of the damned." (Morm. 2:13.)

The key factor in such a situation is the withdrawal of the Lord's Spirit. In the final battle days of the Jaredites, "the Spirit of the Lord had ceased striving with them, and Satan had full power over the hearts of the people . . ." (Eth. 15:19.) And the Nephites at one point continued on in their wickedness until they were left by themselves to "kick against the pricks."

> And they saw that they had become weak, like unto their brethren, the Lamanites, and that the Spirit of the Lord did no more preserve them; yea, it had withdrawn from them because *the Spirit of the Lord doth not dwell in unholy temples* —
>
> Therefore the Lord did cease to preserve them by his miraculous and matchless power, for they had fallen into a state of unbelief and awful wickedness. . . . (Hel. 4:24-25. Italics added.)

Sins Unto Death

In discussing the subject of sin and declaring that the Lord and his Church will forgive transgressions, it must be made clear that there are "sins unto death." John tells us:

> . . . There is a sin unto death: I do not say that he shall pray for it. All unrighteousness is sin: and there is a sin not unto death. (1 John 5:16-17.)

In other words, sins are of different degrees of seriousness. There are those which can be forgiven and those for which one may not promise forgiveness. The sin unto death is of such a serious nature that of those who commit it we are told:

> . . . their end no man knoweth on earth, nor ever shall know, until they come before me in judgment. (D&C 43:33.)

The oft-mentioned unpardonable sin is of monumental import. Of this, the Prophet Joseph Smith has said:

> All sins shall be forgiven, except the sin against the Holy Ghost; for Jesus will save all except the sons of perdition. What must a man do to commit the unpardonable sin? He must receive the Holy Ghost, have the heavens opened unto him, and know God, and then sin against him. After a man has sinned against the Holy Ghost, there is no repentance for him. He has got to say that the sun does not shine while he sees it; he has got to deny Jesus Christ when the heavens have been opened unto him, and to deny the plan of salvation with his eyes open to the truth of it; and from that time he begins to be an enemy. This is the case with many apostates of The Church of Jesus Christ of Latter-day Saints.
>
> When a man begins to be an enemy to this work, he hunts me, he seeks to kill me, and never ceases to thirst for my blood. He gets the spirit of the devil — the same spirit that they had who crucified the Lord of Life — the same spirit that sins against the Holy Ghost. You cannot save such persons; you cannot bring them to repentance; they make open war, like the devil, and awful is the consequence.[1]

As to the shedding of innocent blood, in one sense *innocent blood* might be thought of as the blood of those persons without guile, or of little ones who have not sinned. It might also be thought of as the blood of others whom the murderer deliberately kills. Surely the crucifixion of the perfect Son of God constituted the shedding of innocent blood. Joseph Smith's blood shed in Carthage Jail was innocent — at least he said: "I am void of offense toward God and man." Modern scripture gives the following interpretation:

> The blasphemy against the Holy Ghost, which shall not be forgiven in the world nor out of the world, is in that ye commit murder wherein ye shed innocent blood, and assent unto my death, after ye have received my new and everlasting covenant, saith the Lord God. . . . (D&C 132:27.)

President Joseph Fielding Smith gives us further light on this:

> . . . Shedding innocent blood is spoken of in the scriptures as consenting to the death of Jesus Christ and putting him to shame.

---

[1]Smith, *Teachings of the Prophet Joseph Smith,* p. 358.

For those who have had the witness of the Holy Ghost, fighting with wicked hate against his authorized servants is the same, for if this is done to them, it is also done against him. For men who have had the light of the Holy Ghost to turn away and fight the truth with murderous hate, and those who are authorized to proclaim it, there is no forgiveness in this world, neither in the world to come.[2]

This is in line with the teaching in Hebrews:

For it is impossible for those who were once enlightened, and have tasted of the heavenly gift, and were made partakers of the Holy Ghost,

And have tasted the good word of God, and the powers of the world to come,

If they shall fall away, to renew them again unto repentance; seeing they crucify to themselves the Son of God afresh, and put him to an open shame. (Heb. 6:4-6.)

During the Savior's ministry he made an instructive comment on the sin against the Holy Ghost, which is rendered as follows in Joseph Smith's Inspired Revision of the Bible:

Wherefore, I say unto you, all manner of sin and blasphemy shall be forgiven unto men *who receive me and repent*; but the blasphemy against the Holy Ghost, it shall not be forgiven unto men.

And whosoever shall speak a word against the Son of Man, it shall be forgiven him; but whosoever speaketh against the Holy Ghost it shall not be forgiven him; neither in this world, neither in the world to come. (Inspired Version, Matt. 12:31-32. Italics added.)

The words italicized in the above passage seem to limit the unpardonable sins to those who have received the gospel. Thus "dead works" will not save anyone. Sincerity, faith, repentance, and worthiness must characterize the recipient of the ordinance. "Wherefore, although a man should be baptized an hundred times it availeth him nothing, for you cannot enter in at the strait gate by the law of Moses, neither by your dead works." (D&C 22:2.)

---

[2]Joseph Fielding Smith, "The Sin Against the Holy Ghost," *The Improvement Era*, (July, 1955) p. 494.

Endure to the End

Having received the necessary saving ordinances — baptism, the gift of the Holy Ghost, temple ordinances and sealings — one must live the covenants made. He must endure in faith. No matter how brilliant was the service rendered by the bishop or stake president or other person, if he falters later in his life and fails to live righteously "to the end" the good works he did all stand in jeopardy. In fact, one who serves and then falls away may be in the category spoken of by Peter, "the dog turning to his vomit or the sow returning to her wallowing in the mire." (See 2 Pet. 2:22.)

> And he that endureth not unto the end, the same is he that is also hewn down and cast into the fire, from whence they can no more return, because of the justice of the Father. (3 Ne. 27:17.)

Corianton apparently was in danger of not enduring to the end (having been guilty of immorality) when his father Alma told him:

> For behold, if ye deny the Holy Ghost when it once has had place in you, and ye know that ye deny it, behold, this is a sin which is unpardonable; yea, and whosoever murdereth against the light and knowledge of God, it is not easy for him to obtain forgiveness. . . . (Al. 39:6.)

To what extent must the Holy Ghost have "had a place in you"? President Joseph F. Smith had this to say:

> No man can sin against light until he has it; nor against the Holy Ghost, until after he has received it by the gift of God through the appointed channel or way. To sin against the Holy Ghost, the Spirit of Truth, the Comforter, the Witness of the Father and the Son, wilfully denying him and defying him, after having received him, constitutes this sin. . . .[3]

It is important for all men that they do not even approach the tragic point of the unpardonable sin. Numerous people have lost the Spirit through immorality and through rebellion brought about by the sophistry and philosophy of men, and sometimes through fancied offenses. Bitterness

---

[3]Smith, *Gospel Doctrine*, p. 434.

has a way of poisoning the mind and killing the spirit. One should take no chances of permitting such situations to become sore and gangrenous, for who can tell when one might slip across the line? To do so rather than enduring to the end is perhaps to be in the category Peter described:

> For if after they have escaped the pollutions of the world through the knowledge of the Lord and Saviour Jesus Christ, they are again entangled therein, and overcome, the latter end is worse with them than the beginning.
>
> For it had been better for them not to have known the way of righteousness, than, after they have known it, to turn from the holy commandment delivered unto them. (2 Pet. 2:20-21.)

Sin Against the Holy Ghost

The sins unto death may be thought of as somewhat difficult to define and limit with precision. From the words of Joseph Smith quoted above we note that ". . . many apostates of The Church of Jesus Christ of Latter-day Saints" will fall into this category. We cannot definitely identify them individually since it is impossible for us to know the extent of their knowledge, the depth of their enlightenment, and the sureness of their testimonies before their fall.

When one has received the Holy Ghost he has a companion who will constantly warn and teach and inspire him. (See Moro. 10:5.) If not driven away through uncleanness or other persistent wickedness the Holy Ghost will always bear increasing witness to gospel truth. The potency of his influence is emphasized in this explanation by President Joseph Fielding Smith:

> The reason blasphemy against the Son of God may be forgiven, even if the Son be made manifest in a vision or a dream, is that such manifestation does not impress the soul as deeply as does the testimony of the Holy Ghost. The influence of the Holy Ghost is spirit speaking to spirit, and the indelible impression is one that brings conversion and conviction to the soul as no other influence can. The Holy Spirit reveals the truth with a positiveness wherein there is no doubt and therefore is far more impressive than a vision given to the eye.[4]

---

[4]Smith, *The Improvement Era* (July, 1955), p. 494.

The depth and durability of impressions made by "spirit speaking to spirit" perhaps explains the Lord's statement to Thomas after his resurrection: "Thomas, because thou hast seen me, thou hast believed: blessed are they that have not seen, and yet have believed." (John 20:29.) Here was the reference to the surer witness. The eyes can be deceived, as can the other physical senses, but the testimony of the Holy Ghost is certain.

The sin against the Holy Ghost requires such knowledge that it is manifestly impossible for the rank and file to commit such a sin. Comparatively few Church members will commit murder wherein they shed innocent blood, and we hope only few will deny the Holy Ghost.

Priesthood Oath and Covenant

Relevant to this subject are the Lord's words about the oath and covenant of the priesthood. They say in part:

> For whoso is faithful unto the obtaining these two priesthoods of which I have spoken, *and the magnifying their calling,* are sanctified by the Spirit unto the renewing of their bodies.

> They become the sons of Moses and of Aaron and the seed of Abraham, and the church and kingdom, and the elect of God. (D&C 84:33-34. Italics added.)

In the words "magnifying their calling," far more seems to be implied than the mere attending of priesthood meetings, administering to the sacrament and the sick, and serving in Church work. Faithfulness to warrant the reception of the priesthood is a condition that perhaps all men do not meet. And the magnifying of their calling seems to imply a totalness which few, if any, men reach in mortality. Perfection of body and spirit seems to be included here. Also in the next five verses much is implied which is not amplified fully:

> And also all they who receive this priesthood receive me, saith the Lord;

> For he that receiveth my servants receiveth me;

> And he that receiveth me receiveth my Father;

> And he that receiveth my Father receiveth my Father's king-
> dom; therefore all that my Father hath shall be given unto him.
>
> And this is according to the oath and covenant which be-
> longeth to the priesthood. (D&C 84:35-39.)

The word "receive" in these sentences has deep meaning.
To receive in this connection seems to mean more than
merely to accept casually, but to magnify and develop and
make effective. To receive the servants might mean to
accept calls and responsibilities and to serve well and faithfully; to receive the Lord would mean loving him and
obeying all his commandments; to receive the Father would
mean to leave nothing undone toward arriving at personal
perfection; and all this means exaltation and eternal life,
for the promise is the kingdom and "all that my Father
hath." A moment's reflection will remind us of the infinite
knowledge, power, dominion, kingdoms, exaltations, and
joy offered to us here in an oath and covenant which the
Father cannot break. If we measure up fully we are guaranteed limitless blessings!

And lest the enormous difficulty of the task should dis-
courage one from accepting the priesthood, the Lord
warned: "And wo unto all those who come not unto this
priesthood . . ." (D&C 84:42.) I have known people who
would not be baptized and confirmed and who would not
receive the priesthood because of the grave responsibility
they would assume by accepting. Clearly one will not escape
condemnation by refusing to accept the responsibility.

Likewise the Lord specifies the terms on which we receive the priesthood:

> Therefore, all those who receive the priesthood, receive this
> oath and covenant of my Father, which he cannot break, neither
> can it be moved.
>
> But whoso breaketh this covenant after he hath received it,
> and altogether turneth therefrom, shall not have forgiveness of
> sins in this world nor in the world to come. (D&C 84:40-41.)

Verse 41 might well strike terror to the heart as we
realize its implications, yet in our weaknesses and our failure fully to measure up we rejoice that the word "alto-

gether" has been inserted. It seems to imply rejection, that one who would reject the program and make little or no effort to comply could miss the blessings promised. It seems to imply also that so long as one is bending every effort to measure up yet fails in perfection, there is hope for him.

Sons of Perdition

Those who followed Lucifer in his rebellion in the pre-mortal life and those who in mortality sin against the Holy Ghost are sons of perdition. The ex-mortal sons of perdition will be resurrected, as will everyone else; but they will finally suffer the second death, the spiritual death, for "they are cut off again as to things pertaining to righteousness." (Hel. 14:18.)

In the days of the restoration there apparently were those who taught that the devil and his angels and the sons of perdition should sometime be restored. The Prophet Joseph Smith would not countenance the teaching of this doctrine, and sanctioned the decision of the bishop that any who taught it should be barred from communion.[5]

In the realms of perdition or the kingdom of darkness, where there is no light, Satan and the unembodied spirits of the pre-existence shall dwell together with those of mortality who retrogress to the level of perdition. These have lost the power of regeneration. They have sunk so low as to have lost the inclinations and ability to repent, consequently the gospel plan is useless to them as an agent of growth and development.

> And he who cannot abide the law of a telestial kingdom cannot abide a telestial glory; therefore he is not meet for a kingdom of glory. Therefore he must abide a kingdom which is not a kingdom of glory. (D&C 88:24.)

> Thus saith the Lord concerning all those who know my power, and have been made partakers thereof, and suffered themselves through the power of the devil to be overcome, and to deny the truth and defy my power —

---

[5]See Smith, *Teachings of the Prophet Joseph Smith*, p. 24.

They are they who are the sons of perdition, of whom I say that it had been better for them never to have been born;

For they are vessels of wrath, doomed to suffer the wrath of God, with the devil and his angels in eternity;

Concerning whom I have said there is no forgiveness in this world nor in the world to come —

Having denied the Holy Spirit after having received it, and having denied the Only Begotten Son of the Father, having crucified him unto themselves and put him to an open shame.

These are they who shall go away into the lake of fire and brimstone, with the devil and his angels —

And the only ones on whom the second death shall have any power;

Yea, verily, the only ones who shall not be redeemed in the due time of the Lord, after the sufferings of his wrath. (D&C 76:31-38.)

These deny the Son and the gospel of repentance, and thus lose the power to repent. Their habitation shall be where

. . . the fire is not quenched, which is their torment —

And the end thereof, neither the place thereof, nor their torment, no man knows;

Neither was it revealed, neither is, neither will be revealed unto man, except to them who are made partakers thereof. (D&C 76:44-46.)

The Prophet Joseph Smith gives us this further picture:

. . . Those who commit the unpardonable sin are doomed to Gnolom — to dwell in hell, worlds without end. As they concocted scenes of bloodshed in this world, so they shall rise to that resurrection which is as the lake of fire and brimstone. Some shall rise to the everlasting burnings of God; for God dwells in everlasting burnings and some shall rise to the damnation of their own filthiness, which is as exquisite a torment as the lake of fire and brimstone.[6]

Speculation as to individual sons of perdition is at best unprofitable. Some have consigned Judas Iscariot to this doom, based on certain scriptural passages. (See John 12:6;

---

[6]*Documentary History of the Church,* Vol. 6, p. 317.

6:70; 17:12; Acts 1:20.) President Joseph F. Smith questions this interpretation:

> To my mind it strongly appears that not one of the disciples possessed sufficient light, knowledge nor wisdom, at the time of the crucifixion, for either exaltation or condemnation; for it was afterward that their minds were opened to understand the scriptures, and that they were endowed with power from on high; without which they were only children in knowledge, in comparison to what they afterwards became under the influence of the Spirit.[7]

The Murderer

John wrote that "no murderer hath eternal life abiding in him." The murderer denies himself salvation in the celestial kingdom, and in this sense he cannot be forgiven for his crime.

The instance of the first murder is instructive. Though thoroughly taught the gospel by his parents, Cain "loved Satan more than God." He became rebellious, "carnal, sensual, and devilish." Cain was to become the father of Satan's lies and to be called perdition. His culminating sin was the murder of his brother Abel, which he did by secret covenant with Satan and to gain Abel's possessions. As a punishment the Lord consigned the wicked Cain to be a fugitive and a vagabond and placed a mark upon him which would reveal his identity.

On the sad character Cain, an interesting story comes to us from Lycurgus A. Wilson's book on the life of David W. Patten. From the book I quote an extract from a letter by Abraham O. Smoot giving his recollection of David Patten's account of meeting "a very remarkable person who had represented himself as being Cain."

> As I was riding along the road on my mule I suddenly noticed a very strange personage walking beside me. . . . His head was about even with my shoulders as I sat in my saddle. He wore no clothing, but was covered with hair. His skin was very dark. I asked him where he dwelt and he replied that he had

---

[7]Smith, *Gospel Doctrine*, p. 433.

no home, that he was a wanderer in the earth and traveled to and fro. He said he was a very miserable creature, that he had earnestly sought death during his sojourn upon the earth, but that he could not die, and his mission was to destroy the souls of men. About the time he expressed himself thus, I rebuked him in the name of the Lord Jesus Christ and by virtue of the Holy Priesthood, and commanded him to go hence, and he immediately departed out of my sight. . . .[8]

Another scriptural character responsible for murder — and this in conjunction with adultery — was the great King David. For his dreadful crime, all his life afterward he sought forgiveness. Some of the Psalms portray the anguish of his soul, yet David is still paying for his sin. He did not receive the resurrection at the time of the resurrection of Jesus Christ. Peter declared that his body was still in the tomb. (See Acts 2:29-34.)

President Joseph F. Smith made this comment on David's position:

But even David, though guilty of adultery and murder of Uriah, obtained the promise that his soul should not be left in hell, which means, as I understand it, that even he shall escape the second death.[9]

The Prophet Joseph Smith underlined the seriousness of the sin of murder for David as for all men, and the fact that there is no forgiveness for it.

A murderer, for instance, one that sheds innocent blood, cannot have forgiveness. David sought repentance at the hand of God carefully with tears, for the murder of Uriah; but he could only get it through hell: he got a promise that his soul should not be left in hell.

Although David was a king, he never did obtain the spirit and power of Elijah and the fullness of the Priesthood; and the Priesthood that he received, and the throne and kingdom of David is to be taken from him and given to another by the name of David in the last days, raised up out of his lineage.[10]

---

[8]Lycurgus A. Wilson, *Life of David W. Patten* (Salt Lake City: Deseret News, 1900), p. 50.

[9]Smith, *Gospel Doctrine*, p. 434.

[10]Smith, *Teachings of the Prophet Joseph Smith*, p. 339.

Perhaps one reason murder is so heinous is that man cannot restore life. Man's mortal life is given him in which to repent and prepare himself for eternity, and should one of his fellowmen terminate his life and thus limit his progress by making his repentance impossible, it would be a ghastly deed, a tremendous responsibility for which the murderer might not be able to atone in his lifetime.

Of course, the laws both of the land and of God recognize a great difference between murder or wilful slaughter and manslaughter which was not premeditated. Likewise men unfortunately must take others' lives in war. Some of our conscientious young men have been disturbed and concerned as they have been compelled to kill. There are mitigating circumstances but certainly the blame and responsibility rest heavily upon the heads of those who brought about the war, making necessary the taking of life. It is conceivable that even in war there may be many times when there is a legitimate choice and enemy combatants could be taken prisoner rather than be killed.

Here is an excerpt from the message of the First Presidency dated April 6, 1942:

> The whole world is in the midst of a war that seems the worst of all time. The Church is a world-wide church. Its devoted members are in both camps. They are the innocent war instrumentalities of their warring sovereignties. On each side they believe they are fighting for home, country, and freedom. On each side, our brethren pray to the same God, in the same name, for victory. Both sides cannot be wholly right; perhaps neither is without wrong. God will work out in His own due time and in His own sovereign way the justice and right of the conflict but he will not hold the innocent instrumentalities of the war, our brethren in arms, responsible for the conflict. This is a major crisis in the world-life of man. God is at the helm.

Even among wilful murderers there are grades and categories. There are the Herods and the Eichmanns and the Heydrichs, who kill for sadistic pleasure. There are those who kill in drunkenness, in rage, in anger, in jealousy. There are those who kill for gain, for power, for fear. There are those who kill for lust. They certainly will suffer different degrees of punishment hereafter. The proper earthly penalty for the crime is clearly set out in the scriptures and applied to all ages of the world. This penalty is the prerogative and responsibility of governmental authority, since no unauthorized person may take the law into his own hands and slay a fellow being:

> Whoso sheddeth man's blood, by man shall his blood be shed: for in the image of God made he man. (Gen. 9:6.)

> He that smiteth a man, so that he die, shall be surely put to death. (Ex. 21:12.)

> And he that killeth any man shall surely be put to death. (Lev. 24:17.)

> . . . Thou shalt not kill, but he that killeth shall die. (D&C 42:19.)

Regrettably, too, there are people who, when finally discovered in their defalcations, in misappropriation of funds, in deep transgressions involving immorality and which affect families and friends, and in other sins, begin to think of suicide. Sometimes the temptation toward suicide comes when a person is bowed in grief at bereavement or feeling inadequate to meet and cope with the difficult situations he encounters. To end it all! But this great crime does not end it. In his right mind, only a fool would ever consider taking his own life.

The Church and the Murderer

Occasionally people who have murdered come to the Church requesting baptism, having come to some partial realization of the enormity of the crime. Missionaries do not knowingly baptize such people. Rather than assuming this great responsibility, they refer the problem to their mission presidents who in turn will wish to refer the matter to the First Presidency of the Church. This response is in line with Joseph Smith's comment on murderers, and particularly on those of the Savior:

> Peter referred to the same subject on the day of Pentecost, but the multitude did not get the endowment that Peter had; but

several days after the people asked, "What shall we do?" Peter says, "I would ye had done it ignorantly," speaking of crucifying the Lord, etc. He did not say to them, "Repent and be baptized for the remission of your sins"; but he said, "Repent ye therefore, and be converted, that your sins may be blotted out, when the times of refreshing shall come from the presence of the Lord."

This is the case with murderers. They could not be baptized for the remission of sins, for they had shed innocent blood."[11]

To Church members the word is clear:

And now, behold, I speak unto the church. Thou shalt not kill; and he that kills shall not have forgiveness in this world, nor in the world to come. (D&C 42:18.)

And it shall come to pass, that if any persons among you shall kill they shall be delivered up and dealt with according to the laws of the land; for remember that he hath no forgiveness; and it shall be proved according to the laws of the land. (D&C 42:79.)

When a member of the Church is adjudged guilty of murder or what seems to approach the terrible crime, consideration should be given to excommunication, which in most cases is the penalty required.

Avoid the First Steps

Even unpardonable sins should be repented of. The murderer does not have eternal life abiding in him, but a merciful God will grant to every soul adequate rewards for every good deed he does. God is just. He will compensate for every effort to do good, to repent, to overcome sin. Even the murderer is justified in repenting and mending his ways and building up a credit balance in his favor.

Much better is it to avoid the steps which lead to unforgivable sin. Thus as a preventive measure against murder one should avoid anger and hatred, avarice and greed, and any of the other impulses which can spark the act. Nephi said his brothers were murderers at heart. One usually will commit the deed in his thoughts many times before he will deliberately commit the crime in actuality.

---

[11]*Ibid.*

Similarly the wise Church member will not take the first step in separating himself from the Church, as many do through apostasy. He will pray frequently and regularly, read the scriptures, and generally stay close to the Lord. He will diligently fulfil his Church and family duties and will follow the counsel of his spiritual leaders. By so doing he will always be able to repent of his sins as he pursues the upward road; he will never approach the unforgivable sin; he will never get anywhere near the point of no return.

Chapter Ten

Repent or Perish

> . . . *Except ye repent, ye shall all likewise perish.*
>
> —Luke 13:3

REPENTANCE IS THE KEY TO FORGIVENESS. IT OPENS the door to happiness and peace and points the way to salvation in the kingdom of God. It unlocks the spirit of humility in the soul of man and makes him contrite of heart and submissive to the will of God.

"Sin is the transgression of the law" (1 John 3:4.), and for such transgression a punishment is affixed under eternal law. Every normal individual is responsible for the sins he commits, and would be similarly liable to the punishment attached to those broken laws. However, Christ's death on the cross offers us exemption from the eternal punishment for most sins. He took upon himself the punishment for the sins of all the world, with the understanding that those who repent and come unto him will be forgiven of their sins and freed from the punishment.

Message of the Ages

In these circumstances it is not surprising that through his prophets a loving God has constantly emphasized the call to repentance. It would be interesting if we could have a recording of each dispensation of the gospel in sequence, and hear the pleas and commands for repentance repeated through six millennia. It would be impressive to see the speaker and to hear the intonation of his voice — loud, penetrating, soft, pleading, warning, calling. They would be portentous words.

We would hear the voice of Jacob discharging the responsibility which weighed heavily upon him: ". . . It must needs be that I teach you the consequences of sin." (2 Ne. 9:48.) And from Mars Hill, where the sophisticated Athenians were debating over their numerous gods, we would hear Paul's words denouncing their deities and explaining their "unknown god": "And the times of this ignorance God winked at; but now commandeth all men every where to repent." (Acts 17:30.)

There would be also the voices of Adam, Noah, Lehi, Alma, Abraham and Isaiah and many others, all like a John the Baptist preaching in the wilderness: ". . . Bring forth . . . fruits meet for repentance." (Matt. 3:8.) And prominent would be the voice of Jesus Christ himself giving priority to this all-important call as he ushered in the dispensation of the meridian of time with the words, "Repent: for the kingdom of heaven is at hand." (Matt. 4:17.)

Penalties for Unrepentant

The prophetic message has always carried the same penalty, for no one can reject with impunity the call from the God of law and justice. Hence the alternative the Lord has given — repent or perish!

Abinadi gives solemn warning:

> But behold, and fear, and tremble before God, for ye ought to tremble; for the Lord redeemeth none such that rebel against him and *die in their sins*; yea, even all those that have perished in their sins ever since the world began, that have wilfully rebelled against God, that have known the commandments of God, and would not keep them; these are they that have no part in the first resurrection. (Mos. 15:26. Italics added.)

That endless misery and suffering await the unrepentant sinner is amply attested in the holy scriptures. For instance:

And if their works are evil they shall be restored unto them for evil. Therefore, all things shall be restored to their proper order, every thing to its natural frame—mortality raised to immortality, corruption to incorruption—raised to endless happiness to inherit the kingdom of God, or to endless misery to inherit the kingdom of the devil, the one on one hand, the other on the other. (Al. 41:4.)

Perhaps the best summation of the multitude of scriptures warning of the penalties visited upon the unrepentant is the comparison the Lord makes between these penalties and his own sacrificial suffering:

Therefore I command you to repent—repent, lest I smite you by the rod of my mouth, and by my wrath, and by my anger, and your sufferings be sore—how sore you know not, how exquisite you know not, yea, how hard to bear you know not.

For behold, I, God, have suffered these things for all, that they might not suffer if they would repent;

But if they would not repent they must suffer even as I;

Which suffering caused myself, even God, the greatest of all, to tremble because of pain, and to bleed at every pore, and to suffer both body and spirit. . . (D&C 19:15-18. Italics added.)

Civilizations Destroyed Through Sin

One would have thought that all the pleadings and warnings the Lord has made through his prophets over the centuries would induce a high general level of righteousness. Unfortunately this is not so. Apparently it is easier for man to sin than to live a life of righteousness; therefore, greater effort needs to be put forth to avoid evil and conform our lives to the elevating principles of the gospel. This is understandable, since

. . . the natural man is an enemy to God, and has been from the fall of Adam, and will be, forever and ever, unless he yields to the enticings of the Holy Spirit, and putteth off the natural man and becometh a saint through the atonement of Christ the Lord, and becometh as a child, submissive, meek, humble, patient, full of love, willing to submit to all things which the Lord seeth fit to inflict upon him, even as a child doth submit to his father. (Mos. 3:19.)

This ascendency of the natural man, this rejection of God's call to repentance, has caused the destruction of entire civilizations. In the early generations it is true that those who were sufficiently righteous followed Enoch to a translated life; but only eight, Noah and sons and their four wives, were preserved later through the great flood, all others being drowned. In their debauchery, the unrepentant Babylonians lost their kingdom, and the individuals of the nation placed their souls in serious jeopardy when they did not repent. Likewise Sodom and Gomorrah, the cities of the plain, were destroyed. They had their chance also to repent but ignored the warning voices of the prophets who came to them.

Can one ever forget the tribulations of the tribes of Israel as the foreign nations came upon them and despoiled their cities and their country, ravished their women, blinded their king and took them captive to serve as slaves? Their temple was defiled, their sacred vessels expropriated, their national identity terminated. We read with sad hearts of the song of regret and anguish and loneliness sung by the Jewish survivors:

> By the rivers of Babylon, there we sat down, yea, we wept, when we remembered Zion.
>
> We hanged our harps upon the willows in the midst thereof.
>
> For there they that carried us away captive required of us a song; and they that wasted us required of us mirth, saying, Sing us one of the songs of Zion.
>
> How shall we sing the Lord's song in a strange land?
>
> If I forget thee, O Jerusalem, let my right hand forget her cunning.
>
> If I do not remember thee, let my tongue cleave to the roof of my mouth; if I prefer not Jerusalem above my chief joy. (Ps. 137:1-6.)

Even then, when the exiles were later allowed to return to their native land, the lesson was unheeded, evil dominated the lives of the people, and all the warnings and threats were as nothing. The Jews even rejected and crucified their Lord and Master. Then the heavy weight of the penalties finally came upon them through the Roman legions who crushed them, destroyed their palaces, and killed and scattered the people.

And what of the plight of the posterity of Lehi, who seemingly quickly forgot their afflictions after they had been relieved from them? Persisting in their wickedness, they needed to be chastised numerous times and were finally cut off. We seem to hear the moaning of Mormon as he might weep for them:

> O ye fair ones, how could ye have departed from the ways of the Lord! O ye fair ones, how could ye have rejected that Jesus, who stood with open arms to receive you!
>
> Behold if ye had not done this, ye would not have fallen. But behold, ye are fallen, and I mourn your loss. (Morm. 6:17-18.)

My wife and I spent a holiday one year down in Maya land. We were days in Chichén Itzá and Uxmal climbing the old pyramids and the ruins of an ancient civilization. As we ascended those steep steps, felt our way through those dark passages, and looked out over that vast area, the thought continued to come to me: Why, why aren't these Mayan Indians still building temples and other magnificent structures?

We went into some of the little Mayan homes of today. They are small houses, elliptical in shape, twice as long as they are wide — and having only dirt floors. They are made of sticks plastered with mud. They have thatched roofs made from the grasses that grow in the ubiquitous jungles.

Again, I wondered: Why do they grovel in the earth today when in the long-ago-past they had their observatories and looked into the heavens? The answer comes ringing back with great force: Because they forgot the purpose of life! They forgot the thing for which they had come to earth and they dwelt in the earth and lived an earthy life. And the time came when God could not tolerate it longer and they were permitted to be decimated and destroyed.

When we went abroad, among the interesting things we saw in Italy was the city of Pompeii. When I had been a boy in my early teens I had read from my father's library *The Last Days of Pompeii.* It intrigued me. I read it many times. So when we crossed the border into Italy that day, one of my greatest anticipations was to see Pompeii.

After spending some days among the ruins of Rome we went down to Naples, to climb Vesuvius and to see Pompeii. We went as high on the mountain as we could go in a taxi and then climbed the rest of the way to the top. We stood in the crater and less than a yard under our feet was the boiling, seething mass of lava. We could feel its fiery breath; we could see its rich color. Vesuvius was still active. And then we remembered that back in A.D. 79 the Lord permitted it to "blow its top" literally and figuratively.

This city of Pompeii, as we came to know by first-hand observation, was a worldly city. The politicians, the wealthy, the socialites, came from Rome to Pompeii near the coast of the Mediterranean. There they spent their money and time in lavish and riotous living.

The city of Pompeii has now been excavated. The stone roads show the marks of chariot wheels. The roads are lower than the sidewalks and we could see where the hubs of the chariots had worn into the stones at the corners of the blocks. We went into their bakeries where the food had been prepared. We went into their homes where they had lived. We went into their theaters and into their baths. Their empty brothels and houses of prostitution were locked with padlocks and carried signs in Italian, "For Men Only." These places of shame stood after nineteen centuries, a witness of their degradation; and on the walls in these buildings, in color still preserved for these nearly two millennia, were the pictures of every vice that could be committed by human beings — all the vicious sins that have accumulated since Cain began his evil ways.

Then I came to realize why Pompeii was destroyed. There came a time when it just had to be destroyed. And as Vesuvius erupted, it blew up, and the ashes went into the sky for miles and miles — millions of tons of them. The lava flowed down the edge of that conical structure and pushed before it everything in its path, burning the vineyards, the orchards, and some of the homes. It destroyed everything in its path, and some little cities were completely burned or covered out of existence.

But Pompeii did not all burn. It was not in the way of the lava flow, but the cinders and ashes in the air gradually settled, covering the city completely. The people in their buildings were choked to death. Their bodies were later found clasping each other in deadly embrace. Cats and dogs were there in the buildings. They were found as they died — covered with ashes, so that when the excavation was completed, the houses and contents were in place. There had been no general fire, but many of the roofs had burned off. Pompeii was destroyed. I think I know why. It was because of its wickedness and depravity. I think Pompeii must have been in much the same lamentable situation as Sodom and Gomorrah long before it.

Modern Sinners Invite Similar Penalties

It seems strange that with all these historical examples of peoples who were destroyed because of unrepented sin, so many pursue a similar course today, including many in America. Yet the promise has been given to the great nations of the Americas that they shall never fall if they will but serve God. Those in the service of the Lord in those nations are but a token number. The devil reigns; sin is rampant in political, religious and social circles. Evil is called good, and good evil.

"Let us eat, drink and be merry, for tomorrow we may die," has been the theme song of the worldly wise since time began. "Let's live it up" is a more modern interpretation. It means, have fun today and let tomorrow take care of itself. There are the fun lovers who sit at the banquet table, drink their liquor in their homes and clubs, violate the moral laws. Then there is another class of people who have an obsession to accumulate worldly wealth, even at great costs of spirituality and morality. To such the Lord gave the parable of the rich fool:

> And he spake a parable unto them, saying, The ground of a certain rich man brought forth plentifully:
>
> And he thought within himself, saying, What shall I do, because I have no room where to bestow my fruits?
>
> And he said, This will I do: I will pull down my barns, and build greater; and there will I bestow all my fruits and my goods.
>
> And I will say to my soul, Soul, thou hast much goods laid up for many years; take thine ease, eat, drink, and be merry.
>
> But God said unto him, Thou fool, this night thy soul shall be required of thee: then whose shall those things be, which thou hast provided?
>
> So is he that layeth up treasure for himself, and is not rich toward God. (Luke 12:16-21.)

Some are deceived by the prosperity of the wicked. They argue that many people gain their riches through crime, and that by ignoring the Lord's commandments they show a constant profit. This concept wrongly focuses on the short-term. The wicked may appear to be temporarily triumphant, as those seemed who crucified the Master, but the Savior's Parable of the Tares allows for this situation. Like the tares, the wicked are allowed to ripen — for eventual destruction.

Sin Brings Natural Consequences

Should there be readers who think of the Lord as an angry, cruel God who brings vengeance on people for not complying with his laws, let them think again. He organized a plan which was natural — a cause-and-effect program. It is inconceivable that God would desire to punish or to see his children in suffering or pain or distress. He is a God of peace and tranquility. He offers joy and growth and happiness and peace. Through Ezekiel the Lord asks: "Have I any pleasure at all that the wicked should die? saith the Lord God: and not that he should return from his ways, and live?" (Ezek. 18:23.) And the Psalmist adds: "Let the wicked fall into their own nets . . ." (Ps. 141:10.)

Yes, causes inevitably bring effects. One may avoid high tension wires, having been told they are dangerous, or he may touch them and suffer the consequences. Similarly, one may learn by obeying God's laws gracefully or he may learn by suffering. And this applies in any era — 4000 B.C., 2000 B.C., in the Savior's time, or in the twentieth century.

Many people have a difficult time in assuming the blame for their misfortunes. There must always be a scapegoat. If they fall, they look about to see who pushed them. If they fail, they assess the failure to others who prevented them or did not help them. Thus if what they call "bad luck" attends them, they are prone to blame fortune rather than themselves. And in the ultimate, the Lord gets blamed for many of our woes and seldom gets thanked for our achievements.

Two Book of Mormon prophets help to set the record straight on this. Alma told his son, Corianton: ". . . And thus they stand or fall; for behold, they are their own judges, whether to do good or do evil." (Al. 41:7.) And from Mormon we learn that "it is by the wicked that the wicked are punished." (Morm. 4:5.)

But however he tries, a man cannot escape the consequences of sin. They follow as the night follows the day. Sometimes the penalties are delayed in coming, but they are as sure as life itself. Remorse and agony come. Even ignorance of the law does not prevent, though it may mitigate, the punishment. Remorse may be pushed aside with bravado and brainwashing, but it will return to prick and pinch. It may be drowned in alcohol or temporarily shocked into numbness in the increasing sins which follow, but the conscience will eventually awaken, and remorse and sorrow will be followed by pain and suffering and finally torture and distress in the exquisite degree spoken of by the Lord in the passage quoted previously in this chapter. And the longer repentance is pushed into the background the more exquisite will be the punishment when it finally comes to the fore.

The words of Alma give us what is perhaps the best scriptural account of the exquisite suffering of the sinner.

> But I was racked with eternal torment, for my soul was harrowed up to the greatest degree and racked with all my sins.
>
> Yea, I did remember all my sins and iniquities, for which I was tormented with the pains of hell; yea, I saw that I had rebelled against my God, and that I had not kept his holy commandments.
>
> Yea, and I had murdered many of his children, or rather led them away unto destruction; yea, and in fine so great had been my iniquities, that the very thought of coming into the presence of my God did rack my soul with inexpressible horror.
>
> Oh, thought I, that I could be banished and become extinct both soul and body, that I might not be brought to stand in the presence of my God, to be judged of my deeds.
>
> And now, for three days and for three nights was I racked, even with the pains of a damned soul. (Al. 36:12-16.)

If men would only let their sins trouble them early when the sins are small and few, how much anguish would be saved them! Those who have never suffered the pain and "gnashing of teeth" which the sinner goes through would hardly understand. Church leaders have many come to them who are beginning to have a realization of the seriousness of their errors. To see them mentally writhe and seethe in their suffering is to know something of what the Lord meant when he said their sufferings would be sore and exquisite. Unfortunately, many transgressors sear the conscience and continue on in their sins until a judgment day comes.

Unfortunately too, the natural consequences of sin are not confined to the transgressor. One of the saddest features of wrongdoing is that it grievously affects the lives of those who love the wrongdoer — innocent children, dutiful wife, wronged husband, and aged parents. All such suffer the penalties.

Consequences Are Inescapable

That person who attempts to escape from reality and to avoid the penalties, to avoid coping with the situation, is somewhat like that escapist who had committed serious crime and was incarcerated in the penitentiary with a life sentence. He felt he had been very clever in his manipulations and that only through some error or trick of fate had he been caught.

In the long, merciless hours behind the bars, he planned his escape. With much organization and effort he created a tiny saw, and with this he worked almost ceaselessly in the dead of night until he eventually sawed a bar through. He waited until what he thought was a propitious moment in the stillness of the night to pull the bar aside and to squeeze his body out through the aperture, and as he cleared the bars the thought came into his mind, "Ah, at last I am free!" And then he realized that he was only in the inner passageways, and he had not yet freed himself.

He stealthily moved down the hallway to the door and stood in the darkness of the corner until the guard came along. He knocked the guard unconscious and took his keys and opened the door. As he got a breath of the cool outside air the thought came to him again, "I am free! I am clever. No one can hold me; no one can force me to pay the penalties." As he quietly stepped out he noted that he was still in the outer courts of the prison compound. He was still a prisoner.

But he had planned well. He found a rope, threw it over the wall and got the end caught, and pulled himself up by the rope to the top of the wall. "At last I am free," he thought, "I do not need to pay penalties. I am clever enough to evade the pursuers." About this time the lights went on from the wall towers, and guns began to shoot, and the alarm was given. He dropped quickly down on the outside in the dark and ran for cover. As he got farther from the prison he heard the bloodhounds baying, but his scent was lost for the dogs as he waded a distance in the creek.

He found a hiding place in the city until his pursuers had lost his tracks.

Eventually he found his way out into the eastern part of the state and hired himself out to a stockman, herding sheep. He was far out in the hills. No one had seemed to recognize him. He changed his appearance by letting his hair and beard grow. The months passed. At first he reveled in his freedom and prided himself on his cunning — on how he had eluded all pursuers and now had no witnesses and no accusers, and he was free and did not have to answer to anyone. But the months were barren and stale, the sheep were monotonous, time was limitless; his dreams would never terminate. He came to realize that he could not get away from himself and his accusing conscience. He came to know that he was not free, that he was in fact in fetters and bondage; and there seemed to be ears that heard what he said, eyes that saw what he did, silent voices that were always accusing him of what he had done. The freedom in which he had reveled had changed to chains.

Finally this escapist left his sheep, went into town and terminated his employment. Then he found his way back to the big city and to the officers of the law and told them he was ready to pay so that he could be free.

This man learned the cost of sin. Many do not learn that cost in this life, simply because the payments may be deferred. What effect would it have if the payments were always "in cash"? A thoughtful comment whose authorship I do not know considers that point:

> I am convinced that if each thing we did wrong had a price tag on it, the world would experience a phenomenal change. That is to say, if we could see what each such wrongdoing is costing, we might think twice before committing the act. Unfortunately, we often have only a vague notion of the terrible cost or allow Satan to sugar-coat our concept of circumstances. But, let us stop and look at some of these prices. It is quite certain that if all rewards for goodness were immediately available and all the penalties for evil were immediately assessed and suffered there would

seldom be a second evil—but then, that would tamper with one's precious free agency.

We might add that one's position makes no difference to the inescapability of the consequences of sin. In the Church, the bishop, the stake president, the apostle — all are subject to the same laws of right living, and penalties follow their sins just as for the other members of the Church. None are exempt from the results of sin, as regards either Church action against the offender or the effects of sin upon the soul.

Do Not Die in Sin

When we think of the great sacrifice of our Lord Jesus Christ and the sufferings he endured for us, we would be ingrates if we did not appreciate it so far as our power made it possible. He suffered and died for us, yet if we do not repent, all his anguish and pain on our account are futile. In his own words:

> For behold, I, God, have suffered these things for all, that they might not suffer if they would repent;
>
> But if they would not repent they must suffer even as I.
>
> Which suffering caused myself, even God, the greatest of all, to tremble because of pain, and to bleed at every pore, and to suffer both body and spirit. . . (D&C 19:16-18.)

Abinadi expressed the danger of delaying repentance:

> But remember that he that persists in his own carnal nature, and goes on in the ways of sin and rebellion against God, remaineth in his fallen state and the devil hath all power over him. Therefore, he is as though there was no redemption made, being an enemy to God; and also is the devil an enemy to God. (Mos. 16:5.)

This only underlines the vital importance of repenting *in this life,* of not dying in one's sins. In an interview with a young man in Mesa, Arizona, I found him only a little sorry he had committed adultery but not sure that he wanted to cleanse himself. After long deliberations in which I seemed to make little headway against his rebellious spirit

I finally said, "Goodbye, Bill, but I warn you, don't break a speed limit, be careful what you eat, take no chances on your life. Be careful in traffic for *you must not die before this matter is cleared up. Don't you dare to die.*" I quoted this scripture:

> Wherefore, if they should die in their wickedness they must be cast off also, as to the things which are spiritual, which are pertaining to righteousness; wherefore, they must be brought to stand before God, to be judged of their works. . .

> . . . And there cannot any unclean thing enter into the kingdom of God; wherefore there must needs be a place of filthiness prepared for that which is filthy. (1 Ne. 15:33-34.)

A slow death has its advantages over the sudden demise. The cancer victim who is head of a family, for instance, should use his time to be an advisor to those who will survive him. The period of inactivity after a patient learns there is no hope for his life can be a period of great productivity. How much more true this is of one who has been involved in deliberate sin! He must not die until he has made his peace with God. He must be careful and not have an accident.

The Way from Sin

The saddest part about sinning, perhaps, is that our wrongdoing grievously affects the lives of others. Innocent children, wronged wives, parents, husbands — all feel the keenness of the sorrow. Elder Adam S. Bennion felt this in respect to one of his friends. I heard him tell the story when I was very young and it has clung to me all through the years. His former friend was in death row in the penitentiary. Brother Bennion visited him and, before leaving, asked him this question: "What message may I take from you to the young people in Zion?" The answer was quick and positive. "Tell them," said the doomed man, "to keep their lives so full of good works that there will be no room for evil."

Fortunately, for most of us there is a way out from the pall of sin. A wise and a just God has provided a way whereby the moral deterioration that comes to human beings because of sin can be eliminated. In other words, the Great Physician has made the remedy of repentance adequate to counteract the sickness of sin.

The story is told of a vessel stranded off the coast of South America whose Captain signalled to a passing ship to share their water with his passengers as they were suffering from thirst. The passing ship signalled back telling him to let down his bucket into the water in which they were floundering, because they were in the mouth of the Amazon River and the water was fresh.

The message of the ages to all people stranded in their sins is that they are in friendly territory and all they need to do is to let down their buckets and have their thirst quenched. The Master is ready always to listen to the cry of a repentant person and let him drink of the fountain of life freely.

Chapter Eleven

Conviction — the Awakening

*The awakening of the conscience
is the grandeur of the soul.*

—Charles A. Callis

REPENTANCE IS A KIND AND MERCIFUL LAW. IT IS FAR-reaching and all-inclusive. Contrary to common thinking it is composed of many elements, each one indispensable to complete repentance. This is well brought out in the following definition by President Joseph F. Smith:

> True repentance is not only sorrow for sins, and humble penitence and contrition before God, but it involves the necessity of turning away from them, a discontinuance of all evil practices and deeds, a thorough reformation of life, a vital change from evil to good, from vice to virtue, from darkness to light. Not only so, but to make restitution, so far as it is possible, for all the wrongs we have done, to pay our debts, and restore to God and man their rights—that which is due them from us. This is true repentance, and the exercise of the will and all the powers of body and mind is demanded, to complete this glorious work of repentance. . .[1]

There is *no royal road to repentance,* no privileged path to forgiveness. Every man must follow the same course whether he be rich or poor, educated or untrained, tall or short, prince or pauper, king or commoner. "For there is no respect of persons with God." (Rom. 2:11.) There is one way only. It is a long road spiked with thorns and briars and pitfalls and problems. It is a way which must

---

[1]Smith, *Gospel Doctrine,* pp. 100-101.

be kept open, otherwise the wasteland, the badland, will invade it again and take over, just as the forest has invaded flourishing cities and cultivated areas of bygone days.

The First Step

Before the many elements of repentance are set in motion there has to be a first step. That first step is the turning point at which the sinner consciously recognizes his sin. This is the awakening, the conviction of guilt. Without this there can be no true repentance because there is no acknowledgement of sin.

There are many souls too stubborn to admit their sins even to themselves. They have no escape. They have yet much to learn. Of such people, Jeremiah asks the searching question:

> Were they ashamed when they had committed abomination? nay, they were not at all ashamed, neither could they blush: therefore they shall fall . . . saith the Lord. (Jer. 6:15.)

This failure to recognize our faults holds us back, makes life stagnant. The Prophet David O. McKay expresses the thought in these words:

> What progress can there be for a man unconscious of his fault? Such a man has lost the fundamental element of growth, which is the realization that there is something bigger, better, and more desirable than the condition in which he now finds himself. In the soil of self-satisfaction, true growth has poor nourishment. Its roots find great succor in discontent.
>
> "Our pleasures and our discontents
> Are rounds by which we may ascend."
>
> Heaven pity the man who is unconscious of a fault! Pity him also who is ignorant of his ignorance! Neither one is the road to salvation.

When we have become aware of the gravity of our sin, we can condition our minds to follow such processes as will rid us of the effects of the sin. Alma tried to convey this to Corianton when he said: ". . . Let your sins trouble you, with that trouble which shall bring you down unto repen-

tance . . . Do not endeavor to excuse yourself in the least
point . . ." (Al. 42:29-30.)

The Stirrings of Conscience

To avoid the unpleasant recognition of their sins, many
rationalize. Some blame God or his laws for their downfall,
and by eliminating God and his Church from their lives
they seem to think they will get relief. But rationalizing
and minimizing sin betrays disregard for or ignorance of
the scriptures and the program of God, for Samuel the
Lamanite said: "And if ye believe on his name ye will
repent of all your sins, that thereby ye may have a remission
of them through his merits." (Hel. 14:13.) Someone
has said: "Rationalizing is the bringing of ideals down to
the level of one's conduct. Repentance is the bringing of
one's conduct up to the level of his ideals."

However much the lips may deny the sin it is difficult
to escape the accusations of the conscience. Many times I
have had people say to me, "I have never done anything
wrong," when in reality they were deep in transgressions
which they had not catalogued. People generally know
when they are doing wrong. Certainly all people who
possess the Holy Ghost and who live worthy of its promptings will know when they enter the portals of sin. Moroni
says: ". . . By the power of the Holy Ghost ye may know
the truth of all things." (Moro. 10:5.) Until and unless
one has seared his conscience this influence is a dependable
guide.

The birth or rebirth of conscience is effected by teaching and training. Parents must train their children to know
the Lord and his laws. To be sorry for sin one must know
something of its serious implications, and to learn this too
we have the scriptures, the Church leaders, and teachings
of parents. It is a grave matter if parents fail to instruct
their children, as the Lord tells us in Doctrine and Covenants 68:25-28. Likewise we are to be exhorted constantly
by our leaders: "But exhort one another daily, while it is

called To day; lest any of you be hardened through the deceitfulness of sin." (Heb. 3:13.)

Even very small children when properly taught in right-eous homes come to know good from evil to a considerable degree, and the Lord says that when children are eight years old they are accountable for their acts and thoughts. At that point, in the providence of God children may be bap-tized and receive the Holy Ghost, thus opening the way to receive the guidance, comfort and truth promised through that heavenly influence. And as the child grows, his con-science is stimulated and his knowledge of right and wrong developed by the family home evening, the home teaching program, and the other organizations and programs of the Church.

How wonderful that God should endow us with this sensitive yet strong guide we call a conscience! Someone has aptly remarked that "conscience is a celestial spark which God has put into every man for the purpose of saving his soul." Certainly it is the instrument which awakens the soul to consciousness of sin, spurs a person to make up his mind to adjust, to convict himself of the transgression with-out soft-pedaling or minimizing the error, to be willing to face facts, meet the issue and pay necessary penalties — and until the person is in this frame of mind he has not begun to repent. To be sorry is an approach, to abandon the act of error is a beginning, but until one's conscience has been sufficiently stirred to cause him to move in the matter, so long as there are excuses and rationalizations, one has hardly begun his approach to forgiveness. This is what Alma meant in telling his son Corianton that "none but the truly penitent are saved." (Al. 42.24.)

The Holy Ghost can play an important role in convinc-ing the sinner of his error. He helps in making known "the truth of all things" (Moro. 10:5); in teaching all things and bringing all things to one's remembrance (John 14:26); and in reproving the world of sin (John 16:8).

Sorrow Not Enough

Often people indicate that they have repented when all they have done is to express regret for a wrong act. But true repentance is marked by that godly sorrow that changes, transforms, and saves. To be sorry is not enough. Perhaps the felon in the penitentiary, coming to realize the high price he must pay for his folly, may wish he had not committed the crime. That is not repentance. The vicious man who is serving a stiff sentence for rape may be very sorry he did the deed, but he is not repentant if his heavy sentence is the only reason for his sorrow. That is the sorrow of the world.

The truly repentant man is sorry before he is apprehended. He is sorry even if his secret is never known. He desires to make voluntary amends. The culprit has not "godly sorrow" who must be found out by being reported or by chains of circumstances which finally bring the offense to light. The thief is not repentant who continues in grave offenses until he is caught. Repentance of the godly type means that one comes to recognize the sin and voluntarily and without pressure from outside sources begins his transformation. Paul put it this way to the Corinthian saints:

> Now I rejoice, not that ye were made sorry, but that ye sorrowed to repentance: for ye were made sorry after a godly manner, that ye might receive damage by us in nothing.
>
> For godly sorrow worketh repentance to salvation not to be repented of: but the sorrow of the world worketh death. (2 Cor. 7:9-10.)

How Wrong Is Wrong?

Sometimes we hear a youth in the Church say with regard to sex sins, "I did not know it was wrong." This is unthinkable. Where were the teachings of the home, of Primary, of Sunday School, of MIA, and so on. Where were the whisperings of conscience, the guidance of the Holy Ghost to which he was entitled until he drove that

Spirit away by sin? Some at least of these influences and promptings must have lingered in his heart to tell him that the act was wrong! Even if he did not know *how* wrong it was he knew it was sin. Otherwise, why would he hide the act and keep secret the error?

I had a young couple come to me with a problem. In the interview I said to them: "Yes, it is wrong for two members to marry out of the temple. But the thing which you did which prohibited you from going into the temple was infinitely worse." And the very fact that they still expected and insisted on an early entrance into the temple was an indication that they had not yet come to a realization of the seriousness of their sin.

This transgression of which they were guilty is not merely a breach in etiquette. It is not only bad manners and a thing that "just is not done." It is breaking a law of God, a law that always since the beginning has been named by the Lord as most heinous. This is not something that can be set aside with a brushing-off gesture, or even with feigned sorrow, or even with a determination never to repeat the error. This is the violation of a fundamental law.

Apparently these two young people had been taught through the years, quite properly, that they must be married in the temple. But they had not grasped the point that failure to do this at this time was a small error compared to the sin of fornication, and that the value of their temple marriage could be jeopardized by unrepentant sex sin. That heinous sin concerned them only little. Their values were distorted. There are many like them who, when the sin is as long as a mile, call it a yard, when the sin is as heavy as a ton, they call it a pound, when the sin is as voluminous as a hundred-gallon drum, they call it a pint. The soft-pedaling process is a damaging one, for it keeps people from repentance. And until there is real repentance there can never be forgiveness.

"You mean that we cannot be married in the temple?" the couple asked. And I replied with a question, "Do you honestly think you should be permitted in the temple after such a despicable transgression? Do you not realize what you have done? If I were to give you the total responsibility with freedom to go, would you go? If you committed murder and then merely felt a little sorry, would you feel that you should be permitted immediately all privileges of freedom you formerly possessed, merely because you intended never to repeat the act? Do you think you should pay no price? no penalty? no adjustment? Analyze it. Do you think you yourselves would be better off if you went free?"

If adultery or fornication justified the death penalty in the old days, and still in Christ's day, is the sin any less today because the laws of the land do not assess the death penalty for it? Is the act less grievous? There must be a washing, a purging, a changing of attitudes, a correcting of appraisals, a strengthening toward self-mastery. And these cleansing processes cannot be acomplished as easily as taking a bath or shampooing the hair, or sending a suit of clothes to the cleaners. There must be many prayers, and volumes of tears. There must be more than a verbal acknowledgement. There must be an inner conviction giving to the sin its full diabolical weight. "My sins are disgusting — loathsome" one could come to think about his baser sins, like the Psalmist who used these words: "My wounds stink and are corrupt because of my foolishness." (Ps. 38:5.)

There must be increased devotion and much thought and study. There must be a re-awakening, a fortification, a re-birth. And this takes energy and time and often is accompanied with sore embarrassment, heavy deprivations and deep trials, even if indeed one is not excommunicated from the Church, losing all spiritual blessings.

Another young couple showed a similar unawareness of the gravity of sin, and especially of sexual sin. They came to me in June, having become formally engaged with a ring the previous December, and in the six months' interval their sexual sin had been repeated frequently. In June they went to their respective bishops seeking recommends to the temple. The girl's bishop, knowing that she had always been active, did not searchingly question her as to cleanliness, and a recommend was soon tucked away in her purse for use in the planned June marriage. The bishop of the other ward questioned the young man carefully and learned of the six months of transgression.

In my office the couple frankly admitted their sin and shocked me when they said: "That isn't so very wrong, is it, when we were formally engaged and expected to marry soon?" They had no comprehension of the magnitude of the sin. They were ready to go into the holy temple for their marriage without a thought that they were defiling the Lord's house. How lacking was their training! How insincere was their approach! They were very disturbed when their marriage had to be postponed to allow time for repentance. They had rationalized the sin nearly out of existence. They pressed for a date, the first possible one they could set up and on which they could plan their temple marriage. They did not understand that forgiveness is not a thing of days or months or even years but is a matter of intensity of feeling and transformation of self. Again, this showed a distortion of attitude, a lack of conviction of the seriousness of their deep transgression. They had not confessed their serious sin. They had but admitted it when it had been dug out. There is a wide difference between the two situations.

This couple seemed to have no conception of satisfying the Lord, of paying the total penalties and obtaining a release and adjustment which could be considered final and which might be accepted of the Lord. I asked them the question: "As you weigh this transgression, do you feel that you should be excommunicated from the Church?" They were surprised at such a question. They had thought of their heinous sin as nothing more than an indiscretion. They had been born and reared in the Church and had received the gift of the Holy Ghost at eight years of age. But in the successive nights of their perfidy they had driven the Holy Spirit away. They had made him unwelcome.

They were not listening to his promptings. It is inconceivable that they did not know how wrong their sin was but they had convinced themselves against the truth. They had seared their consciences as with a hot iron.

Conviction Opens Door to Repentance

When we come to recognize our sin sincerely and without reservations, we are ready to follow such processes as will rid us of sin's effects. Enos sets us a good example. As he began to realize his true status before his Maker, he pondered upon his condition — how he had been born in the faith and trained by a good father who had taught him righteousness and the nurture and admonitions of the Lord. When he found himself far out of hearing, deep in the forest where he was alone with himself, he began to convict himself of his sins. Eternal life began to loom up as something much to be desired, and he says: ". . . the words [of] . . . eternal life, and the joy of the saints, sunk deep into my heart, and my soul hungered . . ."

Now that he had convinced himself that he was in desperate straits, he began to put his mind in order. ". . . I kneeled down before my Maker," he said, "and I cried unto him in mighty prayer and supplication for mine own soul . . ."

The sincerity of his change of heart is manifested in his extended efforts to make his adjustment and get forgiveness: ". . . And all the day long did I cry unto him; yea, and when the night came I did still raise my voice high that it reached the heavens." (Enos 3-4.)

When this spirit is in the transgressor and he has placed himself at the mercy of the Lord, he begins to receive the relief which will eventually develop into total repentance.

Young Alma was so deep in his sin that it was most difficult for him to humble himself toward repentance, but when his experiences broke down his resistance, softened his rebellion and overcame his stubbornness, he began to see himself in his true light and appraise his situation as it really was. His hard heart was softened. His repentance was being born. Listen to his words of confession. Though these words of Alma are used in this book in connection with other phases of the gospel, they are repeated here as an indication of conviction of guilt:

> But I was racked with eternal torment, for my soul was harrowed up to the greatest degree and racked with all my sins.
>
> Yea, I did remember all my sins and iniquities, for which I was tormented with the pains of hell; yea, I saw that I had rebelled against my God, and that I had not kept his holy commandments.
>
> Yea, and I had murdered many of his children, or rather led them away unto destruction; yea, and in fine so great had been my iniquities, that the very thought of coming into the presence of my God did rack my soul with inexpressible horror.
>
> Oh, thought I, that I could be banished and become extinct both soul and body, that I might not be brought to stand in the presence of my God, to be judged of my deeds.
>
> And now, for three days and for three nights was I racked, even with the pains of a damned soul. (Al. 36:12-16.)

Conviction brought "sorrow to repentance" through torment-racking memory. His sin pains were exquisite and bitter. Alma had convinced himself.

The great assurance came to him that his repentance had been accepted, and a great peace came to his soul:

> For, said he, I have repented of my sins, and have been redeemed of the Lord; behold I am born of the Spirit.
>
> And the Lord said unto me: Marvel not that all mankind, yea, men and women, all nations, kindreds, tongues and people, must be born again; yea, born of God, changed from their carnal and fallen state, to a state of righteousness, being redeemed of God, becoming his sons and daughters; . . . . (Mos. 27:24-25.)

How far would Enos and Alma have progressed without this recognition of their sinful state? A young man was brought to me by his worried father to consider the sex perversions to which the youth was addicted. The young man was not convinced that his practice was so wrong. He had read in books published by deviates that it was a normal activity. The scriptures meant little to him — he felt that they did not specify as forbidden the particular thing he was doing. He thought his father was old-fashioned and was not up on the newer trends. He had talked to other deviates who had convinced him that he belonged to a third sex — a normal situation. Generally, we can easily believe the things we wish to believe. For four hours we considered the matter from every point of view — logic, common sense, scripture — and finally the young man admitted he was convinced. Now, but not until now, could he move forward toward repentance.

Humility the Key

Of course, even the conviction of guilt is not enough. It could be devastating and destructive were it not accompanied by efforts to rid oneself of guilt. Accompanying the conviction, then, must be an earnest desire to clean up the guilt and compensate for the loss sustained through the error.

The recognition of guilt should give one a sense of humility, of a "broken heart and a contrite spirit," and bring him to the proverbial "sackcloth and ashes" attitude. This does not mean that one must be servile and self-effacing to the destructive point, but rather one must have an honest desire to right the wrong.

Conviction would incorporate within it the recognition that the broken law was God's law, that all his laws are designed for the ultimate benefit and glory of man, and that in his loving omniscience God knows what is best for each of us. Then with respect and reverence and a developing love for God we generate a desire to please him and eventually to be like him and near him. This gives the incentive and willingness to move along the path which will accomplish those purposes, including doing whatever is necessary to get the forgiveness which will make possible the eventual realization of these goals. This is true humility in the context of conviction of guilt.

This humility needs to be voluntary, as it normally will be when the offender becomes convinced of his sin without outside pressures.

> Yea, he that truly humbleth himself, and repenteth of his sins, and endureth to the end, the same shall be blessed—yea, much more blessed than they who are compelled to be humble. . .

> Therefore, blessed are they who humble themselves without being compelled to be humble. . . . (Al. 32:15-16.)

Whatever our predispositions when influenced by the pride of our hearts, the person convinced of his sin and suffering godly sorrow for it in humility is reduced — or rather in this case elevated — to tears. Thus he expresses anguish for his folly and for the grief it has brought to the innocent. Those who have not been through the experience may not comprehend this reaction, but the scriptural writers with their deep insight understood that there is a healing balm in tears for the humble soul who is reaching toward God. Jeremiah wrote: "Oh that my head were waters, and mine eyes a fountain of tears, that I might weep day and night . . . (Jer. 9:1.) The Psalmist cried in his anguish: "I am weary with my groaning; all the night make I my bed to swim; I water my couch with my tears." (Ps. 6:6.) And again he pleaded: "Turn thee unto me, and have mercy upon me; for I am desolate and afflicted." (Ps. 25:16.)

Test of Conviction

A total return to the spiritual experiences seems a vital step to repentance. Loss of faith runs parallel to loss of virtue and righteousness. "Whom we serve, we love." We hate those we ignore, whose laws we break. Many seem to feel that if they eliminate God and his Church from their lives they can solve their problems, little realizing that by so doing they are discarding the life-saving apparatus and the "iron rod" that could save them.

There is a good verbal test to apply to determine the depth of one's conviction of sin and hence of his start on the road to repentance. A brother who had committed heinous transgressions was trying to tell me he had repented. I was far from convinced and I asked him some questions. Long before I ceased asking the questions his head dropped and he admitted that he had hardly begun his repentance. He had not thought it so all-inclusive. These were the questions.

Do you wish to be forgiven?

Could you accept excommunication for the sin if deemed necessary? Why do you feel you should not be excommunicated? If you were, would you become bitter at the Church and its officers? Would you cease your activities in the Church? Would you work your way back to baptism and restoration of former blessings even through years?

What have you done to prove your repentance? How much did you pray before the sin? How much during? How much since your admission of it?

How much did you study the scriptures before your trouble? How much since?

Are you attending meetings? paying tithing?

Have you told your wife or parents? Have you confessed your total sins?

Are you humble now? Is it the result of "being forced to be humble"?

Have you wrestled with your problems as did Enos? Has your soul hungered for your soul's sake? Did you "cry unto him" a day-long prayer and into the night and raise your voice high that it reached the heavens, as did Enos?

How much have you fasted?

How much suffering have you endured? Is your guilt "swept away"?

Take the First Step

The implications of these questions are not pretty, not pleasant — as Satan makes the sin appear to be. But they are inevitable implications when the first steps of repentance from grievous sin are taken, and some of them — as in the instance of Enos — apply to all of us who are still short of sanctification.

That is why, through the great gospel message, our loving Father makes this emphasis: Abstain from grievous sin. Repent of it if you have committed it. Steadily and consistently repent of and conquer your sins and weaknesses, and thus receive the forgiveness which will ease and beautify the upward journey.

And the first step in all this is awareness of one's sins.

Chapter Twelve

Abandonment of Sin

> *By this ye may know if a man re-*
> *penteth of his sins — behold, he*
> *will confess them and forsake*
> *them.*
>
> Doctrine & Covenants 58:43

THERE IS ONE CRUCIAL TEST OF REPENTANCE. THIS IS abandonment of the sin. Providing that a person discontinues his sin with the right motives — because of a growing consciousness of the gravity of the sin and a willingness to comply with the laws of the Lord — he is genuinely repenting. This criterion has been set by the Lord: "By this ye may know if a man repenteth of his sins — behold, he will confess them and *forsake them.*" (D&C 58:43. Italics added.)

Desire Is Not Sufficient

In other words, it is not real repentance until one has abandoned the error of his way and started on a new path. Someone has said that there is only one way to quit a bad habit and that is to stop. The saving power does not extend to him who merely *wants* to change his life. True repentance prods one to action.

One must not be surprised that effort is required, and not merely desire. After all, it is work which develops our moral as well as our physical muscles. Ralph Parlette puts it this way:

> Strength and struggle go together. The supreme reward of struggle is strength. Life is a battle and the greatest joy is to overcome. The pursuit of easy things makes men weak. Do not equip yourselves with superior power and hope to escape the responsibility and work. It cannot be done. It is following the lines of least resistance that makes rivers and men crooked.

Trying Is Not Sufficient

Nor is repentance complete when one merely *tries* to abandon sin. To try with a weakness of attitude and effort is to assure failure in the face of Satan's strong counteracting efforts. What is needed is resolute action. A story will perhaps illustrate this.

An army officer called a soldier to him and ordered him to take a message to another officer. The soldier saluted and said, "I'll try, sir! I'll try!" To this the officer responded: "I don't want you to *try,* I want you to deliver this message." The soldier, somewhat embarrassed, now replied: "I'll do the best I can, sir." At this the officer, now disgusted, rejoined with some vigor: "I don't want you to *try* and I don't want you to 'do the best you can.' I want you to deliver this message." Now the young soldier, straightening to his full height, approached the matter magnificently, as he thought, when he saluted again and said: "I'll do it or die, sir." To this the now irate officer responded: "I don't want you to die, and I don't want you merely to do the best you can, and I don't want you to try. Now, the request is a reasonable one; the message is important; the distance is not far; you are able-bodied; you can do what I have ordered. Now get out of here and accomplish your mission."

It is normal for children to try. They fall and get up numerous times before they can be certain of their footing. But adults, who have gone through these learning periods, must determine what they will do, then proceed to do it. To "try" is weak. To "do the best I can" is not strong. We must always do *better* than we can. This is true in every walk of life. We have a companion who has promised: "Ask, and it shall be given you; seek, and ye shall find; knock, and it shall be opened unto you." (Matt. 7:7.) With the inspiration from the Lord we can rise higher than our individual powers, extend far beyond our own personal potential.

No Forgiveness Without Repentance

This connection between effort and the repentance which attracts the Lord's forgiveness is often not understood. In my childhood, Sunday School lessons were given to us on the 8th chapter of John wherein we learned of the woman thrown at the feet of the Redeemer for judgment. My sweet Sunday School teacher lauded the Lord for having forgiven the woman. She did not understand the impossibility of such an act. In my years since then I have repeatedly heard people praise the Lord for his mercy in having forgiven the adulteress. This example has been used numerous times to show how easily one can be forgiven for gross sin.

But did the Lord forgive the woman? Could he forgive her? There seems to be no evidence of forgiveness. His command to her was, "Go, and sin no more." He was directing the sinful woman to go her way, *abandon her evil life, commit no more sin, transform her life.* He was saying, Go, woman, and start your repentance; and he was indicating to her the beginning step — to *abandon her transgressions.*

The Lord's prophet Amulek had said emphatically: ". . . Ye cannot be saved *in* your sins." (Al. 11:37. Italics added.) It was this same Lord Jesus Christ who made the laws, and he must observe them. Accordingly, how could he have forgiven the woman in her deep sin? When she had had time to repent; when she had abandoned her evil ways and evil associates; when she had made restitution so far as she could; and when she had proved by her works and the living of the commandments that she was "born again" and was a new creature — when she had done these things the forgiveness of the Savior could overshadow her and claim her and give her peace.

Another mistaken idea is that the thief on the cross was forgiven of his sins when the dying Christ answered: "Today shalt thou be with me in paradise." (Luke 23:43.) These men on the cross were thieves. How could the Lord forgive a malefactor? They had broken laws. There was no doubt of the guilt of the two men, for the one voluntarily confessed their guilt.

The Lord cannot save men *in* their sins but only *from* their sins, and that only when they have shown true repentance. The one thief did show some compassion, whether selfishly with hope we are not sure. He was confessing, but how could he abandon his evil practices when dungeon walls made evil deeds impossible? How could he restore the stolen goods when hanging on the cross? How could he, as John the Baptist required, "bring forth fruits meet for repentance"? How could he live the Lord's commands, attend his meetings, pay his tithing, serve his fellowmen? All these take time. Time was the one thing he was running out of very rapidly. "No unclean thing can enter the kingdom of heaven." This thought has been repeated throughout the scriptures numerous times and is a basic truth. We may be sure that the Savior's instructions to the thief on the cross were comparable to his instructions to the woman caught in adultery: "Go your way and transform yourself and repent."

As the hours passed, the thief's life would ebb out and his spirit would abandon the lifeless body and go into the spirit world, where Christ was going to organize his missionary program. (See 1 Pet. 3:18-20; 4-6.) There he would live along with the antediluvians and all others who had died in their sins. All the Lord's statement promised the thief was that both of them would soon be in the spirit world. The thief's show of repentance on the cross was all to his advantage, but his few words did not nullify a life of sin. The world should know that since the Lord himself cannot save men *in* their sins, no man on earth can administer any sacrament which will do that impossible thing. Hence the mere display of death-bed faith or repentance is not sufficient.

When the Lord, in his dying moments, turned to the Father and requested, "Father, forgive them; for they know not what they do" (Luke 23:34), he was referring to the soldiers who crucified him. They acted under the mandate of a sovereign nation. It was the Jews who were guilty of the Lord's death. Again how could he forgive them, or how could his Father forgive them, when they were not repentant. These vicious people who cried, ". . . His blood be on us, and on our children" (Matt. 27:25) had not repented. Those who "reviled him" on Calvary (Matt. 27:39) had not repented. The Jewish leaders who tried Jesus illegally, demanded his crucifixion from Pilate, and incited the mob to their vilest actions had not repented. Nor had the Roman soldiers who, though no doubt obligated under their military law to crucify Jesus as instructed, were under no compulsion to add the insults and cruelties to which they subjected the Savior prior to his crucifixion.

Could the Lord forgive Pilate? Certainly he could not without Pilate's repentance. Did Pilate repent? We do not know what Pilate did after the scripture drops him. He had a desire to favor the Savior. He did not display full courage in resisting the pressures of the people. Could he have saved the life of the Lord? Again, we do not know. We leave Pilate to the Lord as we do all other sinners, but remember that "to know and not to do" is sin.

Repentance Takes Time

Repentance is inseparable from time. No one can repent on the cross, nor in prison, nor in custody. One must have the opportunity of committing wrong in order to be really repentant. The man in handcuffs, the prisoner in the penitentiary, the man as he drowns, or as he dies — such a man certainly cannot repent totally. He can wish to do it, he may intend to change his life, he may determine that he will, but that is only the beginning.

That is why we should not wait for the life beyond but should abandon evil habits and weaknesses while in the flesh on the earth. Elder Melvin J. Ballard pinpointed this problem:

> A man may receive the priesthood and all its privileges and blessings, but until he learns to overcome the flesh, his temper, his tongue, his disposition to indulge in the things God has forbidden, he cannot come into the celestial kingdom of God — he must overcome either in this life or in the life to come. But this life is the time in which men are to repent. Do not let any of us imagine that we can go down to the grave not having overcome the corruptions of the flesh and then lose in the grave all our sins and evil tendencies. They will be with us. They will be with the spirit when separated from the body.[1]

Clearly it is difficult to repent in the spirit world of sins involving physical habits and actions. There one has spirit and mind but not the physical power to overcome a physical habit. He can desire to change his life, but how can he overcome the lusts of the flesh unless he has flesh to control and transform? How can he overcome the tobacco or the drink habit in the spirit world where there is no liquor nor tobacco and no flesh to crave it? Similarly with other sins involving lack of control over the body.

Repentance Easier Before Sin Is Entrenched

While repentance is possible at any stage in the process of sin it is certainly easier in the early stages. Sinful habits may be compared to a river which flows slowly and placidly at first then gains speed as it nears the falls over the precipice. Where it is slow and quiet, one can cross it in a rowboat with relative ease. As the stream flows faster it be-

---

[1]Ballard, "Three Degrees of Glory."

comes more difficult to cross, but this is still possible. As the water nears the falls, it becomes almost a superhuman effort to row across without being swept mercilessly over the falls. The rowboat and its passenger have little chance when the speeding stream prepares to take its leap to the gorge below. But even now, with much external help, one might still be saved from destruction. Likewise, in the stream of sin, it is relatively easy to repent at first, but as the sin becomes more and more entrenched the overcoming becomes increasingly difficult.

If one ignores the roar of the falls below, he is doomed; if he will not listen to the warnings given him, he is sucked into the swift current to destruction.

We can use another analogy from nature. Early settlers in the Gila Valley in Arizona stated that when they first arrived they could jump across the little trickle of water running down the San Simon Valley, a small tributary of the Gila River. But the overgrazed valley yielded to erosion. The little freshets of water followed the cow trails and cut deep ruts. Each succeeding storm stream undermined the dirt walls, making the gorge ever deeper and wider. The undercut walls caved in and the cow trail became a rut. The rut became a deep wash, and the wash became a very wide and very deep and almost uncrossable chasm.

So it is with transgression. When a sin is repeated again and again, the channel gets deeper and deeper. And even though the gash in the earth may be filled, any flood of water is likely again to find the bed of the wash and follow it, making it even deeper. Similarly, even though sin be abandoned and forgiven, careless or deliberate action can bring it back.

Forgiveness Cancelled on Reversion to Sin

Old sins return, says the Lord in his modern revelations. Many people either do not know this or they conveniently forget it. "Go your ways and sin no more," the Lord warned.

And again, ". . . Unto that soul who sinneth shall the former sins return, saith the Lord your God." (D&C 82:7.)

Would this mean that the person who has returned to the sins he has professedly abandoned must start the process of repentance again from the beginning? that one cannot return to sin and then start repentance from where he left off?

To return to sin is most destructive to the morale of the individual and gives Satan another hand-hold on his victim. Those who feel that they can sin and be forgiven and then return to sin and be forgiven again and again must straighten out their thinking. Each previously forgiven sin is added to the new one and the whole gets to be a heavy load.

Thus when a man has made up his mind to change his life, there must be no turning back. Any reversal, even in a small degree, is greatly to his detriment. The reformed alcoholic who takes "just a little sip" again may have lost all the ground he has gained. The pervert who relaxes and returns to old companions or situations is in grave danger again. The former cigarette addict who smokes just one more cigarette is on his way back to addiction. It was Mark Twain who said he knew he could quit smoking because he had done it a thousand times. When one quits, he must quit. Generally, those who try to taper off find it an impossible task.

One man who had been a slave to alcohol most of his adult life became convinced through the various Church programs that he must give up the habit and prepare himself for the temple program. With great effort he quit drinking. He moved many miles away from the area where his drinking friends lived and, though his body craved and ached and gnawed for the long-depended-on stimulant, he finally conquered. He was at all his Church meetings, and was paying his tithing. His new friends in the Church seemed to fortify him. He felt good in the new activity, and life was glorious. His wife was beaming, because now the whole family were always together. This is what she had dreamed about all their married life.

They got their temple recommends and the happy day arrived and they drove to the temple city for this great event. They arrived early and each had some errands to do. As it happened, the husband ran into some old friends. They urged him to go with them to the tavern. No, he would not, he said, he had other important things to do. Well, he could just take a soft drink, they urged. With the best of intentions he finally relented. But by the time he was to meet his wife at the temple he was so incapacitated that the family went home in disgrace and sorrow and disappointment.

Months passed and a new reformation had taken place and he was ready again for the temple. Unfortunately the previous experience was repeated. He knew he was strong enough now to resist, but again the temple opportunity had to wait. And, sadly enough, he had passed away before another reformation could come.

Having been reared on the farm, I know that when the pigs got out, I looked first for the holes through which they had previously escaped. When the cow was out of the field looking for greener pastures elsewhere, I knew where to look first for the place of her escape. It was most likely to be the place where she had jumped the fence before, or where the fence had been broken. Likewise the devil knows where to tempt, where to put in his telling blows. He finds the vulnerable spot. Where one was weak before, he will be most easily tempted again.

In abandoning sin one cannot merely wish for better conditions. He must make them. He may need to come to hate the spotted garments and loathe the sin. He must be certain not only that he has abandoned the sin but that he has changed the situations surrounding the sin. He should avoid the places and conditions and circumstances where the sin occurred, for these could most readily breed it again. He must abandon the people with whom the sin was committed. He may not hate the persons involved but he must avoid them and everything associated with the sin. He must dispose of all letters, trinkets, and things which will remind him of the "old days" and the "old times." He must forget addresses, telephone numbers, people, places and situations from the sinful past, and build a new life. He must eliminate anything which would stir the old memories.

Does this mean that the man who has quit smoking or drinking or had sex pollutions finds life empty for a time? The things which engaged him and caught his fancy and occupied his thoughts are gone, and better substitutions have not yet filled the void. This is Satan's opportunity. The man makes a start but may find the loss of the yesterday's habits so great that he is enticed to return to his evil ways, and his lot thus becomes infinitely worsened. The Savior had this kind of situation in mind when he said:

> When the unclean spirit is gone out of a man, he walketh through dry places, seeking rest; and finding none, he saith, I will return unto my house whence I came out.
>
> And when he cometh, he findeth it swept and garnished.
>
> Then goeth he, and taketh to him seven other spirits more wicked than himself; and they enter in, and dwell there: and the last state of that man is worse than the first. (Luke 11:24-26.)

Victory in the fight to abandon sin depends on constant vigilance.

The importance of this watchfulness is exemplified too in the story of my apricot tree. The lawn had been extended under this favored tree. All other trees had been removed. The apricot tree had been pruned and one rather sharp stump of a lower limb was partly hidden in the foliage. The new lawn had done well and was ready to be mowed. Having gone around and around with the mower, I came under the tree and ran straight into the sharp end of the limb. My forehead took the bump and I reeled and fell to the ground. As I recovered, I said to myself: "What a stupid trick! I'll never do that again."

Throughout the summer, I mowed the lawn and re-membered the tree and skirted the offending limb. Then the winter came and went, and returning spring called for yard work. I had forgotten my pain. I was not vigilantly watching, and again I ran headlong into the sharp limb and took another fall. I had let down my guard. I had not fortified myself sufficiently. The pain brought me again to my senses and I now protected myself against a repetition.

In relation to sin, many people are constantly running into that sharp limb. They return again and again to make the same error. Knowing the danger point, they still return. The girl, knowing the hazard of a date that has given her concern, takes another chance and another until the injury could be fatal. The person who married out of the Church and had a broken marriage returns to marry again out of the Church and the temple, having learned but little. After a while, the "forehead" will not heal again. He who cannot learn by others' mistakes is stupid. He who cannot learn by his own errors is a fool.

Many who have discontinued bad habits have found that substitution is part of the answer, and have conquered a bad habit by replacing it with a good or harmless one. The classic case is giving up the habit of chewing tobacco while acquiring the habit of chewing gum.

In Australia, I was struck by a statement used often there: "He dropped his bundle." When speaking of one who had become inactive or had retrogressed and gone back to his former habits of life, some applied this colloquial expression and said with disgust: "He dropped his bundle."

All that has been said and written on this subject should warn the worthy from the beginning not to get entangled in iniquity, but it should not be construed to suggest that it is futile to start again when one has reverted to sin. Being a god in embryo with the seeds of godhood neatly tucked away in him, and with the power to become a god even-tually, man need not despair. He should not give up. If he has had problems and slipped from the path of rectitude and right, he must stop in his headlong slipping and turn and transform himself. He must begin again. If he slips, he must regain his footing and protect himself from further slipping and return to the sin no more. If in his weakness he fails time and time again, he still should not despair but should make each new effort stronger than the last.

Human weakness seems to lead people to forget. Having once been in bondage to sin and having finally thrown off the yoke, many are deeply repentant for a time and transform their lives to meet all requirements for forgiveness. But time has a way of dimming impressions and some fall back into sin again.

> But when the righteous turneth away from his righteousness, and committeth iniquity, and doeth according to all the abominations that the wicked man doeth, shall he live? All his righteousness that he hath done shall not be mentioned: in his trespass that he hath trespassed, and in his sin that he hath sinned, in them shall he die. (Ezek. 18:24.)

Satan Desires Church Leaders

What a sad day when men who have been granted much knowledge, many ministrations of the Spirit, even heavenly visions, then turn away from their righteousness! We have the heart-breaking examples of many men in the early days of the Church who were destined for high places and great rewards, but who became disaffected, left the faith and became estranged from all that could sanctify them and give them eternal life.

One such example was Oliver Cowdery, who shared some of the most spectacular of all blessings that have come to man on the earth. For reasons which he seemed to think sufficient, he dissociated himself from the Brethren and the fast-moving Church. After he had been away for a long time, the Prophet Joseph had compassion and wanted him to come back. Writing to his brethren in his journal of Wednesday, April 19, 1843, Joseph Smith wrote:

> Write to Oliver Cowdery and ask him if he has not eaten husks long enough? If he is not almost ready to return, be clothed

with robes of righteousness, and go up to Jerusalem? Orson Hyde hath need of him. (A letter was written accordingly.)[2]

But this great man, who had more than a dozen revelations from the Lord addressed to him and as many concerning him, and who had received heavenly visitors many times, turned away from his blessings and opportunities.

Lucifer desires all good people. He even tempted the Savior on at least three recorded occasions. He had designs upon Peter, who was soon to be the number one man in the world of righteousness. The Lord warned Peter to be on his guard, for, said he:

> Simon, Simon, behold, Satan hath desired to have you, that he may sift you as wheat:
>
> But I have prayed for thee, that thy faith fail not: and when thou art converted, strengthen thy brethren. (Luke 22:31-32.)

Satan wants all men, but especially is he anxious for the leading men who have influence. Perhaps he might try much harder to claim men who are likely to be his greatest opposition, men in high places who could persuade many others not to become servants to Satan.

It seems that missionaries are special targets. The young man is going to spend two years exclusively in the service of converting people from error to truth, of teaching men to leave the employ of Lucifer and serve the Lord, of bringing people out of the dark where they are most vulnerable into the light where there is a measure of protection and where new strengths can be developed. Satan takes a special interest in all such workers.

We Can Do What We Will

While changing one's life from evil to good is admittedly not easy, we cannot emphasize too strongly that every person endowed with normal faculties can do it. Elder Richard L. Evans has said:

---

[2] *Documentary History of the Church*, Vol. 5, p. 368.

> . . . In life no road can be retraveled just as once it was. We can't begin where we were. But we can begin where we are, and in an eternity of existence, this is a reassuring fact. There is virtually nothing that a man cannot turn away from if he really wants to. . . . There is virtually no habit that he cannot give up if he sincerely sets his will to do so. . . .

Setting the will is the key. There must be resoluteness and determination. Discontinuance of sin must be permanent. The *will to do* must be strong and kept strengthened. Napoleon is said to have coined the phrase: "He who fears being conquered is sure of defeat." If one fears he cannot win, if he merely tries, he may fail.

Someone gave us this truth:

> The height of a man's success is gauged by his self-mastery; the depth of his failure by his self-abandonment. There is no other limitation in either direction and this law is the expression of eternal justice. He who cannot *establish a dominion over himself will have no dominion over others.* He who *masters himself shall be king.*

The Spirit Aids the Repentant

James gave a formula for conquering: "Submit yourselves therefore to God. Resist the devil, and he will flee from you." (Jas. 4:7.) In abandoning evil, transforming lives, changing personalities, molding characters or remolding them, we need the help of the Lord, and we may be assured of it if we do our part. The man who leans heavily upon his Lord becomes the master of self and can accomplish anything he sets out to do, whether it be to secure the brass plates, build a ship, overcome a habit, or conquer a deep-seated transgression.

He who has greater strength than Lucifer, he who is our fortress and our strength, can sustain us in times of great temptation. While the Lord will never forcibly take anyone out of sin or out of the arms of the tempters, he exerts his Spirit to induce the sinner to do it with divine assistance. And the man who yields to the sweet influence and pleadings of the Spirit and does all in his power to stay in a repentant attitude is guaranteed protection, power, freedom and joy.

Chapter Thirteen

Lifting Burdens Through Confession

> . . . *I, the Lord, forgive sins, and*
> *am merciful unto those who con-*
> *fess their sins with humble hearts.*
>
> —Doctrine & Covenants 61:2

THE CONFESSION OF SIN IS A NECESSARY ELEMENT IN repentance and therefore in obtaining forgiveness. It is one of the tests of true repentance, for, "By this ye may know if a man repenteth of his sins — behold, *he will confess them* and forsake them." (D&C 58:43. Italics added.)

Confession Required Now, as Formerly

Elders Ezra Taft Benson and Mark E. Petersen of the Council of the Twelve, in a study made for the Brethren, expressed themselves as follows with regard to confession:

It seems to be clearly set forth in the New Testament and in modern scriptures that acknowledgment of sin is an important condition to receiving forgiveness and making restitution. The Apostle James admonished the saints to "confess your faults one to another, and pray for one another." (Jas. 5:16.) The Apostle Paul counseled the Romans as follows: "For with the heart man believeth unto righteousness; and with the mouth confession is made unto salvation." (Rom. 10:10.) Several of the revelations in the Doctrine and Covenants refer to the obligations of those who have sinned, to confess their evil deeds. In Section 59, in which the Lord gives counsel regarding the keeping of the Sabbath Day holy, he mentions the offering of oblations and sacraments "unto the Most High, confessing thy sins unto thy brethren, and before the Lord." (D&C 59:12.) However, Section 42 seems to carry the fullest instruction on this matter found in the holy writ. In this revelation men are not only commanded to love their wives and "cleave unto her and none else," but are condemned for looking "upon a woman to lust after her." The sins of adultery and fornication are emphasized and the principles of confession and forgiveness set forth.

Perhaps confession is one of the hardest of all the obstacles for the repenting sinner to negotiate. His shame often restrains him from making known his guilt and acknowledging his error. Sometimes his assumed lack of confidence in mortals to whom he should confess his sin justifies in his mind his keeping the secret locked in his own heart.

Notwithstanding the difficulty the repenting sinner may experience, the requirement remains, as the Lord has emphasized to his Church in modern days:

> And him that repenteth not of his sins, *and confesseth them not,* ye shall bring before the church, and do with him as the scripture saith unto you, either by commandment or by revelation. (D&C 64:12. Italics added.)

It has been so in all dispensations of the gospel. The Book of Mormon provides us concrete, specific examples. Directly from God, Alma received instructions on dealing with the repentant sinner in the Church, on which point it was later recorded:

> And whosoever repented of their sins and *did confess them,* them he [Alma] did number among the people of the church;
>
> And those that *would not confess* their sins and repent of their iniquity, the same were not numbered among the people of the church, and their names were blotted out. (Mos. 26:35-36.)

And under the pattern established following the Savior's personal ministrations on the American continent the same pattern of Church discipline prevailed:

> And they were strict to observe that there should be no iniquity among them; and whoso was found to commit iniquity,

and three witnesses of the church did condemn them before the elders, and if they repented not, and *confessed not,* their names were blotted out, and they were not numbered among the people of Christ. (Moro. 6:7. Italics added.)

Major Sins Confessed to Church Authority

Knowing the hearts of men, and their intents, and their abilities to repent and regenerate themselves, the Lord waits to forgive until the repentance has matured. The transgressor must have a "broken heart and a contrite spirit" and be willing to humble himself and do all that is required. The confession of his major sins to a proper Church authority is one of those requirements made by the Lord. These sins include adultery, fornication, other sexual transgressions, and other sins of comparable seriousness. This procedure of confession assures proper controls and protection for the Church and its people and sets the feet of the transgressor on the path of true repentance.

Many offenders in their shame and pride have satisfied their consciences, temporarily at least, with a few silent prayers to the Lord and rationalized that this was sufficient confession of their sins. "But I have confessed my sin to my Heavenly Father," they will insist, "and that is all that is necessary." This is not true where a major sin is involved. Then two sets of forgiveness are required to bring peace to the transgressor — one from the proper authorities of the Lord's Church, and one from the Lord himself. This is brought out in the Lord's clarification of Church administration as he gave it to Alma:

> Therefore I say unto you, Go; and whosoever transgresseth against me, him shall ye judge according to the sins which he has committed; and *if he confess his sins before thee* and me, and repenteth in the sincerity of his heart, him shall ye forgive, and I will forgive him also. (Mos. 26:29. Italics added.)

From this, and from the Lord's word to modern Israel — ". . . confessing thy sins unto thy brethren, and before the Lord" (D&C 59:12) — it is plain that there are two confessions to make: one to the Lord and the other to "the brethren," meaning the proper ecclesiastical officers. From the following scriptural passages it might be argued that the confession is to be to the Lord, but in none of them is there evidence that the confession is not also to be made to the local authorities.

> . . . I, the Lord, forgive sins unto those who *confess their sins* before me and ask forgiveness, who have not sinned unto death. . . . (D&C 64:7. Italics added.)

> If we confess our sins, he is faithful and just to forgive us our sins, and to cleanse us from all unrighteousness. (1 John 1:9.)

Confession to Be Complete

In a statement to the Roman saints Paul underlines that the heart should be totally involved in the vocal confession from the lips: "For with the heart man believeth unto righteousness; and with the mouth *confession is made unto salvation.*" (Rom. 10:10. Italics added.) Thus one must not compromise or equivocate — he must make a clean, full confession. When the apples in a barrel rot, it is not enough to throw away half of the spoiled apples from the barrel and replace them with fresh apples on top. This would result in all the apples rotting. Instead it would be necessary to empty the barrel and completely clean and scrub — perhaps disinfect — the entire inside. Then the barrel could be safely filled again with apples. Likewise in clearing up problems in our lives it is well also to go to the bottom and confess all the transgressions so that repentance begins with no half-truths, no pretense, no unclean residue.

The Prophet Joseph Smith counseled:

> Again, let the Twelve and all Saints be willing to confess all their sins, and not keep back a part; and let the Twelve be humble, and not be exalted, and beware of pride, and not seek to excel one above another, but act for each other's good, and pray for one another, and honor our brother or make honorable mention of his name, and not backbite and devour our brother.[1]

[1] Smith, *Teachings of the Prophet Joseph Smith*, p. 155.

Voluntary Confession Is Best

It follows that the ideal confession is voluntary, not forced. It is induced from within the offender's soul, not sparked by being found out in the sin. Such confession, like the voluntary humility of which Alma spoke (Al. 32:13-16), is a sign of growing repentance. It indicates the sinner's conviction of sin and his desire to abandon the evil practices. The voluntary confession is infinitely more acceptable in the sight of the Lord than is forced admission, lacking humility, wrung from an individual by questioning when guilt is evident. Such forced admission is not evidence of the humble heart which calls forth the Lord's mercy: ". . . For I, the Lord, forgive sins, and am merciful unto those *who confess their sins* with humble hearts." (D&C 61:2. Italics added.)

The wicked Cain denied his guilt when first accused. He never did confess his grievous sin, but finally admitted it after he was discovered. Even when he was confronted with his dastardly act he still tried to evade it by saying, "Am I my brother's keeper?"

Years ago, a missionary in South America wrote a long letter of confession. He had broken the law of chastity. No one but the young girl and himself knew of the transgression, but he had promptly gone to his mission president and confessed it in total.

This missionary had been a member of the Church but a few months, and his many years of adulthood while "of the world" had produced a weakness hard to overcome. He quoted, "The spirit is willing but the flesh is weak." He did not excuse himself, nor claim any special immunities, nor rely on extenuating circumstances. He said: "I knew I had to pay the full penalty, I knew that in life or death I had to answer for the sin. I wanted to get it over with and be on my way to eventual forgiveness. I would rather confess, take my punishment, and get back as soon as possible on the road to forgiveness, and I did not want my eternity cluttered with these blemishes."

He was excommunicated from the Church. After what seemed an eternity to him, through his faithfulness and repentance he was baptized and finally his priesthood and temple blessings were restored to him. He found peace through complete repentance of which his total, voluntary confession was a vital part.

Unfortunately, many have to be brought to the involuntary or forced admission of sin. This comes when circumstances and information point to the guilt of the person who is seeking to hide his sin. It often precedes his final admission, and has led through the path of lies, then excuses after his lies have collapsed. This course heaps further sins upon him.

One young man came to me to be interviewed for a mission. He admitted nothing wrong except what he called a "little" masturbation. I had him come again. In the meantime, his conscience had pricked "a little." The next week he admitted he had done a "little" petting, nothing more. In subsequent visits he admitted one error after another, until finally he had admitted fornication.

Even making the admission upon confrontation is better than continuing to lie and evade the truth. In fact, many of those forced sooner or later to admit their sins do come to a full, sincere repentance and a humble desire to receive forgiveness. This again involves the same steps to repentance, with conviction, abandonment of sins, and confession, as fundamental to the process.

Confession to God's Servants

In the Book of Mormon the following warning is given:

> And wo unto them that seek deep to hide their counsel from the Lord! And their works are in the dark; and they say: Who seeth us, and who knoweth us? . . . But behold, I will show unto them, saith the Lord of Hosts, that I know all their works. . . . (2 Ne. 27:27.)

Previously in this book is discussed the principle that we can hide nothing from God. True, it is possible sometimes, by lying and evasion and half-truth, to conceal the truth from God's servants on earth, but to what purpose? It will be impossible to lie to God on judgment day, so the unrepented sins will certainly be revealed then. Far better to confess them and forsake them now, and be rid of their burden!

How can one lie to the Lord or to his servants, especially when he may come to know that the Lord's servants may discern his lie? Section 1 of the Doctrine and Covenants reads: "And the rebellious shall be pierced with much sorrow; for their iniquities shall be spoken upon the housetops, and their secret acts shall be revealed." (D&C 1:3.) The commandment says, "Thou shalt not lie." Jacob proclaimed, "Wo unto the liar, for he shall be thrust down to hell." (2 Ne. 9:34.) And through the Prophet Joseph Smith the Lord gave the warning: ". . . And those who are not pure, and have said they were pure, shall be destroyed, saith the Lord God." (D&C 132:52.)

Those who lie to Church leaders forget or ignore an important rule and truth the Lord has set down: that when he has called men to high places in his kingdom and has placed on them the mantle of authority, a lie to them is tantamount to a lie to the Lord; a half-truth to his officials is like a half-truth to the Lord; a rebellion against his servants is comparable with a rebellion against the Lord; and any infraction against the Brethren who hold the gospel keys is a thought or an act against the Lord. As he expressed it: "For he that receiveth my servants receiveth me; and he that receiveth me receiveth my Father. (D&C 84:36-37.)

And he made it explicit again when he said:

What I the Lord have spoken, I have spoken, and I excuse not myself; and though the heavens and the earth pass away, my word shall not pass away, but shall all be fulfilled, *whether by mine own voice or by the voice of my servants, it is the same.* (D&C 1:38. Italics added. See also 3 Ne. 28:34.)

In connection with men's thoughts I discussed in a previous chapter the discernment often given to God's servants. If they are in sweet attunement, Church leaders are entitled ". . . to have it given unto them to discern . . . lest there shall be any among you professing and yet be not of God." (D&C 46:27.) Not only the General Authorities but bishops and stake and mission presidents have often discerned situations and thereby been enabled to protect the Church and bring the sinner to repentance. Let me quote one instance.

I sat at my desk on one occasion to interview a prospective missionary. When we had covered finance and health and like matters, I approached the moral requirements. I asked him if he was virtuous and free from all immorality.

He replied that he was free from such sins and indiscretions. I had no clear reason to question his word, but a sort of depression and uneasiness weighed heavily upon me. I hesitated a moment then returned to ask again: "Have you been immoral in any way? I must know. This is the final interview." He looked me in the eye and again disclaimed any unworthiness.

I somehow knew that all was not in order with this young man. I folded up the papers, set them on the edge of my desk — unaccepted, unsigned — and said to him, "I will need to see you later." He left the room and I went on about my work. Some hours later, there was a knock on the door and he entered in tears. The recommendation forms were still on the desk untouched. When he ceased his sobbing, he blurted out, "You knew I lied to you. You knew that I was not worthy to fill a mission." It transpired that he had been immoral over a period and had committed fornication many times. He remained home, repented, transformed his life, and became a faithful member of the Church.

The Lord has planned an orderly process in this matter. It is the true way even though there have been distortions and spurious programs advanced. Some have complained at the need for confessing one's sins to Church authorities, stating that this is like the practices of other churches. In many areas in Church service, there are the genuine and the spurious. But the fact that there is priestcraft is no reason for discarding the true priesthood; because there is a distorted form of baptism is no reason for renouncing the true gateway to the Church; because there are presumptuous, spurious claims and practices is no reason for the Church to forfeit the true and correct.

Confession may be made to Church leaders in confidence. A church dignitary is not required by law to reveal in court those matters given to him in total confidence as a spiritual adviser. He will keep sacred the confidences given him. The bishop or stake president will guard confidence as carefully and resolutely as he would want another to guard his own confidences if the situation were reversed. For instance, it would be wholly unwarranted for the ecclesiastical officer to confide in his wife or friends the secrets of another's heart, at least without the direction and permission of the confider.

Confession to Other People

While the major sins such as those listed earlier in this chapter call for confession to the proper Church authorities, clearly such confession is neither necessary nor desirable for all sins. Those of lesser gravity but which have offended others — marital differences, minor fits of anger, disagreements and such — should instead be confessed to the person or persons hurt and the matter should be cleared between the persons involved, normally without a reference to a Church authority. And if one confesses his sins, there is an obligation on the part of the Church membership to accept and forgive, to eradicate from their hearts the memory of the transgression or ill feelings. The Lord said in modern revelation through Joseph Smith:

> And if thy brother or sister offend thee, thou shalt take him or her between him or her and thee alone; and if he or she confess thou shalt be reconciled.

And if he or she confess not thou shalt deliver him or her up unto the church, not to the members, but to the elders. . . .

And if thy brother or sister offend many, he or she shall be chastened before many.

And if any one offend openly, he or she shall be rebuked openly, that he or she may be ashamed. And if he or she confess not, he or she shall be delivered up unto the law of God.

If any shall offend in secret, he or she shall be rebuked in secret, that he or she may have opportunity to confess in secret to him or her whom he or she has offended, and to God. . . .

And thus shall ye conduct in all things. (D&C 42:88-93.)

And to the Church in former days these words were given: *"Confess your faults* one to another, and pray one for another, that ye may be healed . . ." (Jas. 5:16. Italics added.)

When one has wronged another in deep transgression or in injuries of lesser magnitude, he, the aggressor, who gave the offense, regardless of the attitude of the other party, should immediately make amends by confessing to the injured one and doing all in his power to clear up the matter and again establish good feelings between the two parties.

Confession Not to Be Repeated

President Brigham Young spoke out on the matter of confession of sin as follows:

I believe in coming out and being plain and honest with that which should be made public, and in keeping to yourselves that which should be kept. If you have your weaknesses, keep them hid from your brethren as much as you can. You never hear me ask the people to tell their follies . . . do not tell about your nonsensical conduct that nobody knows of but yourselves.[2]

President Young's statement suggests that he was annoyed by many people coming to confess follies of a minor nature. In my own experience there have been those who seemed to have an obsession to confess their weaknesses,

---

[2]*Journal of Discourses*, Vol. 8, p. 326.

and time and time again they have returned to my office to add another little confession or another little detail of the earlier confession. Undoubtedly, President Young had people like this who would be willing to confess sins to be able to get an audience with the Prophet. His advice here is to keep to oneself follies which do not concern others. Certainly it is not necessary to parade one's minor errors. However, a major sin involves more than the two contracting parties. The law of God has been broken; the law of the Church has been involved. The transgressors have offended their God, the Church, the people of the Church. Thus the confession of major sins should be made to the appropriate Church leaders, while less grave sins should be confessed to the persons offended.

Generally it is unwise and quite unnecessary to confess the same sin over and over again. If a major transgression has been fully confessed to and cleared by the proper authority, the person may usually clear himself in any future interview by explaining that this is so and giving the authority's name. Providing there has been no repetition of the offense, nor a commission of any other serious transgression, usually the matter may be considered settled.

Peace Through Confession

Confession brings peace. How often have people departed from my office relieved and lighter of heart than for a long time! Their burdens were lighter, having been shared. They were free. The truth had made them free.

Having warned of excruciating pain and punishments, the Lord said: ". . . Confess your sins, lest you suffer these punishments of which I have spoken . . ." (D&C 19:20.) There is substantial psychological strength in confession. Confession is not only the revealing of errors to proper authorities, but the sharing of burdens to lighten them. One lifts at least part of his burden and places it on other shoulders which are able and willing to help carry the load. Then there comes satisfaction in having taken another step in doing all that is possible to rid oneself of the burden of transgression.

Those who take the course of honest confession of their sin further the process of repentance, of adjustment in their lives, of reconciliation with God. To illustrate this I quote below a letter received from one young transgressor who, following excommunication, was finding his way back to the blessings of the gospel and the Church.

> I am writing this letter hoping I may soon be rebaptized into the Church. I was excommunicated. . . .

> I was very sorry for my sins and sickened by them. I read a great deal in the Book of Mormon, seeking somewhat to justify myself not going to the mission president to confess. I read about Alma and Corianton and tried to convince myself that, since I had repented (I thought), I would not need to confess to anyone but God. I did pray a great deal. After everyone else had gone to bed, I would remain up reading and praying. Finally one night, a voice from within me said, "You know what you must do, so do it."

> A few days later at a conference, I confessed to the mission president. . . . I had no choice if I was to ever obtain forgiveness.

> After I had confessed, even knowing I would be excommunicated, I felt an extremely sweet peace in my soul . . . and I thank God . . . that he gave me courage to do it.

> When I came home, humiliated and fearful, my family was extremely kind and understanding as was the bishop who . . . gave me an opportunity to get up in priesthood meeting . . . and . . . ask . . . forgiveness. It was extremely difficult . . . but I am thankful I did it. Then the bishop told me I should . . . shake hands with the people and not slink away. I'm thankful I did that also for it made things easier for me. They seemed to forgive me and they accepted me back. Their true Christianity helped me to have strength to go to all the meetings I could attend.

> Since this weekend was fast Sunday, I started fasting Friday after supper and Saturday I went into the mountains and spent about five hours by myself, thinking and praying, and I read part of the Book of Mormon, particularly the Book of Enos.

> While praying aloud to my Father, I tasted the most bitter sorrow that I have ever felt. I had a slight indication of what it really is to suffer godly sorrow for sin. . . . I had pleaded that

I would be forgiven for my sins and for being such a great cause of suffering to my family and to the Lord Jesus Christ. I understood ever so vaguely that Christ did take upon himself my sins and he suffered untold sorrow for me. I begged for forgiveness, and for release from the deadening, prisoner-like effects of sin, and to know that I was forgiven.

I felt impressed . . . that I would receive forgiveness if I did continue to be humble, fast, and pray. I fear I will have to suffer sorrow as I did yesterday many times again before all the evil effects of sin will be lifted out of me and I will feel that freedom that my spirit craves.

I ask in all humility, realizing that the responsibilities of membership are great, that I might be accepted back into the Church and back onto the path I departed from. I know God lives and that his Son Jesus Christ really did take upon himself our sins and that he lives today. I know the Church was restored through the beloved Joseph Smith and that all the keys remain with the Church today. . . .

Sincerely,

P.S. I observe the Word of Wisdom and I have been giving my tithing to my mother. She pays it to the bishop in my father's name. I felt that the money was the Lord's and I could not steal it. I have also been clean in mind and act since my excommunication.

This young man had received a conviction of his guilt; he had abandoned the sin; he had confessed the transgression in the proper way. He was well on the way to complete forgiveness and to the peace of soul which it brings.

Chapter Fourteen

Restitution

> *If the wicked restore the pledge,*
> *give again that he had robbed,*
> *walk in the statutes of life, with-*
> *out committing iniquity; he shall*
> *surely live, he shall not die.*
>
> *None of his sins that he hath*
> *committed shall be mentioned un-*
> *to him. . .*
>
> —Ezekiel 33:15-16

IN PREVIOUS CHAPTERS WE HAVE TRACED SOME OF WHAT are perhaps the more obvious steps in repentance — the awakening conviction of sin, the renouncing or abandoning of sin, the confession of sin. When a person has experienced the deep sorrow and humility induced by a conviction of sin; when he has cast off the sin and resolutely determined to abhor it henceforth; when he has humbly confessed his sin to God and to the proper persons on earth — when these things are done there remains the requirement of restitution. He must restore that which he damaged, stole, or wronged.

President Joseph F. Smith put restitution in its proper place as a part of the pattern of repentance. His statement is quoted previously in this book but is repeated here by way of emphasis:

> True repentance is not only sorrow for sins, and humble penitence and contrition before God, but it involves the necessity of turning away from them, a discontinuance of all evil practices and deeds, a thorough reformation of life, a vital change from evil to good, from vice to virtue, from darkness to light. Not only so, but *to make restitution,* so far as it is possible, for all the wrongs we have done, to pay our debts, and to restore to God and man their rights — that which is due them from us.[1]

Restitution Always Part of Repentance

There are many scriptures which show that restitution is an important part of true repentance. Some of them even go so far as to prescribe the amount of restitution which should be made in return for a wrong. For example, Moses taught:

> If a man shall steal an ox, or a sheep, and kill it, or sell it; *he shall restore five oxen for an ox,* and *four sheep for a sheep.*
>
> If the theft be certainly found in his hand alive, whether it be ox, or ass, or sheep; he shall *restore double.*
>
> If a man shall cause a field or vineyard to be eaten, and shall put in his beast, and shall feed in another man's field; of the best of his own field, and of the best of his own vineyard, *shall he make restitution.*
>
> If fire break out, and catch in thorns, so that the stacks of corn, or the standing corn, or the field, be consumed therewith; he that kindled the fire shall surely *make restitution.* (Exod. 22:1, 4, 5, 6. Italics added.)

It is true that Moses was concerned with governing and controlling a population larger than many of our modern cities, and to that extent some think of his laws as being secular in purport. But observe that in the quotation which follows, the Lord equates actions against one's neighbor with committing "a trespass against the Lord" — or, as he goes on to say, with sin. Thus the restoration spoken of was to be not merely a legal requirement for the mainte-

---

[1]Smith, *Gospel Doctrine,* pp. 100-101.

nance of earthly justice but also part of the process of repentance from sin.

> If a soul sin, and commit a trespass against the Lord, and lie unto his neighbour in that which was delivered him to keep, or in fellowship, or in a thing taken away by violence, or hath deceived his neighbour;

> Or have found that which was lost, and lieth concerning it, and sweareth falsely; in any of all these that a man doeth, sinning therein:

> Then it shall be, because he hath sinned, and is guilty, that he shall restore that which he took violently away, or the thing which he hath deceitfully gotten, or that which was delivered him to keep, or the lost thing which he found,

> Or all that about which he hath sworn falsely; he shall even restore it in the principal, and shall add the fifth part more thereto, and give it unto him to whom it appertaineth, in the day of his trespass offering. (Lev. 6:2-5.)

There is frequent mention of a four-fold restitution for wrongdoing. In a law given in previous gospel dispensations and reiterated in our own time the Lord provides as follows:

> And again, verily I say unto you, if after thine enemy has come upon thee the first time, he repent and come unto thee praying thy forgiveness, thou shalt forgive him, and shalt hold it no more as a testimony against thine enemy —

> And so on unto the second and third time; and as oft as thine enemy repenteth of the trespass wherewith he has trespassed against thee, thou shalt forgive him, until seventy times seven.

> And if he trespass against thee and repent not the first time, nevertheless thou shalt forgive him.

> And if he trespass against thee the second time, and repent not, nevertheless thou shalt forgive him.

> And if he trespass against thee the third time, and repent not, thou shalt also forgive him.

> But if he trespass against thee the fourth time thou shalt not forgive him, but shalt bring these testimonies before the Lord; and they shall not be blotted out until he repent and *reward thee four-fold* in all things wherewith he has trespassed against thee.

And if he do this, thou shalt forgive him with all thine heart; and if he do not this, I the Lord, will avenge thee of thine enemy an hundred-fold. (D&C 98:39-45. Italics added.)

One may trespass in ignorance. Should anyone be in sin yet be unaware of the evil nature of his actions, he should be required to make restitution so far as possible when brought to a realization of his sin.

A classic example of restitution as part of repentance is that of Zacchaeus. This rich publican was small of physical stature but mighty in moral size. From his special vantage point in the sycamore tree he could see the Lord who was passing that way in the midst of a multitude. Not only was he to see the Master but to be actually his host, for the Savior commanded him to climb down in haste, ". . . for today I must abide at thy house." (Luke 19:5.)

The inhabitants of Jericho who saw this incident complained that Christ was to be guest in the home of a sinner. As if to reassure the Savior that his confidence was not misplaced:

. . . Zacchaeus stood, and said unto the Lord; Behold, Lord, the half of my goods I give to the poor; and if I have taken anything from any man by false accusation, *I restore him fourfold.*

And Jesus said unto him, This day is salvation come to this house, forsomuch as he also is a son of Abraham. (Luke 19:8-9. Italics added.)

Complete Restitution Sometimes Impossible

From these quotations and examples it is quite clear that the repentant sinner is required to make restitution insofar as it is possible. I say "insofar as it is possible" because there are some sins for which no adequate restitution can be made, and others for which only partial restitution is possible.

A thief or burglar may make partial restitution by returning that which was stolen. A liar may make the truth known and correct to some degree the damage done by the lie. A gossip who has slandered the character of another may make partial restitution through strenuous effort to restore the good name of the person he harmed. If by sin or carelessness the wrongdoer has destroyed property, he may restore or pay for it in full or in part.

If a man's actions have brought sorrow and disgrace to his wife and children, in his restitution he must make every effort to restore their confidence and love by an overabundance of filial devotion and fidelity. This is true also of wives and mothers. Likewise if children have wronged their parents, a part of their program of repentance must be to right those wrongs and to honor their parents.

As a rule there are many things which a repentant soul can do to make amends. "A broken heart and a contrite spirit" will usually find ways to restore to some extent. The true spirit of repentance demands that he who injures shall do everything in his power to right the wrong.

A man who had confessed infidelity was forgiven by his wife, who saw much in him to commend and believed in his total repentance. To him, I said: "Brother Blank, you should from this day forward be the best husband a woman ever had. You should be willing to forgive her little eccentricities, overlook her weaknesses, for she has forgiven you the ten-thousand-talent sin and you can afford to forgive numerous little hundred-pence errors."

No Adequate Restoration for Murder

As to crimes for which no adequate restoration is possible, I have suggested in a previous chapter that perhaps the reason murder is an unforgivable sin is that, once having taken a life — whether that life be innocent or reprobate — the life-taker cannot restore it. He may give his own life as payment, but this does not wholly undo the injury done by his crime. He might support the widow and children; he might do many other noble things; but a life is gone and the restitution of it in full is impossible. Repentance in the ordinary sense seems futile.

Murder is so treacherous and so far-reaching! Those who lose their possessions may be able to recover their wealth. Those defamed may still be able to prove themselves above reproach. Even the loss of chastity leaves the soul in mortality with opportunity to recover and repent and to make amends to some degree. But to take a life, whether someone else's or one's own, cuts off the victim's experiences of mortality and thus his opportunity to repent, to keep God's commandments in this earth life. It interferes with his potential of having "glory added upon [his head] for ever and ever." (Abraham 3:26.)

Restitution for Loss of Chastity

Also far-reaching is the effect of loss of chastity. Once given or taken or stolen it can never be regained. Even in a forced contact such as rape or incest, the injured one is greatly outraged. If she has not cooperated and contributed to the foul deed, she is of course in a more favorable position. There is no condemnation where there is no voluntary participation. It is better to die in defending one's virtue than to live having lost it without a struggle.

As stated throughout this book, while one may recover in large measure from sexual sins they are nevertheless heinous, and because of their gravity the Lord has placed them very close to the unpardonable ones in order of seriousness.

The principle of restitution is brought into focus where two unmarried young people have entered into sin by which both lives are damaged, and especially if virtue has been taken. In such circumstances serious consideration should be given to a marriage which will hold the sin in one family. Why should they not marry when by their iniquitous act they have plunged themselves into an adult role?

This is especially true if pregnancy results from the sin. In this situation it is the girl who suffers most. She must not have an abortion, for that would add serious sin to serious sin. She carries most of the burdens, while the boy often goes penalty-free. The girl must go through the uncomfortable nine months with its distress, deprivations, limitations and embarrassments, and then the pain and expense of delivery and the difficult life afterward. It is a cowardly boy who would not propose marriage, pay the costs, share the deprivations and embarrassment. Yet many young men have walked away and abandoned the girl to all the devastating payments for the sin of them both. Parents frequently excuse the son on one pretext or another, and leave the girl to suffer for the sins of them both. Sometimes, parents of the boy curiously feel magnanimous when they offer to pay the actual financial costs of the delivery, not taking into account that the financial is a one-time experience, while the girl has the problems throughout her life, and they are heavy burdens.

To buy the girl off or abandon her to her lifelong problem is not courageous, nor fair, nor right. The time will come when every individual will pay full price, and perhaps with interest, every obligation incurred, even though it was hidden or covered at the time.

The young girl who sins should realize that all the sorrows, inconvenience and suffering she goes through incident to the carrying and bearing of a child do not fully constitute forgiveness for her sin. She must repent and make her proper adjustment. Let the boy realize too that none of the suffering of the girl minimizes his guilt, but rather magnifies it. For many reasons he may not be prepared to settle down to family life, but he has by his immoral act projected himself into adulthood and has brought upon himself responsibilities which he will do well to accept and discharge as honorably as he can. Like the girl, he needs to find his way to total repentance, and the road leads through acceptance of responsibility, not away from it.

The prophets understood clearly the weaknesses of men and the likelihood of their running away from their responsibilities in this area. Moses recorded the law:

> And if a man entice a maid that is not betrothed, and lie with her, he shall surely endow her to be his wife. (Exod. 22:16.)

And again:

> If a man find a damsel that is a virgin, which is not betrothed, and lay hold on her, and lie with her, and they be found;
>
> . . . She shall be his wife; because he hath humbled her, he may not put her away all his days. (Deut. 22:28-29.)

For the boy, perhaps the matter can be glossed over and covered up by parents who seek to avoid publicity and a scandal, but have they realized what they have done for their son's soul when he doubles his transgression by failing in his repentance? True repentance means restitution, meeting every obligation and restoring every damage so far as is possible. Yet it is strange how many times parents of the boy decide that the girl who was good enough for him to date suddenly became promiscuous and therefore is now unworthy of their son; strange also how few of the parents charge the boy with promiscuity and consequently encourage their son to pass up his responsibilities, even to his own detriment; strange how many parents charge the girl with having trapped their son and now rate their boy "holier than thou" and the girl not worthy of further consideration in the matter!

I have known many young couples who had been loose in morals and who, having prostituted each other's bodies, found they were to become parents. In some instances, each party accused the other; each began to distrust the other; each began to hate the other. They both admitted their sin but now the boy was trying to "crawl out." His parents were encouraging him to get out of it. They knew the many problems which marriage brings.

In my office I talked to a partly-repentant young couple about marriage — a quiet, immediate marriage with no frills, no pomp and no publicity. They had moved to forfeit many of those things when they disregarded the law of chastity. He was quite willing to marry when the two came in alone at first, but when he came the second time he had been brainwashed by his parents and he would not consider it.

I urged marriage by the bishop at the home. The girl, beginning now to realize her predicament, was willing in spite of her fast-diminishing respect or affection for the weakening, selfish boy. Not so the boy! He asked: "Why? Why should we marry? How could we marry? I have no job. I haven't finished my education. Where would we live? How could I pay doctor and hospital bills? How could we get along without a car? How could we assume the responsibilities of a family and parenthood?"

Then I asked some questions: "Why did you precipitate yourselves into this demanding situation? Why did you do the act which would make you parents? Why did you engage in associations which demand home, employment, status? Your completely irresponsible act and your reaction to it brand you immediately as immature. You do not know the meaning of responsibility. You seem to be highly interested in yourself and your conveniences, and your desires. Are you going to run and leave the girl to carry your baby with all your penalties too? It is time you both grew up and matured and faced realities. This situation is not the intention of either of you but it is the result of your loose actions. You made the choice when you broke the law of chastity. You knew it was wrong. You knew this problem could result. Now if you are going to grow up and meet life's issues; if you are going to be fair and just; if you are going to start out a good life on a straight road, start now to meet your responsibilities. When you gave up your virtue — that hour your freedom was replaced with tyrannical fetters (for transgression is a ball and chain, it is handcuffs, hard and heavy) — you accepted shackles and limitations and sorrows and eternal regrets when you could have had freedom with peace.

"Today is a good day to start a new life of mature responsibility. Cease blaming others, start to accept your own responsibility. Make up your own mind. You brought this about together, now solve your problems together. Forgive each other and move along and make the best of a difficult situation, but do not run away from it.

"You two have committed a heinous sin. Do you wish to carry this terrible burden all your days or would you like to be forgiven for it? To be forgiven one must repent. Repentance means not only to convict yourselves of the horror of the sin, but to confess it, abandon it, and restore to all who have been damaged to the total extent possible; then spend the balance of your lives trying to live the commandments of the Lord so he can eventually pardon you and cleanse you."

Restoring and Forgiving

I have known many young couples who slipped in their courtship and committed the serious sin, but who married and made a good life of it and largely "lived down" the embarrassment of their youth. In a difficult situation wherein complete restitution was impossible they did the best they could at that point and, having repented, were forgiven.

In the process of repentance we must restore completely where possible, otherwise restore to the maximum degree attainable. And through it all we must remember that the pleading sinner, desiring to make restitution for his acts, must also forgive others of all offenses committed against him. The Lord will not forgive us unless our hearts are fully purged of all hate, bitterness and accusation against our fellowmen.

Chapter Fifteen

Keeping God's Commandments Brings Forgiveness

> *Nevertheless, he that repents and does the commandments of the Lord shall be forgiven.*
>
> —Doctrine & Covenants 1:32
>
> *And in nothing doth man offend God, or against none is his wrath kindled, save those who confess not his hand in all things, and obey not his commandments.*
>
> —Doctrine & Covenants 59:21

IN HIS PREFACE TO MODERN REVELATION, THE LORD OUT-lined what is one of the most difficult requirements in true repentance. For some it is the hardest part of repentance, because it puts one on guard for the remainder of his life. The Lord says:

> . . . I the Lord cannot look upon sin with the least degree of allowance;
> Nevertheless, he that repents and *does the commandments of the Lord* shall be forgiven. (D&C 1:31-32. Italics added.)

This scripture is most precise. First, one repents. Having gained that ground he then must live the commandments of the Lord to retain his vantage point. This is necessary to secure complete forgiveness.

No step in the process of repentance is universally easy, which is one reason why it is preferable to stay clear of the chains of sin. The degree of difficulty in each step varies with the participant.

Devotion and Effort Required

Under the humiliation of a guilty conscience, with perhaps the possibility of detection and consequent scandal and shame, with a striving spirit urging toward adjustment — with such motivation the first steps of sorrow, abandonment, confession and restitution may be less difficult for some. But keeping God's commandments is a challenge to the faith and will power of the most resolute soul.

Doing the Lord's commandments, as the above scripture requires, is an effort extending through the balance of life. "Unto the end" is a phrase used often in the scriptures, and it means, literally, to the end of life. This phrase now takes on new and added meaning and significance to the repentant one: ". . . He only is saved who endureth unto the end." (D&C 53:7.) And again: *"If thou wilt do good,* yea, and *hold out faithful to the end,* thou shalt be saved in the kingdom of God . . ." (D&C 6:13. Italics added.)

Since all of us sin in greater or lesser degree, we are all in need of constant repentance, of continually raising our sights and our performance. One can hardly do the commandments of the Lord in a day, a week, a month or a year. This is an effort which must be extended through the remainder of one's years. To accomplish it every soul should develop the same spirit of devotion and dedication to the work of the Lord as the bishop and the Relief Society president enjoy. Most often theirs is near total devotion.

This devotion needs to be applied as much in mental as in spiritual and physical effort. To understand the gospel so that true obedience can be intelligently given to its requirements takes time and application. The child born in the Church goes to Primary and Sunday School; later attends MIA and seminary and institute; works in scouting and exploring; later participates in Relief Society and much other specialized works, besides serving and attending and participating in other meetings and conferences, and all this in addition to the study of the gospel and many hours on his knees in prayer. The adult convert can make up much of this training by intensive study and pondering and prayer.

Yet many people expect to get a knowledge and understanding of the whole gospel plan and its eternities of implications and associations in a very short period of time. They are quite willing to go years and years with intense study to partly master one of the rudiments of total knowledge — to become a dentist, a doctor, a judge, a professor, a specialist in any line — yet many reject the gospel because it may not be discerned and understood in a few easy lessons. They are not "doing the commandments," hence they do not repent.

Repentance Must Be Wholehearted

In connection with repentance, the scriptures use the phrase, "with all his heart" (see D&C 42:25). Obviously this rules out any reservations. Repentance must involve an all-out, total surrender to the program of the Lord. That transgressor is not fully repentant who neglects his tithing, misses his meetings, breaks the Sabbath, fails in his family prayers, does not sustain the authorities of the Church, breaks the Word of Wisdom, does not love the Lord nor his fellowmen. A reforming adulterer who drinks or curses is not repentant. The repenting burglar who has sex play is not ready for forgiveness. God cannot forgive unless the transgressor shows a true repentance which spreads to all areas of his life.

The Lord knows, as does the individual concerned, the degree of contrition exhibited, and the reward will be received accordingly, for God is just. He knows the heart.

He knows whether or not one is making but a show of repentance. Feigning repentance or bluffing is futile, for both the transgressor and the Lord know the degree of sincerity.

Bringing Gospel to Others Aids Repentance

"Doing the commandments" includes the many activities required of the faithful, only a few of which are mentioned above. General good works and devotion accompanied by constructive attitudes are what is needed. In addition, a sound way to neutralize the effects of sin in one's life is to bring the light of the gospel to others who do not now enjoy it. This can mean working with both inactive members of the Church and nonmembers — perhaps more usually the latter. Note how the Lord has related the forgiveness of sins to the bearing of testimony respecting the latter-day work:

> For I will forgive you of your sins with this commandment — that you remain steadfast in your minds in solemnity and the spirit of prayer, *in bearing testimony to all the world* of those things which are communicated unto you. (D&C 84:61. Italics added.)

The Lord seemingly is disappointed with many who fail to bear their testimonies, as he says:

> But with some I am not well pleased, for they will not open their mouths, but they hide the talent which I have given unto them, because of the fear of man. Wo unto such, for mine anger is kindled against them. (D&C 60:2.)

This failure to bear testimony would be particularly serious with those who have deadly sins to overcome and neutralize. Of special note is the scripture given in 1831 through the Prophet Joseph Smith to himself and his associated elders en route to Zion. Addressing them, the Lord said:

> Nevertheless, ye are blessed, for the testimony which ye have borne is recorded in heaven for the angels to look upon; . . . and your sins are forgiven you. (D&C 62:3.)

Here he promises a forgiveness of sins to those elders who had been valiant in proselyting and bearing testimony.

The angels as well as the Father in heaven would certainly rejoice over those members who with great sincerity would overcome their sins and receive remission of them, partly through their efforts to raise the spiritual standard of their fellow creatures by bearing testimony of the restored gospel.

Another statement of the Lord — this one through James — reinforces the value of the testimony in overcoming sins. The testimony comes from study, prayer, and living the commandments, and the repetition of the testimony builds and stabilizes it. James says that through this missionary work of saving souls of others, one comes to the point of bringing salvation and sanctification to himself.

> Brethren, if any of you do err from the truth, and one convert him;
>
> Let him know, that he which converteth the sinner from the error of his way shall save a soul from death, and shall hide a multitude of sins. (Jas. 5:19-20.)

Every person who is beginning the long journey of emancipating himself from the thralldom of sin and evil will find comfort in the thought expressed by James. We could expand it somewhat and remind the transgressor that every testimony he bears, every prayer he offers, every sermon he preaches, every scripture he reads, every help he gives to stimulate and raise others — all these strengthen him and raise him to higher levels.

The proper motivation for missionary work of any kind, as for all Church service, is of course love for fellowmen, but always such work has its by-product effect on one's own life. Thus as we become instruments in God's hands in changing the lives of others our own lives cannot help being lifted. One can hardly help another to the top of the hill without climbing there himself.

Not all of us can engage in full-time missionary work, where one might have opportunity to explain the gospel and bear testimony of its divinity many times every day. Nor can we all be formally set apart as stake missionaries, where opportunities like those of the full-time missionaries occur, though to a somewhat lesser degree. But what every member most definitely *can* do is follow President McKay's inspired slogan, "Every member a missionary." He can befriend and fellowship nonmember neighbors, friends and acquaintances, and by his interest and association strive to bring those nonmembers to the point where they will willingly receive the stake or full-time missionaries. No one needs to be concerned lest he cannot properly teach his friends the gospel. The set-apart missionaries are equipped to do that. What every member ought to do, by good example and by bearing testimony, is to portray to nonmembers the joys of gospel living and understanding, and thus help to bring them to the stage where they will accept more formal teaching.

In addition to the possibilities in missionary work, in areas such as quorum and auxiliary and committee work of the Church almost limitless opportunities are afforded to lift others, thus blessing oneself. Monthly there are testimony meetings held where each one has the opportunity to bear witness. To by-pass such opportunities is to fail to that extent to pile up credits against the accumulated errors and transgressions.

Faith and Works

In view of the emphasis thus far made on the importance of good works in returning from sin and establishing a repentant life, it may be well to say a word about the idea of salvation by faith alone. Some people not of our Church like to quote, in support of that concept, the following words of Paul:

> For by grace are ye saved through faith; and that not of yourselves: it is the gift of God:
>
> Not of works, lest any man should boast. (Eph. 2:8-9.)

One of the most fallacious doctrines originated by Satan and propounded by man is that man is saved alone by the grace of God; that belief in Jesus Christ alone is all that is needed for salvation. Along with all the other works necessary for man's exaltation in the kingdom of God this could rule out the need for repentance. It could give license for sin and, since it does not require man to work out his salvation, could accept instead lip service, death-bed "repentance," and shallow, meaningless confession of sin.

Church members are fortunate indeed to have scriptures brought forth in this age which clarify this and other doctrinal questions beyond all doubt. One passage in the Book of Mormon, written perhaps with the same intent as Paul's statement above — to stress and induce appreciation for the gracious gift of salvation offered on condition of obedience — is particularly enlightening:

> For we labor diligently to write, to persuade our children, and also our brethren, to believe in Christ, and to be reconciled to God; for we know that it is by grace that we are saved, *after all we can do.* (2 Ne. 25:23. Italics added.)

And the Lord further emphasized the fact:

> And no unclean thing can enter into his kingdom; therefore nothing entereth into his rest save it be those who have washed their garments in my blood, because of their faith, and the repentance of all their sins, and their faithfulness unto the end.

> Now this is the commandment: Repent, all ye ends of the earth, and come unto me and be baptized in my name, that ye may be sanctified by the reception of the Holy Ghost, that ye may stand spotless before me at the last day. (3 Ne. 27:19-20.)

This makes clear the two facets, neither of which alone would bring the individual salvation — the grace of Christ, particularly as represented by his atoning sacrifice, and individual effort. However good a person's works, he could not be saved had Jesus not died for his and everyone else's sins. And however powerful the saving grace of Christ, it brings exaltation to no man who does not comply with the works of the gospel.

Of course we need to understand terms. If by the word "salvation" is meant the mere salvation or redemption from the grave, the "grace of God" is sufficient. But if the term "salvation" means returning to the presence of God with eternal progression, eternal increase, and eventual godhood, for this one certainly must have the "grace of God," as it is generally defined, plus personal purity, overcoming of evil, and the good "works" made so important in the exhortations of the Savior and his prophets and apostles.

Few, if any, have understood these matters better than the Apostle Paul, who would have been surprised that any other construction should be put upon his words. Throughout his writings he stresses the importance of deeds of righteousness. He preaches against sin of any kind, urging repentance and indicating that forgiveness is a necessary element of salvation. He declares in his Epistle to the Romans that "the wrath of God is revealed from heaven against all . . . unrighteousness of men . . ." (Rom. 1:18.) He not only condemns all evil things but promises that God "will render to every man according to his deeds." (Rom. 2:6.) He promises eternal life to those "who by patient continuance in well doing seek for glory and honour and immortality." (Rom. 2:7.) He emphasizes, "For not the hearers of the law are just before God, but the doers of the law shall be justified." (Rom. 2:13.) And as discussed previously in this book, he points out specific sins in considerable number and calls on men to repent of them.

Repentant Life Seeks Perfection

One could multiply references almost indefinitely but enough has been said to establish the point that the repentant life, the life which constantly reaches for perfection, must rely on works as well as on faith. The gospel is a program of action — of *doing* things. Man's immortality and eternal life are God's goals. (Moses 1:39.) Immortality has been accomplished by the Savior's sacrifice. Eternal life hangs in the balance awaiting the works of men.

This progress toward eternal life is a matter of achieving perfection. Living all the commandments guarantees total forgiveness of sins and assures one of exaltation through that perfection which comes by complying with the formula the Lord gave us. In his Sermon on the Mount he made the command to all men: "Be ye therefore perfect, even as your Father which is in heaven is perfect." (Matt. 5:48.) Being perfect means to triumph over sin. This is a mandate from the Lord. He is just and wise and kind. He would never require anything from his children which was not for their benefit and which was not attainable. Perfection therefore is an achievable goal.

The Savior voiced the same instruction to his Nephite leaders when he told them the requirements of the gospel: to be like himself. (3 Ne. 12:48.) The Savior had lived the commands of his gospel; now it was required of all men to likewise live the commandments. Nephi quoted the Savior along the same line:

> And also, the voice of the Son came unto me, saying: He that is baptized in my name, to him will the Father give the Holy Ghost, like unto me; wherefore, follow me, and do the things which ye have seen me do. (2 Ne. 31:12.)

The Lord amplified his statement somewhat to the Nephites when, after long dissertations on growing perfect through living the gospel, he asked his disciples the pertinent question: "Therefore, what manner of men ought ye to be?" He may have been merely trying to impress them further with the truth and reinforce it, or he may have been asking in order to note how well they had been grasping the vital truths he was teaching them. He did not wait for their response, but followed the question quickly with the answer: "Verily I say unto you, even as I am." (3 Ne. 27:27.)

Perfection really comes through overcoming. The Lord revealed through John: "To him that overcometh will I grant to sit with me in my throne, even as I also overcame, and am set down with my Father in his throne." (Rev. 3:21.)

It seems that evil is always about us. It has been speculated by one of the earlier Brethren that there are hundreds of evil spirits working against each of us. Accordingly, we must be alert constantly. We catalogue our weaknesses and move in against them to overcome them. Christ became perfect through overcoming. Only as we overcome shall we become perfect and move toward godhood. As I have indicated previously, the time to do this is now, in mortality.

Someone once said: "A fellow who is planning to reform is one step behind. He ought to quit planning and get on with the job. Today is the day." Certainly self-mastery is a continuous program — a journey, not a single start. Men do not suddenly become righteous any more than a tiny acorn suddenly becomes an oak. Advancement to perfection can nevertheless be rapid if one resolutely strides toward the goal.

Perspective Is Important

In the march to perfection through the conquering of sin, it is important to have the right perspective. For example, some people get means and ends reversed. Many feel that the Word of Wisdom is for the principal purpose of increasing our health, increasing our mortal life, but a more careful study of the revelation (D&C 89) reveals that there is a deeper purpose. Of course, total observance will strengthen one's body, make it survive longer so that there will be a longer time in which to perfect the body and, especially, the spirit — looking toward eternal status and eternal joys. The Lord made solemn promises to ". . . all Saints who remember to keep and do these sayings, walking in *obedience to the commandments* . . ." (D&C 89:18. Italics added.) Here the commitments of the Lord were two-fold. First, he promised to such who obey that they shall ". . . receive health in their navel and marrow to their bones . . . ," that as a consequence of good health physically they "shall run and not be weary, and shall walk and not faint." This is a glorious promise.

But the spiritual promises greatly exceed the physical. For those who observe these particular instructions and are obedient to all the Lord's commandments, the blessings really are increased and magnified. Such saints, he promises, shall be passed over by the angel of death and shall not be slain. This promise returns us to Exodus where we read that the Lord tested the faith of the children of Israel to see if they would follow the great Moses.

Now the promise in the revelation above quoted is similar and dissimilar to ancient Israel's test, as comparisons generally are. In both circumstances there would be the element of passover, the element of obedience of faith without knowing all the reasons why. The "obedience of faith" is basic. Without it the miracle cannot happen. Had Israel not obeyed, their firstborn sons would not have been protected.

For observing the Word of Wisdom the reward is life, not only prolonged mortal life but life eternal. No promise is made through the Word of Wisdom that the faithful observer will not die: "For as in Adam all die, even so in Christ shall all be made alive." (1 Cor. 15:22.) With ancient Israel it was physical life or physical death. In our modern promise, it is spiritual life or spiritual death. If one ignores "these sayings" and fails in "obedience to the commandments" his death is certain, but if he obeys implicitly, his eternal life through perfection is assured. The angel of death cuts one short of mortal life for disobedience; the angel of light makes the way clear for the spiritual life eternal.

Initiative Is With the Individual

We have discussed elsewhere that other class of people who are basically unrepentant because they are not "doing the commandments." They are Church members who are steeped in lethargy. They neither drink nor commit the sexual sins. They do not gamble nor rob nor kill. They are good citizens and splendid neighbors, but spiritually speaking they seem to be in a long, deep sleep. They are doing nothing seriously wrong except in their failures to do the right things to earn their exaltation. To such people as this, the words of Lehi might well apply:

> ⁀ O that ye would awake; awake from a deep sleep, yea, even from the sleep of hell, and shake off the awful chains by which ye are bound, which are the chains which bind the children of men, that they are carried away captive down to the eternal gulf of misery and woe. (2 Ne. 1:13.)

The third chapter of the Book of Revelation contains these words of the Savior:

> Behold, I stand at the door, and knock: if any man hear my voice, and open the door, I will come in to him, and will sup with him, and he with me. (Rev. 3:20.)

Holman Hunt, the artist, felt inspired to capture this stirring scripture on canvas. One day he was showing his picture of "Christ Knocking at the Door" to a friend when the friend suddenly exclaimed: "There is one thing wrong about your picture."

"What is it?" inquired the artist.

"The door on which Jesus knocks has no handle," replied his friend.

"Ah," responded Mr. Hunt, "that is not a mistake. You see, this is the door to the human heart. It can only be opened from the inside."

And thus it is. Jesus may stand and knock, but each of us decides whether to open. The Spirit is powerless to compel a man to move. The man himself must take the initiative. He must himself desire to repent and take the specific steps. He must, as Paul counseled, "put on the whole armour of God," and thus insure that he is "able to stand against the wiles of the devil." (Eph. 6:11.) That armor is incomplete without steadfast effort to live God's commandments. Without such effort repentance too is incomplete. And incomplete repentance never brought complete forgiveness.

Chapter Sixteen

Avoiding Pitfalls

> *Watch and pray, that ye enter not into temptation: the spirit indeed is willing, but the flesh is weak.*
>
> —Matthew 26:41

PAUL SPEAKS IN THESE WORDS ABOUT THE NEED FOR raising positive, unequivocal voices in the cause of truth:

> For if the trumpet give an uncertain sound, who shall prepare himself to the battle?
>
> So likewise ye, except ye utter by the tongue words easy to be understood, how shall it be known what is spoken? for ye shall speak into the air.
>
> There are, it may be, so many kinds of voices in the world, and none of them is without signification. (1 Cor. 14:8-10.)

Trumpets have sounded, warnings have been given, voices have been recorded in the chapters of this book. Pitfalls which beset youth and others, lurking dangers and forbidden paths for all have been pointed out. To know where the danger is and to be able to recognize it in all of its manifestations provides protection. The evil one is alert. He is always ready to deceive and claim as his victims every unwary one, every careless one, every rebellious one. Paul warned the Ephesians, "For we wrestle not against flesh and blood, but against principalities, against powers, against the rulers of the darkness of this world, against spiritual wickedness in high places." (Eph. 6:12.)

Insidiousness of Sin

Whether or not one is repenting from grave sin, the true spirit of repentance which all should exhibit embraces a desire to stay away from sin. One cannot simultaneously be repentant and flirt with transgression.

Sin, like a journey, begins with the first step; and wisdom and experience teach that it is easier to resist the first temptation than later ones, when a pattern of transgression has begun to develop. This is demonstrated in the story of the lark. Sitting in the high branches of a tree safe from harm, he saw a traveler walking through the forest carrying a mysterious little black box. The lark flew down and perched on the traveler's shoulder. "What do you have in the little black box?" he asked.

"Worms," the traveler replied.

"Are they for sale?"

"Yes, and very cheaply, too. The price is only one feather for a worm."

The lark thought for a moment. "I must have a million feathers. Surely, I'll never miss one of them. Here is an opportunity to get a good dinner for no work at all." So he told the man he would buy one. He searched carefully under his wing for a tiny feather. He winced a bit as he pulled it out, but the size and quality of the worm made him quickly forget the pain. High up in the tree again he began to sing as beautifully as before.

The next day he saw the same man and once again he exchanged a feather for a worm. What a wonderful, effortless way to get dinner!

Each day thereafter the lark surrendered a feather, and each loss seemed to hurt less and less. In the beginning he had many feathers, but as the days passed he found it more difficult to fly. Finally, after the loss of one of his primary feathers, he could no longer reach the top of the tree, let alone fly up into the sky. In fact he could do no more than flutter a few feet in the air, and was forced to seek his food with the quarrelsome, bickering sparrows.

The man with the worms came no more, for there were no feathers to pay for the meals. The lark no longer sang because he was so ashamed of his fallen state.

This is how unworthy habits possess us — first painfully, then more easily, until at last we find ourselves stripped of all that lets us sing and soar. This is how freedom is lost. This is how we become enmeshed in sin.

Serious sin enters into our lives as we yield first to little temptations. Seldom does one enter into deeper transgression without first yielding to lesser ones, which open the door to the greater. Giving an example of one type of sin, someone said, "An honest man doesn't suddenly become dishonest any more than a clean field suddenly becomes weedy."

It is extremely difficult, if not impossible, for the devil to enter a door that is closed. He seems to have no keys for locked doors. But if a door is slightly ajar, he gets his toe in, and soon this is followed by his foot, then by his leg and his body and his head, and finally he is in all the way.

This situation is reminiscent of the fable of the camel and his owner who were traveling across the desert sand dunes when a wind storm came up. The traveler quickly set up his tent and moved in, closing the flaps to protect himself from the cutting, grinding sands of the raging storm. The camel was of course left outside, and as the violent wind hurled the sand against his body and into his eyes and nostrils he found it unbearable and finally begged for entrance into the tent.

"There is room only for myself," said the traveler.

"But may I just get my nose in so I can breathe air not filled with sand?" asked the camel.

"Well, perhaps you could do that," replied the traveler, and he opened the flap ever so little and the long nose of the camel entered. How comfortable the camel was now!

But soon the camel became weary of the smarting sand on his eyes and ears, and he was tempted to ask again:

"The wind-driven sand is like a rasp on my head. Could I put just my head in?"

Again, the traveler rationalized that to acquiesce would do him no damage, for the camel's head could occupy the space at the top of the tent which he himself was not using. So the camel put his head inside and the beast was satisfied again — but for a short while only.

"Just the front quarters," he begged, and again the traveler relented and soon the camel's front shoulders and legs were in the tent. Finally, by the same processes of pleading and of yielding, the camel's torso, his hind quarters and all were in the tent. But now it was too crowded for the two, and the camel kicked the traveler out into the wind and storm.

Like the camel, Lucifer readily becomes the master when one succumbs to his initial blandishments. Soon then the conscience is stilled completely, the evil power has full sway, and the door to salvation is closed until a thorough repentance opens it again.

The Savior's Example

The importance of not accommodating temptation in the least degree is underlined by the Savior's example. Did not he recognize the danger when he was on the mountain with his fallen brother, Lucifer, being sorely tempted by that master tempter? He could have opened the door and flirted with danger by saying, "All right, Satan, I'll listen to your proposition. I need not succumb, I need not yield, I need not accept — but I'll listen."

Christ did not so rationalize. He positively and promptly closed the discussion, and commanded: "Get thee hence, Satan," meaning, likely, "Get out of my sight — get out of my presence — I will not listen — I will have nothing to do with you." Then, we read, "the devil leaveth him."

This is our proper pattern, if we would prevent sin rather than be faced with the much more difficult task of curing it. As I study the story of the Redeemer and his temptations, I am certain he spent his energies fortifying himself against temptation rather than battling with it to conquer it.

Don't Flirt with Temptation

Bringing this into practical, modern terms, what does the principle mean? Among other things it means that to be unequivocally a teetotaler, one does not frequent bars or taverns, one never takes the first drink. To avoid the tobacco habit, one does not tamper with it nor associate in his leisure hours with those who smoke. One may perhaps work with sex deviates and be little damaged, but to play and relax with them is to invite temptation which may eventually be overpowering.

It means that the boy who dates a girl of questionable morals, even just for once, is taking chances. He is dealing with a powerful temptation. The girl who has even one date with a vicious fellow is in danger. The youth who takes one cigarette or one drink is "playing with fire." The young person who begins to yield to sexual intimacies is in a perilous position. One step calls for another, and to turn back is not easy.

To emphasize further by analogy the dangers of flirting with temptation there is an oft-told story of three men who applied for the job of driving the coaches for a transportation company. The successful applicant would be driving over high, dangerous and precipitous mountain roads. Asked how well he could drive, the first one replied: "I am a good, experienced driver. I can drive so close to the edge of the precipice that the wide metal tire of the vehicle will skirt the edge and never go off."

"That is good driving," said the employer.

The second man boasted, "Oh, I can do better than that. I can drive so accurately that the tire of the vehicle will lap over, half of the tire on the edge of the precipice, and the other half in the air over the edge."

The employer wondered what the third man could offer, and was surprised and pleased to hear, "Well, sir, I can keep just as far away from the edge as possible." It is needless to ask which of the men got the job.

Watch for Vulnerable Spots

Carelessness about proximity to sin makes us vulnerable to Satan's wiles. The mythical Achilles was physically vulnerable only in the heel his mother had held as she dipped him in the magic river to immunize him against physical harm; and a poisoned arrow in this heel ended a life of great valor on the field of battle. Like Achilles, most of us have vulnerable spots through which disaster can overtake us unless we are properly safeguarded and immunized.

Even the giant Goliath had a vulnerable spot. Elder Sterling W. Sill, in one of his delightful addresses, told us about this. I quote him:

> In the historic battle of David and Goliath, the giant from Gath had covered himself with a heavy coat of mail weighing 5,000 shekels of brass. He had a helmet of brass upon his head and greaves of brass upon his legs. The staff of his spear was like a weaver's beam and his spear's head weighed six hundred shekels of iron. Goliath must have felt very confident of success as he went out to meet the son of Jesse who was not yet even of military age. But Goliath made the mistake of trusting in his strength rather than protecting his vulnerability. His giant body and huge legs were enclosed in brass, but his large, broad forehead was left uncovered. This was the place at which David successfully aimed his slingshot, and Goliath fell as Achilles had fallen, because he was assaulted where he was unprotected.[1]

History provides many other examples of strength and pride, both individual and national, which succumbed to attack on the vulnerable spot. While these spots were often, on the surface at least, physical, Lucifer and his followers know the habits, weaknesses, and vulnerable spots of every-

---

[1] Sterling W. Sill, *The Way of Success* (Salt Lake City: Bookcraft, 1964), p. 278.

one and take advantage of them to lead us to spiritual destruction. With one person it may be thirst for liquor; another may have an insatiable hunger; another has permitted his sex urges to dominate; another loves money, and the luxuries and comforts it can buy; another craves power; and so on.

At the MIA June Conference of 1959, Elder Delbert L. Stapley of the Council of the Twelve made some comments which bear on this topic. Among other things he then said:

> Light dissipates and takes the place of darkness. The darkness cannot take the place of light. It is only when the light goes out, the darkness prevails. . . . To recognize inherent weaknesses and to do nothing to overcome them . . . is an evidence of character instability.

Pitfall of Rationalization

Some of the matters discussed in this chapter as pitfalls to watch for have been referred to elsewhere in the book. One such is the evil of rationalization. Perhaps Alexander Pope had this kind of mental dexterity in mind when he wrote, perceptively:

> Vice is a monster of so frightful mien,
> As to be hated needs but to be seen;
> Yet seen too oft, familiar with her face,
> We first endure, then pity, then embrace.

It is easy to rationalize oneself into sinful habits. For example, the person released from restraint, perhaps for the first time, thinks he will investigate some of the things he has heard about and try them out to satisfy his curiosity. Of course it is the forbidden things which seem to have the greatest appeal. He takes his first cigarette, his first drink. He enters into the various forbidden sexual fields. He tries his first theft or small robbery. He gambles just a little. He perhaps rationalizes that it is right to try just once, "just for the experience." He certainly never thinks he will go further into the sin, nor permit himself to repeat the acts. But even though these forbidden things are followed by feelings of regret and even of shame and sorrow, he has now become so good at rationalizing that he talks himself out of repenting.

When one falls into deep sin there apparently are only these two alternative courses available, to repent and do what is necessary to clean it all up or to rationalize away the consequences and the sting of conscience. Repentance seems a very difficult, long, agonizing process and is usually embarrassing. The rationalization road is much easier, temporarily. It hides transgressions. The conscience which at first agonized becomes more and more easily seared over until it retires to leave one at the full mercy of the evil, tempting powers. Clearly, the first step in rationalizing sin is a pitfall to avoid.

Pitfalls for Youth

In this book I have deliberately made frequent reference to sexual sins, and this because of their gravity and prevalence. In the present chapter one could hardly fail to emphasize these errors in relation to avoiding pitfalls of sin, especially as they affect the youth of the Church in an era of increasing immorality, permissiveness and commercial enticement.

Our wise Creator fashioned the soul of man, the body and spirit, incorporating timed growth and desires and urges appropriate to the age reached so that there is a proper unfolding of life in a normal way. There is a time for infancy, with its total dependency on others, a time for childhood, with its carefree existence, a time for early youth, with its widening interests and responsibilities. There is a time for more mature youth, with its increasing decisions and accountabilities. There is a time for the young married, with their mutual responsibilities and broadening interests; a time for middle age, with its autumn harvesting of experience; a time for older folks in the winters by the fireside, with memories, happy associations and satisfactions. All these phases of growth, when pursued in harmony with the divine plan, lead the soul firmly and unwaveringly along the path to eternal life.

No stage in life is more significant to the end result than the years of youth. Decisions and activities of this period place what can be an ineradicable impress upon the future, particularly as it affects one's marriage and subsequent family life. Activities and associations at this point often are of vital influence.

The urge for group activity is normal to the younger set, when they are not prematurely and immaturely stimulated in other ways, and the recreational and social activities of the crowd can be wholesome and entertaining. Physical and moral safety is increased in the multiplicity of friends. Group homemade recreation activities can be not only great fun but most beneficial. Firesides may create friendships, and inspire the spirit and train the mind. Group picnics can discipline youth in gentle manners and fellowship and extend circles of intimate friends.

Sports can develop the body in strength and endurance. They can train the spirit to meet difficulties and defeats and successes, teach selflessness and understanding, and develop good sportsmanship and tolerance in participant and spectator. Drama can develop talent, teach patience, and foster fellowship and friendliness. Group music activities have similar effects, and also can soften and mellow the spirit and satisfy the aesthetic needs.

The properly conducted dancing party can be a blessing. It provides opportunity to spend a pleasant evening with many people to the accompaniment of music. It can create and develop friendships which will be treasured in later years. Alternatively it can become a restricting experience.

Well-ordered dances provide favorable places, pleasing times and auspicious circumstances in which to meet new people and to enlarge circles of friends. They can be an open door to happiness. In an evening of pleasurable dancing and conversation, one can become acquainted with many splendid young folk, every one of whom has admirable traits and may be superior to any one companion in at least some qualities. Here partners can begin to appraise and evaluate, noting qualities, attainments and superiorities by comparison and contrast. Such perceptive friendships can be the basis for wise, selective, occasional dating for those of sufficient age and maturity, this to be followed later in proper timing by steady dating, and later by proper courtship which culminates in a happy, never-ending marriage.

On the other hand, for a youth to dance all evening with one partner, which we might call "monopolistic" dancing, is not only anti-social but it circumscribes one's legitimate pleasures and opportunities. Also it can encourage improper intimacies by its exclusiveness. Dancing with dates, single or steady, should presuppose the exchange of partners, which we could call "multiple" dancing.

Serious minds will recognize the wisdom of this course. Young people who pair off early in dating and monopolistic dancing are opening wide one door into dangerous caverns and closing numerous doors which lead to interesting, wholesome, and progressive experiences.

To skip the proper, natural experiences of youth, or to ignore the warning signals, is to bring distortion in life with its troubles and tribulations, and to limit and damage, if not ruin, the later periods of the normal life and development.

To be more specific, for children to receive undue, untimely pressure to assume the role of youth; for the younger teen-ager to skip the days of that period and rush into the experiences of the later teen-age; or for the later teen-agers to enter into the marriage state before proper preparation — these things bring frustration and the loss of an important part of one's life.

Dangers of Steady Dating

Steady dating of people too young leads to early marriage before adequate preparation is made for the future, before one's education is even near complete, and before the young life has had its many glorious training experiences.

Someone wrote an extended article entitled "Marriage Is Not for Children," which gave much evidence of the need for mature planning and charting for youth. It stated that up to 90 percent of the high school marriages end in divorce. It pointed out that very youthful marriages tend to terminate educational and vocational preparation of the participants and that resultant unemployment brings to the acute level the already serious problems of a youthful marriage.

Dating in the earlier teen-age years leads to early steady dating with its multiplicity of dangers and problems, and frequently to early and disappointing marriage. This too-young dating is not uncommon and is often done with parental approval. Yet it is near criminal to subject a tender child to the temptations of maturity. Early marriages, which are almost certain of failure, are usually the result of steady, early dating, whereas a proper preparation for marriage is a well-timed courtship.

My heart bleeds almost every day when I see the children involved in too early dating. Two parents came to me with a problem. They did not know what to do with their little girl. She was only sixteen years old, yet she was a "woman" who had been through deep sin, youthful marriage, humiliating childbirth, and searing divorce. What was left in life for her? Questions came to my mind such as: "Mother, where were you when she was dating steady at fourteen? Were you off to work or were you just asleep? Or were you trying to have another young romance for yourself, by proxy? Where were you when your little girl started dating?"

Automobile — Blessing and Curse

Early dating usually demands a car and seems to imply exclusive mutual possessiveness in date and dance. What an erroneous and stultifying concept! In former days, youth walked with their dates; later they rode horseback or rode in carriages; but now they seem to need the automobile. Some girls are like the one who asked the boy who requested a date: "Do you have a car?" The answer was negative. She responded, "Come around again when you have one." I can only reflect that if a youth's desirability and popularity lie in dangling earrings, money to spend, and a glamorous car, indeed a thin and perishable veneer has been substituted for standards of basic goodness and character.

Since the ultimate goal in every young life should be successful and happy marriage and family life, the dating period becomes the important era in which to appraise and evaluate, and to find the companion who will be compatible, agreeable, and engaging, and has the other necessary qualities. Perhaps those with wealth, convertibles and feigned vivacity suffer the greatest disadvantage in the real courting values. Does not the young man with the most luxurious car have the greatest handicap? How can he determine how much of his popularity is the result of the car, and how much of his own personality and character? The girl who has wealth, a luxurious car, and "money to burn" may have difficulty in knowing how much of her popularity is due to the veneer and how much to her own personal charm and loveliness.

The automobile may be a blessing or a curse — like water which can save a dying man or drown him; like fire which can warm freezing bodies or burn them to death; like atomic power which can drive vessels or despoil cities. The car can transport its occupants to home, school or temple. It can also take them to remote places, to moral dangers where consciences are silenced, righteous inhibitions deadened and guardian angels anesthetized. In short order, the car can transport a couple, youthful or otherwise, great distances from safe harbors. It can impart dangerous privacy and stimulate temptation.

The car is properly for drivers mature in judgment. Lawmakers have sensed this in denying licenses to those

under certain ages. Teen-age car accidents far exceed those
for other ages. But these physical hazards are the lesser ones.
The dead may live again, the crippled may be resurrected
with whole bodies; but the blighted soul, the scarred life,
the violated youth with virtue lost — these are the real
tragedies.

Lane ends, canyon defiles, desert wastes, and quiet
streets at late hours — these are places where people discuss
little of art, music, or gospel doctrines, but where they think
often of baser things, talk in lower veins. And when talk
wears thin there are things to do, the doing of which brings
dust and ashes where roses should be blooming. In interviewing repenting young folks, as well as some older ones, I am
frequently told that the couple met their defeat in the dark,
at late hours, in secluded areas. Troubles, like photographs,
are developed in the dark. The car was most often the confessed seat of the difficulty. It became their brothel. At
first they intended no evil, but the privacy made easy the
passionate intimacies which crept upon them stealthily as
a snake slithers through the grass.

"Where have you been?" asked the fond parent. The
answer was startling. "Up to a drive-in, the 'passion-pit,'
and oh, boy, was that picture a hot number!" There in
the car, in dark privacy, with suggestive, voluptuous acting
on the screen, was Satan's near-perfect setting for sin. With
outward appearances of decency and respectability, with
an absence of holy influences and with legions of vicious,
hovering tempters, even good youth are trapped into immoral acts — acts which would at least be much less likely in
the living room or in the formal theater on Main Street.

No one but the participants witnesses the sin done in the
dark — no one on earth, that is. But the prophets have
had a word to say about sin done in the dark. Job, for
instance, recorded the words of Eliphaz: "And thou sayest,
How doth God know? can he judge through the dark
cloud?" (Job 22:13.) Isaiah warned: "Woe unto them
that seek deep to hide their counsel from the Lord, and

their works are in the dark, and they say, Who seeth us? and who knoweth us?" (Isa. 29:15.) Likewise our Lord suggested that men "loved darkness rather than light, because their deeds were evil. For every one that doeth evil hateth the light . . ." (John 3:19-20.)

Immodesty

Other things besides cars and darkness encourage unchastity and immorality. One of them is immodesty. The young people today seem to talk about sex glibly. They hear it in the locker rooms and on the street, they see and hear it in shows and on television, they read it in the pornographic books everywhere. Those who do not resist this influence absorb and foster it. The spirit of immodesty has developed until nothing seems to be sacred.

One factor contributing to immodesty and the breakdown of moral values is the modern dress worn by our young women and their mothers. I see young women, and some older ones, on the streets wearing shorts. This is not right. The place for women to wear shorts is in their rooms, in their own homes, in their own gardens. I see some of our LDS mothers, wives, and daughters wearing dresses extreme and suggestive in style. Even some fathers encourage it. I wonder if our sisters realize the temptation they are flaunting before men when they leave their bodies partly uncovered or dress in tight-fitting, body-revealing, form-fitting sweaters.

There is no reason why a woman needs to wear an immodest gown because it is the style. We can be in style yet not be extreme. We can create styles of our own. A woman is most beautful when her body is properly clothed and her sweet face adorned with her lovely hair. She needs no more attractions. Then she is at her best and men will love her for it. Men will not love her more because her neck is bare. Girls, if the young man is decent and worthy of you, he will love you the more when you are properly dressed. Of course, if he is a vicious man he will have other ideas.

It would almost seem that some phases of immodesty in dress, in both men and women, border on exhibitionism, the perverted behavior in which people satisfy their lustful desires in displaying their bodies to others. One has indeed slipped a long way down the ladder when he resorts to this detestable expression, though fortunately he can regenerate and restore and transform himself with total repentance, and can be forgiven. Still, no one but a depraved person could approve of the practice or grant its acceptance.

But is this ugly displaying of one's private body to others so far removed from those instances of men who do their yard work wearing only pants and shoes, and those who drive about in cars with the upper part of their bodies uncovered? Is this exhibitionism so different and far removed from that of those young and older women who resort to wearing tight-fitting clothes which accentuate the human body, and those who show their backs and bosoms and lower limbs? Style is blamed for these extremes, but we wonder again if there might not be some satisfactions, sexual and otherwise, in what seems a wanton disregard of modest decency. Are the very scant bathing suits worn for style or to shock or stir or tempt? Can there be in all these expressions total innocence and total modesty? There are laws against indecent exposure, but why jail the man who exhibits his body so very little more than the women who show so little less? Is it possible that in all these immodesties there might be at least some of the same desires which prompt the exhibitionist to uncover his body and flaunt it before people?

We cannot overemphasize immodesty as one of the pitfalls to be avoided if we would shun temptation and keep ourselves clean.

Lewdness, Written and Spoken

Closely allied to the pitfall of immodesty, and partly springing from it, is that of pornography.

Pornography has become a most profitable business in the peddling of ugly, vicious, sexy magazines, books and pictures. There is an immense trade in such things, and very often the boys and girls of our high schools and of younger ages are the victims of this vicious business. Of recent years, this same lewdness has been found in the evil songs and stories put onto phonograph records. An editorial writer in the *Deseret News* wrote:

> The pernicious prongs of pornography, clawing into the phonograph records business . . . presents a new and ugly angle to this nagging problem.
>
> Repressive action by aroused parents and organizations has greatly reduced the amount of obscene literature on the magazine racks hereabouts, but the filth peddlers seem to have found another alluring and remunerative field.
>
> In circulation now are upward of a score of recordings in songs and recitations containing the vilest material. One such record was discovered in her home by a zealous mother. The waxing had been hidden in the room of her daughter, age 15. It was placed in the hands of members of the Youth Protection Committee in consideration of its fight against pornography. It was so obscene that some of the listeners could bear to hear no more than one or two of the ten selections of the two sides of the record. Yet this filthy thing had been purchased by two 15-year-old girls at a supposed reputable music store.

Parents should be warned of these evils, and do all they can to protect their sons and daughters from a corruption which is designed to stimulate sex passions and open the doors to more serious offenses. By a cooperative effort, they can eradicate these things from the newsstands and from the mails, and bring to justice those who would sell the morals of a generation for personal gain.

Lewd talk and jokes constitute another danger which lurks seeking as its prey any who will entertain it as the first step to dirtying the mind and thus the soul.

A magazine told of an entertainer in a New York night club who was tipped off that police were going to tape his program. He had been "revving himself up to give the customers an hour of unleavened, four-letter words plus gross assaults on motherhood, the Testaments, Old and New, and vivid descriptions of the more basic physical and sexual processes." Now he was warned by his boss to "take it easy." As a result the program was a solid hour of comedy without using "so much as darn," and was antiseptically clean. Someone commented that this entertainer could work clean, and the answer was: "Sure. His programs in night clubs and burlesque were clean and his take was $100 a week. But turning all his efforts to a filthy show, he gets $5,000 a week. So he peddles filth." The difference is $4,900 a week.

Who is to blame? The filth peddler, of course, but even more than this vulgar entertainer, the filth consumer, the public. So long as men are corrupt and revel in sewer filth, entertainers will sell them what they want. Laws may be passed, arrests may be made, lawyers may argue, courts may sentence and jails may harbor men of corrupt minds, but pornography and allied insults to decency will never cease until men have cleansed their minds and cease to require and pay for such vile stuff. When the customer is sick and tired of being drowned in filth by the comedians, he will not pay for that filth and its source will dry up.

Of course, only relatively few people get to the night clubs, but at the coffee break, in the locker room, at the banquet table, almost everywhere, there are vulgar people who prolong the life of the coarse and indecent by their retelling and their applause. But when there is no laugh to encourage, no ear to listen, no lips to applaud or repeat the vulgarity, the story-teller will tire of his unappreciated recitals.

Degrading Shows

Other danger spots likely to have most appeal among the youth, and which should be shunned as one would shun a poisonous serpent, are undesirable movies and improper TV programs. Of such, a *Deseret News* editorial stated:

Though it is heartening indeed to note the increasing volume of protests raised throughout the country against the undesirable movies and TV programs being meted out to the American public and particularly to the youngsters who make up a large part of the audiences for both, it is sickening to note the number of questionable productions still being made by the studios.

Juvenile court judges, officers in anti-vice squads, and social workers are united in saying that a high percentage of the crimes of today are traceable to the low grade entertainment watched by so many of the younger generation.

But because evil, with all the "Hollywood trimmings," glitters like gold, and because the suggestive is always attractive to many, the producers of these entertainments find it profitable to continue this line of shows.

After discussing this problem in some detail, the editorial concluded:

There probably is not sufficient public resentment to force the movie and TV producers to clean up their own product because money talks louder than the protesting public.

But certainly church and home can do something about teaching standards to their children. They surely can regulate what young people see by the persuasion which any good home can exercise.

Good taste can be developed, and with it a desire to eliminate filthy entertainment, just as we would eliminate liquor, cigarettes, and petting from the lives of our youth.

Finest Youth Can Fall

Now our Latter-day Saint boys and girls are the finest in the world. There is no group anywhere from ocean to ocean that can even compare with them. I believe practically all our boys and girls grow up with a desire to be righteous. I think they are fundamentally good. And yet, there are too many misfortunes among them. There are too many who have lost themselves.

The devil knows how to destroy them. He knows, young men and women, that he cannot tempt you to commit adultery immediately, but he knows too that he can soften you up by lewd associations, vulgar talk, immodest dress, sexy movies, and so on. He knows too that if he can get them to drink or if he can get them into his "necking, petting" program, the best boys and the best girls will finally succumb and will fall.

It is important to understand this pitfall. This subject is not easy to talk or to write about; but when bishops come to me with sad stories of broken homes, of frustrated lives, of heartbreak, sorrow, and remorse; when I interview people who have fallen into the trap, I say to them in near desperation: "What can we do? What can the Church do to help avoid this? What can we do to protect the next generation, the younger ones who are coming along? Tell me."

In reply, often the boy or girl will say, "We are not taught frankly enough. We get much sex education from many sources but it damages us. We hear the vulgar all the time. We need warnings — frank warnings." I sincerely hope that the warnings given in this book are frank and clear enough.

On the positive side, if our young people would avoid the pitfalls they would be firm in principle, not wobbly as the drunken man. They would enjoy their childhood and early teen-age with their folks at home, then for years the group activities. At dancing parties, they would exchange partners for the happiness of it, and the advantage of it. There would be no dating in early teens, only casual dating in middle teens, and no steady dating until they were ready to look for an eternal mate in proper marriage. Associations would be kept free from all improprieties. Kissing would be saved at least until these later hallowed courtship days when they could be free from sex and have holy meaning. And in all this they would preserve a healthy, constructive attitude toward home, school and Church and toward other people generally. Thus they would grow up free from the contaminations of the world.

Stay on the Lord's Side

The difference between the good man and the bad man is not that one had the temptations and the other was spared them. It is that one kept himself fortified, and resisted temptation, and the other placed himself in compromising places and conditions and rationalized the situations. Hence it is obvious that to remain clean and worthy, one must stay positively and conclusively away from the devil's territory, avoiding the least approach toward evil. Satan leaves his finger prints. They are quite distinguishable to any who are warned. Accordingly, the danger sign is placed prominently where it is always visible to the educated eye. It is like the great hole once made in the street where I live. To drive the car through it would have been flirting with danger or a wreck. I noted that the neighbors' cars moved out of the street on the safe end and avoided the area where the danger lay. I did the same.

In this regard we cannot do better as a conclusion to this chapter than recall the frequent admonition of the late President George Albert Smith, who said:

> My grandfather used to say to his family, "There is a line of demarkation, well defined, between the Lord's territory and the devil's. If you will stay on the Lord's side of the line, you will be under his influence and will have no desire to do wrong; but if you cross to the devil's side of the line one inch, you are in the tempter's power, and if he is successful, you will not be able to think or even reason properly, because you will have lost the Spirit of the Lord.
>
> When I have been tempted sometimes to do a certain thing, I have asked myself, "Which side of the line am I on?" If I determined to be on the safe side, the Lord's side, I would do the right thing every time. So when temptation comes, think prayerfully about your problem, and the influence of the Spirit of the Lord will enable you to decide wisely. There is safety for us only on the Lord's side of the line.

Chapter Seventeen

Charting a Safe Course

> *When a man does not know which harbour he is making for, none is the right one.*
>
> —Anonymous

I F WE WOULD AVOID THE DANGER SPOTS WHICH LEAD TO transgression and sorrow and to forfeiture of our chances for exaltation, the wise way is to chart the course of our lives.

Of course, we cannot know every circumstance of life or plan every detail in advance. But we can so chart a general course that there will be little or no deviation from the "strait and narrow way." Such planning involves establishing worthy ideals and goals. The person who has such goals and then works steadily toward them is the one most likely successfully to negotiate the hazards and bypass the pitfalls which would change the course from a road of happiness to a pathway of destruction.

Plan Early in Life

Such planning must begin early. It has been said that "even the very longest journey begins with a single first step." So when that first step is made it must be on a properly charted course. Otherwise, habits come upon us unawares, and sin has us in its clutches before we realize it.

As well as establishing worthy goals, charting the course prevents one from living an unplanned, haphazard life — a

tumbleweed existence. Over the Utah plains, upon the hill-
sides and along the fence-lines of the valleys, grows the
tumbleweed. When mature and dry, the plant breaks from
its roots and, as a rounded tangle of light stiff branches,
rolls about like a ball. If the wind blows west, the weed rolls
against the western fences. With each direction change in
the wind, the rounded weed rolls with it, following lines of
least resistance until stopped by fences or walls or ditch
banks. As the wind blows down the road, the tumbleweeds
go rolling like mammoth marbles thrown from a giant hand.

Many people, and particularly many of our youth, live
a "tumbleweed" existence. They tend to follow leadership
which is dominant and powerful, regardless of whether it
is right or wrong. They want to know what the other "kids"
are doing. What kind of sweaters are they wearing? What
kind of shoes? Are the dresses long or short, tight or flar-
ing? Do the leader girls wear their hair short, boyish or
windswept, in pony tails or Italian or French styles? Do
the boys preen before mirrors with their ducktail haircuts,
their crewcuts and Mohawks, flattops and beatles, or hair
dropped over the forehead?

These may be just minor things, but there are major
and more hazardous areas in which our young people especially are led by their desire to keep up with the gang. What
must one do to prevent being called a "square," a "sissy,"
a "drip"? Must the youth date early; enter into the kissing
and necking practices; dance all evening with one partner?

The Smart Person Plans

On the other hand, smart young people will discipline
themselves early in youth, charting long-range courses to
include all that is wholesome and nothing that is ruinous.
The bridge builder, before starting construction, draws
charts and plans, makes estimates of strains and stresses,
costs and hazards; the architect, even before excavation,
makes a blueprint of the building from foundation to pinnacle. Similarly the smart person will plan carefully and

blueprint his own life from his first mental awakening to the end of life. "Just as a builder will wish his structure to stand through storm and disturbances of the elements, so the young and old alike will wish a life unharmed by adversities, calamities, and troubles throughout eternity. Having planned such a course, prudent men will gear their lives, activities, ambitions and aspirations so that they may have every advantage in total fulfillment of a righteous destiny."

Life gives to all the choice. You can satisfy yourself with mediocrity if you wish. You can be common, ordinary, dull, colorless; or you can channel your life so that it will be clean, vibrant, progressive, useful, colorful, rich. You can soil your record, defile your soul, trample underfoot virtue, honor, and goodness, and thus forfeit an exaltation in the kingdom of God. Or you can be righteous, commanding the respect and admiration of your associates in all walks of life, and enjoying the love of the Lord. Your destiny is in your hands and your all-important decisions are your own to make.

Of course, your choices will not be the right ones, the ones which carry you unhesitatingly along the path to the great eternal reward, unless they are made under the proper controls. In this matter the greatest control is self-control. The following comment, whose authorship I do not know, comes from a perceptive writer:

> The greatest battle of life is fought out within the silent chambers of the soul. A victory on the inside of a man's heart is worth a hundred conquests on the battlefields of life. To be master of yourself is the best guarantee that you will be master of the situation. Know thyself. The crown of character is self-control.

The world and its people need guidance and controls. Imagine an automobile in motion without a driver, a train without an engineer, a plane without a pilot at the controls. In this day of guided missiles, perhaps we should give more thought to guiding souls. To fire missiles into the air without guidance and controls could kill people, destroy property and spread terror, but its long-term effect would be relatively small compared to that of permitting souls to fire off and run without guidance and controls.

Thus our young people should drive down stakes early, indicating their paths. The stakes are of two kinds: "This I *will do*" and "This I *will not do*." These decisions pertain to general activities, standards, spiritual goals, and personal programs. They should include anticipations for marriage and family. Very early, youth should have been living by a plan. They are the wise young man and the wise young woman who will profit by the experience of others, and who early set a course in their education, a mission, the finding of a pure, clean sweetheart to be a life's companion, their temple marriage and their Church service. When such a course is charted and the goal is set, it is easier to resist the many temptations and to say "no" to the first cigarette, "no" to the first drink, "no" to the car ride which will take one into the dark, lonely and hazardous places, "no" to the first improper advances which lead eventually to immoral practices.

Charting Course Toward Marriage

By the time our youth are old enough to comprehend and plan the charting of their lives the major decision of their lives — marriage — is but a few years hence. For this reason this chapter is concentrated upon the course toward and in marriage. And I might add here that, while its benefits are greatest if it begins early, planning is good for all stages of life.

Plans and decisions relating to marriage for a Church member should be geared to the goal of exaltation and to a program for the unborn children who can bring glory to the parents. When children come into a true Latter-day Saint home, through a marriage sealed by the Holy Spirit of Promise, into a home where there is peace and contentment, common ideals and common standards, life has great promise. Children who are fortunate enough to come into homes where the priesthood presides, where the Spirit of the Lord is ever present, where family prayers unite and where real family love rules, are blessed indeed.

If couples live their married lives properly, training their children in the fear and admonition of the Lord as they themselves will live, it is quite unlikely that their home will produce delinquents, transgressors, or criminals. Most people agree that the problems in life start or get encouragement in the home. Wars would cease, criminal courts would close, jails and penitentiaries would remain largely unused, if all children were taught by the precept and example of worthy parents who loved each other and devoted themselves in total fidelity to each other.

Obviously then, of greatest importance are those acts which contribute to this happy condition. It is of vital significance for every youth to chart his course carefully to be sure there is no ugliness nor error in his life. The dating must be safeguarded, the courting, the marriage and the family life. There must be no mistake as to the persons courted, the protection of the process. The married life must be affectionate and kindly and selfless.

Folly of Inter-Faith Marriages

Our youth often ask the vital question: "Whom shall I marry?" The proper answer to that question brings a proper answer to many others. If you marry the proper "whom," you are sure to marry in the proper "where," and you have an infinitely better chance of happiness here and in eternity. By far the greatest cause of unhappiness, broken homes, wrecked lives, sinfulness and sorrow among the Latter-day Saints is the failure to marry the right person in the right place by the right authority. This is evident in a survey made many years ago.

Approximately 1,500 marriages, involving 3,000 people, most of whom were members of the Church, were considered in that survey. Of these 1,500 couples, nearly a thousand couples or 2,000 people married out of the temple, and some of them out of the Church. Through the years there has been much unhappiness in many of these out-of-faith, out-of-temple families, much disruption in the lives of parents, much frustration in the lives of many children who are growing up without a religious concept of the truth. There were many broken homes — 204 of the couples, involving 408 people, were divorced in fifteen years.

A few of these people, having suffered sorrow and disillusionment, may have learned their lessons and may have remarried within the Church and in the temple and to proper people, but many of them did not learn, remarried out of the Church, and continued their distress. Of the original 3,000 people, nearly 2,000 have lost their way. Their eyes have been covered with spiritual cataracts and they are groping in the fogs and mists, unable to see clearly. They are lost in the labyrinths, and many may never find themselves. The great majority of them have not yet, in the years that followed, recovered themselves but are still wandering and groping in spiritual darkness and marital discomfort. There is not here an implication that all members of the Church are worthy and nonmembers unworthy, but study continues to point out the error of marriage between persons of different faiths. Different standards, ideals, backgrounds and faiths increase the problems of marriage.

Mixed marriages with spouses of different faiths generally bring loss of spirituality; and divorce results very often, with much unhappiness even if there is no divorce. Even with people of faiths other than our own, studies have shown that mixed marriages make adjustment of religious tensions difficult and that frequently one or both partners give up religious practices altogether. As parents give up their religions, an increasing number of children are brought up without any kind of church attachment and the faith it could engender.

The Church member contemplating marriage outside the Church frequently thinks, "Oh, the religious aspect doesn't matter. We'll get along. We'll adjust. We'll each give a little. My spouse will permit me to do as I please, or I will make adjustment. We'll both live and worship according to our own patterns." This is a fallacy. So seldom does it work that it is too hazardous to take the chance. Some people say, "But I believe in being broad-minded about these matters." This is not broad-mindedness, but even if it were, to be broad-minded with the Lord's eternal program is somewhat like being generous with someone else's money.

Researchers seem to agree that even in marriages which do not dissolve, disagreement on religious matters is a definite cause of unhappiness. Many good men and women are lost to the Church and diverted from the straight and narrow path because of these ill-advised marriages. In the survey mentioned above, it was found that nearly half of those who married out of the Church lost their activity in the Church. Twice as many of these parties of mixed marriages are inactive in the Church as even those who married out of the temple but married within the Church. This is significant. Only about twenty-nine percent of the Church members who married members, even in civil marriage, were inactive, whereas about forty-six percent of the mixed-marriage people were inactive.

Marry in the Church

The counsel Church members have received on this is unequivocal. President Joseph F. Smith said:

> We say to our young people, "Get married, and marry aright. Marry in the faith, and let the ceremony be performed in the place God has appointed. Live so that you may be worthy of this blessing. . . . But do not marry those out of the Church, as such unions almost invariably lead to unhappiness. . . .
>
> I would rather go myself to the grave than to be associated with a wife outside the bonds of the new and everlasting covenant. . . . I would like to see Latter-day Saint men marry Latter-day Saint women; and Methodists marry Methodists, Catholics marry Catholics, and Presbyterians marry Presbyterians, and so on to the limit. Let them keep within the pale of their own faith and church. . . .[1]

---

[1] Smith, *Gospel Doctrine,* pp. 275, 279.

Paul told the Corinthians, "Be ye not unequally yoked together . . ." Perhaps Paul wanted them to see that religious differences are fundamental differences. Religious differences imply wider areas of conflict. Church loyalties and family loyalties clash. Children's lives are often frustrated. The nonmember may be equally brilliant, well trained and attractive, and he or she may have the most pleasing personality, but without a common faith, trouble lies ahead for the marriage. There are some exceptions but the rule is a harsh and unhappy one.

There is no bias nor prejudice in this doctrine. It is a matter of following a certain program to reach a definite goal. A fond and lovely Protestant wife says of her good Protestant husband, "But my husband is gracious, honorable, worthy, a good provider, and he is better than many members of The Church of Jesus Christ of Latter-day Saints. I am sure he will receive the blessings and we shall be united through eternity." There is no brief for the unfaithful members of the Church who fail in their obligations. They also will miss the eternal blessings — that is sure — but the person who is not a member of the Lord's Church, who has not received the celestial ordinances, cannot receive the celestial kingdom. The Savior made this clear when he said: "Except a man be born of water and of the Spirit, he cannot enter into the kingdom of God." (John 3:5.)

Marrying outside the faith has always been forbidden. For example, the Lord inspired Abraham to marry a near relative rather than a Gentile. In respect of his son's bride, Abraham commissioned his servant to go on a long and uncomfortable journey to obtain a girl of Isaac's own faith:

> And I will make thee swear by the Lord . . . that thou shalt not take a wife unto my son of the daughters of the Canaanites, among whom I dwell:

> But thou shalt go unto my country, and to my kindred, and take a wife unto my son Isaac. (Gen. 24:3-4.)

Likewise Isaac himself, saddened by his son Esau's marriages with Gentile women, forbade Jacob to do the same and sent him back to Haran to marry in the faith. (See Gen. 28:1-2.) Centuries later the Lord made specific commandment to the Israelites as follows:

> Neither shalt thou make marriages with [Gentiles]; thy daughter thou shalt not give unto his son, nor his daughter shalt thou take unto thy son.
>
> For *they will turn away thy son from following me,* that they may serve other gods. . . . (Deut. 7:3-4. Italics added.)

And in the meridian of time, as partially quoted above, the same word was given: "Be ye not unequally yoked together with unbelievers." (2 Cor. 6:14.)

Many times, women have come to me in tears. How they would love to be able to train their children in the gospel of Jesus Christ! But they are unable to do so because of religious incompatibility with a nonmember husband. How they would like to accept for themselves positions of responsibility in the Church! How they would like to pay their tithing! How they would appreciate going to the temple for their own endowments and to do work for the dead! How they wish they could be sealed for eternity and have the promise of having their own flesh and blood, their children, sealed to them for eternity! Sometimes it is men in this predicament. But they have locked the doors, and the doors have often rusted on their hinges.

Importance of Proper Dating

Clearly, right marriage begins with right dating. A person generally marries someone from among those with whom he associates, with whom he goes to school, with whom he goes to church, with whom he socializes. Therefore, this warning comes with great emphasis. Do not take the chance of dating nonmembers, or members who are untrained and faithless. A girl may say, "Oh, I do not intend to marry this person. It is just a 'fun' date." But one cannot afford to take a chance on falling in love with someone who may never accept the gospel. True, a small percentage have finally been baptized after marrying Church members. Some good women and some good men have joined the Church after the mixed marriage and have remained devout and active. We are proud of them and grateful for them. They are our blessed minority. Others who did not join the Church were still kind and considerate and cooperative and permitted the member spouse to worship and serve according to the Church patterns. But the majority did not join the Church and, as indicated earlier, friction, frustration and divorce marked a great many of their marriages.

In isolated instances a lovely young woman might be so far removed geographically from other Church members that she would either have to marry out of the Church or stay unmarried. Some might feel justified in such circumstances in making an exception to the rule and marrying a nonmember but, justification or not, it is important to recognize that the hazards in such a marriage would remain. To minimize the dangers the girl should by all means make sure that she marries a man who is honorable and good, so that even if he cannot at present be brought to accept the gospel there is a fair chance of his being converted later.

Celestial Marriage the Way to Happiness

In the preceding paragraphs I have assumed that marrying in the Church means marrying in the temple, as of course it should for all members who are able to reach a temple. The gateway to the green pastures of eternal bliss is temple marriage and righteous and abundant family life. The married life can be a continuously heavenly state or a perpetual torture, or anywhere between those two extremes. The successful marriage depends in large measure upon the preparation made in approaching it, which is important to our subject of charting a course. One cannot pick the ripe, rich, luscious fruit from a tree that was never planted, nurtured, nor pruned and was not protected against its enemies.

One study conducted among Church members revealed that there was only one divorce in every sixteen marriages which were sealed in the temple, while there was one divorce in every 5.7 marriages of those who were not sealed in the temple. This means that the person sealed in the temple has about 2½ times better chance for successful marriage and consequent happiness than the one with a civil marriage. In other words, he has about 2½ times the chance to continue with his or her mate through mortality in happiness and joy. Not only the ordinance itself, but also the preparation for the ordinance and the deep appreciation of it, help to achieve this end.

A basic reason for eternal marriage is that life is eternal; and marriage, to be in harmony with eternal purposes, must be consistent with life in duration. Marriage by civil officers, or by Church officers outside of the temples, is made for time only, "till death do you part" or "so long as you both shall live." It terminates with death. Only celestial marriage extends beyond the grave. Eternal marriage is performed by the prophet of the Lord or by one of the very few to whom he has delegated the authority. It is performed in holy temples erected and dedicated for that purpose. Only such marriage transcends the grave and perpetuates the husband-wife and parent-child relationships into and through eternity.

Exaltation in the celestial kingdom will be granted to those only who enter and faithfully observe the covenant of celestial marriage. Christ says in unmistakable terms:

> In the celestial glory there are three heavens, or degrees;
>
> And in order to obtain the highest, a man must enter into this order of the priesthood [meaning the new and everlasting covenant of marriage];
>
> And if he does not, *he cannot obtain it.*
>
> He may enter into the other, but that is the *end of his kingdom;* he cannot have an increase. (D&C 131:1-4. Italics added.)

He cannot have an increase! He cannot have exaltation! That means *worlds without end.* After a person has been assigned to his place in the kingdom, either in the telestial, the terrestrial or the celestial, or to his exaltation, he will never advance from his assigned glory to another glory. That is eternal! That is why we must make our decisions early in life and why it is imperative that such decisions be right.

It will be remembered how the Lord answered the hypocritical Sadducees who, trying to trap him, propounded the difficult problem of the wife whose seven husbands predeceased her: "In the resurrection therefore, when they shall rise, whose wife shall she be of them? for the seven had her to wife." (Mark 12:23.) The Redeemer's answer was clear and concise and unmistakable:

> Do ye not therefore err, because ye know not the scriptures, neither the power of God?
>
> For when they shall rise from the dead, they neither marry, nor are given in marriage; but are as the angels which are in heaven. (Mark 12:24-25.)

What does this answer mean? Elder James E. Talmage writes:

> The Lord's meaning was clear, that in the resurrected state there can be no question among the seven brothers as to whose wife for eternity the woman shall be, since all except the first had married her for the duration of mortal life only. . . ."[2]

The Lord makes clear, and attempts to convince his children here below, that they cannot afford to make an error in the matter of these eternal verities. He holds out promise of transcendent glory to those who abide by his laws.

> . . . If a man marry a wife by my word, which is my law, and by the new and everlasting covenant, and it is sealed unto them by the Holy Spirit of promise, by him who is anointed, unto whom I have appointed this power and the keys of this priesthood . . . it . . . shall be of full force when they are *out of the world*; and they *shall pass by the angels, and the gods,* which are set there, to their exaltation and glory in all things . . .

---

[2]Talmage, *Jesus the Christ*, p. 548.

which glory shall be a fullness and a continuation of the seeds forever and ever.

Then shall they be gods, because they have no end . . . then shall they be above all, because all things are subject unto them. Then shall they be gods, because they have all power, and the angels are subject unto them. (D&C 132:19-20. Italics added.)

Then as if to leave no possible doubt on the matter, the Lord continues: "Verily, verily, I say unto you, except ye abide my law ye cannot attain to this glory." (D&C 132:21.)

The Prophet Joseph Smith was given the same keys which Peter held. The Lord told him: ". . . Whatsoever you seal on earth shall be sealed in heaven; and whatsoever you bind on earth, in my name and by my word, saith the Lord, it shall be eternally bound in the heavens . . ." (D&C 132:46.)

Clearly, attaining eternal life is not a matter of goodness only. That is one of the two important elements, but one must practice righteousness *and* receive the ordinances. People who do not bring their lives into harmony with God's laws and who do not receive the necessary ordinances either in this life or (if that is impossible) in the next, have thus deprived themselves, and will remain separate and single in the eternities. There they will have no spouses, no children. If one is going to be in God's kingdom of exaltation, where God dwells in all his glory, one will be there as a husband or a wife and not otherwise. Regardless of his virtues, the single person, or the one married for this life only, cannot be exalted. All normal people should marry and rear families. To quote Brigham Young: "No man can be perfect without the woman, so no woman can be perfect without a man to lead her. I tell you the truth as it is in the bosom of eternity. If he wishes to be saved, he cannot be saved without a woman by his side."

Celestial marriage is that important.

To emphasize the beauty and wonder and glory of it, here is a word-picture by President Lorenzo Snow of the importance and blessing of celestial marriage:

When two Latter-day Saints are united together in marriage, promises are made to them concerning their offspring that reach from eternity to eternity. They are promised that they shall have the power and the right to govern and control and administer salvation and exaltation and glory to their offspring, worlds without end. And what offspring they do not have here, undoubtedly there will be opportunities to have them hereafter. What else could man wish? A man and a woman, in the other life, having celestial bodies, free from sickness and disease, glorified and beautified beyond description, standing in the midst of their posterity, governing and controlling them, administering life, exaltation and glory worlds without end.[3]

As you read this, can you conceive of the vastness of the program? Can you begin to comprehend it? Remember this: Exaltation is available only to righteous members of the Church of Jesus Christ; only to those who accept the gospel; only to those who have their endowments in holy temples of God and have been sealed for eternity and who then continue to live righteously throughout their lives. Numerous members of the Church will be disappointed. All will fail of these blessings who fail to live worthy lives, even though the temple ordinances have been done for them.

Dangers of Delaying Celestial Marriage

Too often, people think that the decisions on celestial marriage can be postponed and taken care of later. Such thoughts are the tools of Satan. He delights in procrastination and uses it much. If he cannot convince people to ignore these important matters, these ordinances in celestial marriage, he will use the strategy of procrastination on the basis that it will achieve his ends eventually.

But the time to act is now. Any mistake will be a costly one. We must not let attractions of the moment bring disaster for the eternities. All contracts that are not made under the sealing power of the priesthood terminate when one is dead.

---

[3]*Deseret News,* March 13, 1897.

Of course, people who have never heard the gospel, have had no opportunity to accept it, will be given that privilege either in this life or the next. They may hear it in the spirit world, the necessary work may be done vicariously for them on the earth, and they may thus receive eternal marriage. But for us who have heard the word of the Lord, who have the scriptures, who have had the many witnesses, who have been informed — for us, tomorrow is so late! We may be angels if we are righteous enough. Even unmarried, we may reach the lower realms in the celestial kingdom, but there we will be ministering angels only, ". . . which angels are ministering servants, to minister for those who are worthy of a far more, and an exceeding, and an eternal weight of glory." The Lord continues:

> For these angels *did not abide my law;* therefore, they *cannot be enlarged,* but remain separately and singly, without exaltation, in their saved condition, to all eternity; and from henceforth are not gods, but are angels of God forever and ever. (D&C 132:16-17. Italics added.)

The same revelation emphasizes the need for celestial marriage now, in this life:

> . . . Except ye abide my law [celestial marriage] ye cannot attain to this glory.
>
> For strait is the gate, and narrow the way that leadeth unto the exaltation and continuation of the lives, and few there be that find it, because ye receive me not *in the world* neither do you know me.
>
> But if ye receive me *in the world,* then shall ye know me, and shall receive your exaltation: that where I am ye shall be also. (D&C 132:21-23. Italics added.)

And the Prophet Joseph Smith said:

> Except a man and his wife enter into an everlasting covenant and be married for eternity, while in this probation, by the power and authority of the Holy Priesthood, they will cease to increase when they die; that is, they will not have any children after the resurrection. But those who are married by the power and authority of the priesthood in this life, and continue without committing the sin against the Holy Ghost, will continue to increase and have children in the celestial glory.[4]

---

[4] *Documentary History of the Church,* Vol. 5, p. 391.

While in this probation and *in this life* certainly mean the period of our mortal lives.

Through the scriptures we have a fairly clear picture of the fate of the people of Noah's day who, like many people today, ignored the testimonies of written scripture and of living prophets. Luke records the words of the Savior:

> And as it was in the days of Noe, so shall it be also in the days of the Son of man.
>
> They did eat, they drank, they married wives, they were given in marriage, until the day that Noe entered into the ark, and the flood came, and destroyed them all. (Luke 17:26-27.)

They were drowned in their sins. Their marriages were for time. They reveled in worldliness. They were possibly like many in the world today who place no curb upon their eating, drinking and licentiousness. Their ignoring the laws of God and the warning of the prophets continued until the very day when Noah and his family entered the ark. Then it was too late. Too late! What finality in that phrase! Following their eternal history, we find Peter telling of them more than two millennia later:

> For Christ also hath once suffered for sins, the just for the unjust, that he might bring us to God, being put to death in the flesh, but quickened by the Spirit:
>
> By which also he went and preached unto the spirits in prison;
>
> Which sometime were disobedient, when once the longsuffering of God waited in the days of Noah, while the ark was a preparing, wherein few, that is, eight souls were saved by water. (1 Pet. 3:18-20.)

At last, they had a chance in the spirit world to hear the voice of missionaries and prophets again. But so late! What sad words! Nearly a further two millennia passed into history and we hear of them again in modern revelation. Of the vision given to Joseph Smith and Sidney Rigdon in 1832, the Prophet writes:

> And again, we saw the terrestrial world, and behold and lo, these are they who are of the terrestrial. . . .
>
> . . . They who are the spirits of men kept in prison, whom the Son visited, and preached the gospel unto them, that they might be judged according to men in the flesh;

Who received not the testimony of Jesus in the flesh, but afterwards received it. (D&C 76:71, 73-74.)

Too late! The terrestrial for them! It could have been the celestial, and it could have been exaltation! But they proscrastinated the day of their preparation. The same lamentable cry of "Too late!" will apply to many of today's Church members who did not heed the warning but who proceeded — sometimes carelessly, sometimes defiantly — to bind themselves through mortality to those who could not or would not prepare for the blessings which were in reserve for them.

The Lord's program is unchangeable. His laws are immutable. They will not be modified. Your opinion or mine does not alter the laws. Many in the world, and even some in the Church, seem to think that eventually the Lord will be merciful and give them the unearned blessing. But the Lord cannot be merciful at the expense of justice.

Make Firm Bride-and-Groom Decisions

Those young people who chart their course to a marriage in the temple have already established a pattern of thought which will make them amenable to mutual planning with the chosen partner once he or she is found. Even before their marriage is solemnized in the holy place they will be planning their life together, and will continue the process as bride and groom when they sit down to chart their way through a happy, successful and spiritual life to exaltation in the kingdom of God. Now they will drive down some "stakes."

One of the "stakes" the husband drives is that he is going to attend priesthood meeting every week in the year, every year of his life. The two of them drive the "stakes" that they will attend Sunday School and sacrament meeting every Sabbath, taking their babies and the children with them, thus firmly entrenching this as a family program which the children will almost certainly carry on in the families they will raise later. Another "stake" is the decision to pay an honest tithing regularly and permanently. Such decisions having been firmly made, the question of attending church will not need to be re-examined every Sunday morning, nor will the couple have to consider each paycheck time whether to pay tithing. It is the same with other worthy goals.

Importance of Observing Marriage Vows

In a properly charted Latter-day Saint marriage, one must be conscious of the need to forget self and love one's companion more than self. There will not be postponement of parenthood, but a desire for children as the Lord intended, and without limiting the family as the world does. The children will be wanted and loved. There will be fidelity and confidence; eyes will never wander and thoughts will never stray toward extra-marital romance. In a very literal sense, husband and wife will keep themselves for each other only, in mind and body and spirit.

Infidelity is one of the great sins of our generation. The movies, the books, the magazine stories all seem to glamorize the faithlessness of husbands and wives. *Nothing is holy*, not even marriage vows. The unfaithful woman is depicted as the heroine and the hero is so built up that he can seemingly do no wrong. It reminds us of Isaiah who said: "Woe unto them that call evil good, and good evil." (Isa. 5:20.)

There are those married people who permit their eyes to wander and their hearts to become vagrant, who think it is not improper to flirt a little, to share their hearts and have desire for someone other than the wife or the husband. The Lord says in definite terms: "Thou shalt love thy wife with *all thy heart,* and shalt cleave unto her and *none else.*" (D&C 42:22. Italics added.)

The words *none else* eliminate everyone and everything. The spouse then becomes pre-eminent in the life of the husband or wife and neither social life nor occupational life nor political life nor any other interest nor person nor thing shall ever take precedence over the companion spouse. We sometimes find women who absorb and hover over the children at the expense of the husband, sometimes even estranging them from him. This is in direct violation of the command: *None else.*

I have discussed previously the sin of romance outside of one's marriage vows, but I emphasize it again here in the context of planning a life in which the first thought in that direction never arises. Marriage presupposes total allegiance and total fidelity. Each spouse takes the partner with the understanding that he or she gives self totally to the spouse — all the heart, strength, loyalty, honor and affection with all dignity.

Those who claim their love is dead should return home with all their loyalty, fidelity, honor, cleanness, and the love which has become embers will flare up with scintillating flame again. If love wanes or dies, it is often infidelity of thought or act which gave the lethal potion. I plead with all people, young and old, bound by marriage vows and covenants to make that marriage holy, keep it fresh, express affection meaningfully and sincerely and often. Thus will one avoid the pitfalls which destroy marriages.

Home-breaking is sin, and any thought, act or association which will tend to destroy one's own home or the home of another is a grievous transgression. A certain young woman was single and therefore free to properly seek a mate, but she gave attention to and received attention from a married man. She was in transgression. She argued that his marriage was "already on the rocks," that the wife of her new boy friend "did not understand him," that he was most unhappy at home, and that he did not love his wife.

But regardless of the state of the married man, the young woman was in serious error to comfort him and listen to his disloyal castigation of his wife. The man was in deep sin. He was disloyal and unfaithful. So long as a man is married to a woman, he is duty bound to protect and defend her and, conversely, the same responsibility is with his wife.

In one of the numerous cases which have come to my attention, husband and wife were quarreling and had reached such a degree of incompatibility that they had flung the threat of divorce at each other and had already seen attorneys with this in mind. Both of them, embittered at each other, had found companionship with other parties. This was sin. No matter how bitter were their differences, neither had any right to begin courting or looking about for friends. Any dating or such association by wedded folks outside the marriage is iniquitous. Even though two people proceed with a divorce suit, to be moral and honorable they must wait until the divorce is final before either is free to develop new romances.

A woman from a broken marriage married within hours after her divorce became final. It was evident that she had been untrue to her marriage vows, for she had been courting while she was still an undivorced wife. If one cannot remarry before the divorce is final, it must be obvious that one is still married. How then can one justify courtship while he or she still has living an undivorced spouse?

Even though these *affaires* begin near innocently, like an octopus the tentacles move gradually to strangle. When dates or dinners or rides or other contact begin, the abyss of tragedy opens wide its mouth. It has reached deep iniquity when physical contacts of any nature have been indulged in. The tragedies which result affect spouses, children, and other loved ones. Through Jacob, the Lord spoke to the Nephite men on this topic:

> For behold, I, the Lord, have seen the sorrow, and heard the mourning of the daughters of my people . . . because of the wickedness and abominations of their husbands.

> . . . Ye have broken the hearts of your tender wives, and lost the confidence of your children, because of your bad examples before them; and the sobbings of their hearts ascend up to God against you . . . many hearts died, pierced with deep wounds. (Jac. 2:31, 35.)

Women too stand condemned for extra-marital irregularities. They often invite men to sensual desire by their immodest clothes, their loose actions and mannerisms, their coy glances, their extreme makeup, and their flattery.

To a young couple in love and starting married life together the warnings may sound superfluous, but unfortunately they are not. Too many fall into this sin. Those who chart their course wisely will include in their planning a firm resolution never to take the first step away from their marriage vows.

Find Time for Family Gospel Living

When one plans properly early in life, one is not going to permit employment or social life or recreation to control and take over, and to make the basic things take a second place. Therefore, time must be budgeted. There will be time for service in the Church organizations and quorums; time for missionary work; time to be a quorum president, auxiliary leader, bishop, Relief Society president, teacher; and time to support the program of the Church in every way.

Devotion and prayer will be an integral part of lives charted on a true spiritual course. There will *always* be time for prayer. There will *always* be the moments of blessed solitude, of closeness to the Heavenly Father, of freedom from worldly things and cares.

When we kneel in family prayer, our children at our side on their knees are learning habits that will stay with them all through their lives. If we do not take time for prayers, what we are actually saying to our children is, "Well, it isn't very important, anyway. We won't worry about it. If we can do it conveniently, we will have our prayer, but if the school bell rings and the bus is coming and employment is calling — well, prayer isn't very important and we will do it when it is convenient." Unless planned for, it never seems to be convenient. On the other hand, what a joyous thing it is to establish such customs and habits in the home that when parents visit their children in the latter's homes after they are married they just naturally kneel with them in the usual, established manner of prayer!

In the Church, we are trying to shift more of the training of and responsibility for the children and young people back to the parents and home as our fundamental concept, and let the Primary, Sunday School and Mutual Improvement Associations, Seminary and other agencies add their blessings. It is the responsibility of the parents to teach their children in the home and rear them righteously and keep them in a proper environment. In the home, the young people should be so indoctrinated and fortified that the problems of children and youth will be minimal. The family home evening is designed and established for this very purpose. As with prayers, there should be no failure to find time and opportunity for this most rewarding activity.

Plan for Mother to Stay Home

Tremendously important to the child's upbringing is the presence of Mother in the home. Of late years, mothers have left their homes to work in such numbers that Church authorities are much concerned, and make a call to mothers: "Come back home, Mothers, come back home." We realize that there is an occasional mother who must go out to work. There are some mothers whose children are all reared, and who are thus free to work. But for mothers to leave children when there is not an absolute necessity is a hazardous thing. Generally, children just cannot grow up properly disciplined under babysitters, no matter how good these may be, as they can under a mother who loves them so much that she would die for them.

I remember an impressive experience which emphasized to me the value of Mother's staying at home. I was in a northwestern city for an evening missionary meeting. I had arrived early in the day on the only available flight. The stake president was a busy man and I said to him, "You go on about your work. Just give me a table and your typewriter, and I have plenty of things to do all afternoon."

So I started to work. Two or three hours passed so rapidly that I hardly realized the time had flown, and it must have been about 3 p.m. when I heard the front door open. While the father was out at work, the mother was upstairs ironing and sewing. Now the front door opened a crack and a child's voice said: "Oh, Mother!" I listened and heard the warm, loving voice from upstairs say, "I'm up here, dear. Do you want something?"

"Nothing, Mother," said the little boy, and he slammed the door and went out to play.

In a few minutes the door opened again and another boy stepped in, and a little older voice called, "Mother!" Again I heard the voice from upstairs say, "Here I am, darling. Do you want something?"

"No," was the reply, and the door closed again and another child went out to play.

In a little while, there was still another voice, that of a fifteen-year-old girl. She came rushing in, quite surprised to find a stranger in the home. She too called, "Oh, Mother!" And to this the response was again, "I'm up here, darling. I'm ironing." That seemed to satisfy this young girl completely and she went about her piano practice.

A little later there was a fourth voice, a seventeen-year-old girl voice. The call upstairs was repeated and the same mother voice responded and invited her to come up if she wanted to. But she just sat down at the living room table and spread out her books and began studying.

Mother was home! That was the important thing! Here was security! Here was everything that the child seemed to need. But suppose they came home and called "Mother!" only to find a silent house, or suppose another voice answered, calling out, "Your mother isn't home. She'll be home at 5:30." If this were repeated day after day, the youngsters would stop calling "Mother!" They would become independent and get along without Mother and lose that sense of security which comes from Mother's being home to answer the greeting and be available to solve their youthful problems.

We must spend more time with the children and less in clubs, bowling alleys, banquets and social gatherings. Fathers and Mothers, we must "come back home." We must sacrifice some of our other interests, and organize our Church programs better so that both parents and youth will not be away from the home so much of the time. We must get more people to work in the Church so that the burden will not fall so heavily on the few. Then we must organize and do the maximum possible in the minimum amount of time, so that there can be more proper home life.

Chart Course for the Children

Young parents should chart a course in their home and family life which will give the children firm but loving guidance and not let the children rule in the home. Children should be given responsibility, and duties to create in them the proper sense of responsibility. As indicated previously, their activities and habits should be in keeping with their ages, and parents should guide them accordingly. When they begin to go into their teens, they must be guided in their social life, into group activities, group picnics, group parties, going to church in groups, having firesides — only groups, no dating. Our little girls and boys should understand this long before they go to Mutual Improvement Association meetings. They must be made to understand that when they become older there will be other activities and interests in their lives that will be equally important, but until then, group activities. Wise parents will understand this and chart the course of group activities for their children until the offspring are more mature.

When young people begin to mature — perhaps in middle teens — parents may relax the rules a little and permit their sons and daughters to do some dating, but only non-steady dating at this point. This age is the time for Mary to get acquainted with many boys to learn the good qualities of each, and for Johnny to get acquainted with many girls to see the fine points of each. It is at this age that they begin to develop a composite figure, the "dream girl" or "dream boy" — and begin to look for the one who will make an ideal husband or a perfect wife.

This type of child direction can be done properly only with a charted course. It is often too late to solve problems when they already rear their ugly heads due to lack of planning and inadequate indoctrination.

In a properly charted Latter-day Saint home, young people, especially young men, will plan a mission. With proper indoctrination, a boy is led to understand the course of his life. He will be a deacon, a teacher, a priest, an elder. He will attend priesthood meetings and seminary, Sunday School and MIA and do his home teaching. He will fill an honorable mission and he will get his education. He will be married in the holy temple to a lovely Latter-day Saint girl who also has these same ideals and whose life has followed a similar planned course in home and Church to prepare her to be a loving wife and mother. Such young people are properly fortified against such evils as early and steady dating. They will grow up with no petting or immorality and none of the serious, damaging things which ruin lives. Parents should chart and guide the course of their children's lives in the early years. Then there will be none of the intimacies that spell sin and ruin.

Parents Must Stay Close to Children

Each mother should plan to stay close enough to her daughter so that she can talk to her before and if she is in trouble. I say to these girls who are in trouble, "Do your mother and father know about this?" Invariably the answer is, "Oh, no, I couldn't talk to my mother about this. I could talk to my bishop and I could talk to my stake president and to you, but I could never talk about it to my mother or my father."

A little Idaho girl came to my office, ready to have her baby. There was no father for the baby and no name for the poor little unfortunate. "I couldn't tell my mother,"

she said. "I'll stay down here in Salt Lake and have my
baby and give it away; but I'll never tell my mother." It
is sad how many times this situation is repeated.

We all realize that communication is a two-way street,
and that youth often build their own barriers. But are
parents charting their course right in this matter? Mothers,
are you so busy with social life, with clubs, with working
out of the home, or with housework, that you have no time
to sit down and talk to your little girls and tell them the
things they should know when they are nine, and ten, and
eleven, and older? Can you be frank and loving to them
so that they in turn can be frank in giving you their confidences?

And you fathers, are you so busy making a living, playing golf, bowling, hunting, that you do not have time to
talk to your boys and hold them close to you and win their
confidence? Or do you brush them off, so that they dare
not come and talk about these things with you?

Parents Accountable for Children's Training

The Lord holds parents accountable for training their
children in righteousness.

> And again, inasmuch as parents have children in Zion, or in
> any of her stakes which are organized, that teach them not to
> understand the doctrine of repentance, faith in Christ the Son
> of the living God, and of baptism and the gift of the Holy Ghost
> by the laying on of the hands, when eight years old, the sin be
> upon the heads of the parents.
>
> And they shall also teach their children to pray, and to walk
> uprightly before the Lord. (D&C 68:25, 28.)

We cannot evade the responsibility. Only by properly
planning and charting our family life can we guide our
children and keep them free from the pitfalls that lead to
sin and destruction, and put them on the pathway to happiness and exaltation. In this, nothing is more powerful
than the example of their own parents and the influence
of their home life. Our children's lives will be much the

same as they see in their own homes as they are growing
to manhood and womanhood. We should therefore chart
our course along the pathway which we would want our
children to follow.

Plan for Happiness

Happiness is an elusive thing. It is like the pot of gold
at the end of the rainbow. If we go out deliberately to find
it, we may have difficulty in catching it. But if we follow
directions closely, charting our course properly, we will not
need to pursue it. It will overtake us and remain with us.

"What is the price of happiness?" One might be surprised at the simplicity of the answer. The treasure house
of happiness is unlocked to those who live the gospel of
Jesus Christ in its purity and simplicity. Like a mariner
without stars, like a traveler without a compass, is the person who moves along through life without a plan. The
assurance of supreme happiness, the certainty of a successful life here and of exaltation and eternal life hereafter,
come to those who plan to live their lives in complete harmony with the gospel of Jesus Christ — and then consistently
follow the course they have set.

Chapter Eighteen

Forgive to Be Forgiven

> *For if ye forgive men their trespasses, your heavenly Father will also forgive you:*
>
> *But if ye forgive not men their trespasses, neither will your Father forgive your trespasses.*
>
> —Matthew 6:14-15
>
> *And forgive us our debts, as we forgive our debtors.*
>
> —Matthew 6:12

EXALTATION, THE PINNACLE OF THE PROPER DESIRE OF man, comes to him only if he is clean and worthy and perfected. Since man is weak and sinful, he must be cleansed before he can reach the exalted state of eternal life, and such cleansing from personal sins comes only through forgiveness following repentance.

Since forgiveness is an absolute requirement in attaining eternal life, man naturally ponders: How can I best secure that forgiveness? One of many basic factors stands out as indispensable immediately: One must forgive to be forgiven. The Lord's prayer emphasizes this:

> Our Father which art in heaven, Hallowed be thy name. Thy kingdom come. Thy will be done in earth, as it is in heaven. Give us this day our daily bread. And *forgive us our debts, as we forgive our debtors.* And lead us not into temptation, but deliver us from evil: for thine is the kingdom, and the power, and the glory, forever. Amen. (Matt. 6:9-13. Italics added.)

The Savior immediately returned to his message as though he might not have emphasized it enough. Now he strengthened it in the positive as well as in the negative, giving reasons as well as the implied command.

> For if ye forgive men their trespasses, your heavenly Father will also forgive you:
>
> But if ye forgive not men their trespasses, neither will your Father forgive your trespasses. (Matt. 6:14-15.)

The Lord must have considered this basic. He had long before made the same statement to his people in the Western world through his great prophet, Alma, when it was given in comparable words:

> And ye shall also forgive one another your trespasses; for verily I say unto you, he that forgiveth not his neighbor's trespasses when he says that he repents, the same hath brought himself under condemnation. (Mos. 26:31.)

Forgiveness Must Be Sincere

The command to forgive and the condemnation which follows failure to do so could not be stated more plainly than in this modern revelation to the Prophet Joseph Smith:

> My disciples, in days of old, sought occasion against one another and forgave not one another in their hearts; and for this evil they were afflicted and sorely chastened.
>
> Wherefore, I say unto you, that ye ought to forgive one another; for he that forgiveth not his brother his trespasses standeth condemned before the Lord; for there remaineth in him the greater sin.
>
> I, the Lord, will forgive whom I will forgive, but of you it is required to forgive all men. (D&C 64:8-10.)

Note the Lord's comment about inadequate forgiveness on the part of his former-day disciples. Just what their sufferings were is not stated, but the penalties and chastisement were sore.

The lesson stands for us today. Many people, when brought to a reconciliation with others, say that they forgive, but they continue to hold malice, continue to suspect the other party, continue to disbelieve the other's sincerity. This is sin, for when a reconciliation has been effected and when repentance is claimed, each should forgive and forget, build immediately the fences which have been breached, and restore the former compatibility.

The early disciples evidently expressed words of forgiveness, and on the surface made the required adjustment, but "forgave not one another in their hearts." This was not a forgiveness, but savored of hypocrisy and deceit and subterfuge. As implied in Christ's model prayer, it must be a heart action and a purging of one's mind. Forgiveness means forgetfulness. One woman had "gone through" a reconciliation in a branch and had made the physical motions and verbal statements indicating it, and expressed the mouthy words forgiving. Then with flashing eyes, she remarked, "I will forgive her, but I have a memory like an elephant. I'll never forget." Her pretended adjustment was valueless and void. She still harbored the bitterness. Her words of friendship were like a spider's web, her rebuilt fences were as straw, and she herself continued to suffer without peace of mind. Worse still, she stood "condemned before the Lord," and there remained in her an even greater sin than in the one who, she claimed, had injured her.

Little did this antagonistic woman realize that she had not forgiven at all. She had only made motions. She was spinning her wheels and getting nowhere. In the scripture quoted above, the phrase *in their hearts* has deep meaning. It must be a purging of feelings and thoughts and bitternesses. Mere words avail nothing.

> For behold, if a man being evil giveth a gift, he doeth it grudgingly; wherefore it is counted unto him the same as if he had retained the gift; wherefore he is counted evil before God. (Moro. 7:8.)

Henry Ward Beecher expressed the thought this way: "I can forgive but I cannot forget is another way of saying I cannot forgive."

I may add that unless a person forgives his brother his trespasses *with all his heart* he is unfit to partake of the sacrament.

> For he that eateth and drinketh unworthily, eateth and drinketh damnation to himself, not discerning the Lord's body.

> For this cause many are weak and sickly among you, and many sleep. (1 Cor. 11:29-30.)

Transgressors Not to Be Hounded

Some people not only cannot or will not forgive and forget the transgressions of others, but go to the other extreme of hounding the alleged transgressor. Many letters and calls have come to me from individuals who are determined to take the sword of justice in their own hands and presume to see that a transgressor is punished. "That man should be excommunicated," a woman declared, "and I'm never going to rest till he has been properly dealt with." Another said, "I can never rest, so long as that person is a member of the Church." Still another said: "I will never enter the chapel so long as that person is permitted to enter. I want him tried for his membership." One man even made many trips to Salt Lake City and wrote several long letters to protest against the bishop and the stake president who did not take summary disciplinary action against a person who, he claimed, was breaking the laws of the Church.

To such who would take the law into their own hands, we read again the positive declaration of the Lord: ". . . there remaineth in him the greater sin." (D&C 64:9.) The revelation continues: "And ye ought to say in your hearts — let God judge between me and thee, and reward thee according to thy deeds." (D&C 64:11.) When known transgressions have been duly reported to the proper ecclesiastical officers of the Church, the individual may rest the case and leave the responsibility with the Church officers. If those officers tolerate sin in the ranks, it is an awesome responsibility for them and they will be held accountable.

One woman called every week to inquire whether her former son-in-law had been excommunicated. I told her to let the matter drop; that she had done her full duty in making the matter known to the proper authorities and now she would do well to forget it and leave the disciplining to the appropriate officials. Another bitter woman almost lost her reason, so determined was she to see that her divorced husband paid the severest penalties. It was obvious that her motive was revenge, not justice. She had problems of her own, but she disregarded them in her frenzy in seeking revenge.

Another couple had had much trouble which culminated in divorce. The woman had acknowledged her guilt of infidelity, and had done all she could to make adjustment through her bishop, and had remarried in what seemed to be a happy marriage. The man, on the other hand, had been most demanding and seemed determined to see that she was disciplined severely. From authority to authority he took the case, rehearsing all her weaknesses and eccentricities, fully embellishing them and demanding that the Church take action.

Bitter vituperation and ugly calumnies came from him. He quoted scripture; he cited the handbook; he rehearsed the policy and practice of the Church in such matters. Revenge seemed to be his obsession. It was necessary to say to him: "You have done your full duty when you have reported the misdeeds to the proper authority. You need not take the matter further." And when he persisted, it was finally necessary to tell him that unless he desisted, action might be taken against him. Revenge is sweet to some, but "revenge is mine, saith the Lord." Again, he that will not forgive is worse than the original culprit.

Revenge Is Foreign to the Gospel

The spirit of revenge, of retaliation, of bearing a grudge, is entirely foreign to the gospel of the gentle, forgiving Jesus Christ. Even the old Mosaic law, which is usually thought of as being harsher, forbade this spirit. From Sinai and the wilderness comes to us the imperishable command, always pertinent in any age:

> Thou shalt not go up and down as a talebearer among thy people: neither shalt thou stand against the blood of thy neighbour: I am the Lord.
>
> Thou shalt not hate thy brother in thine heart: thou shalt in any wise rebuke thy neighbour, and not suffer sin upon him.
>
> Thou shalt not avenge, nor bear any grudge against the children of thy people, but thou shalt love thy neighbour as thyself: I am the Lord. (Lev. 19:16-18.)

Again, James warns against the grudge: "Grudge not one against another, brethren, lest ye be condemned: behold, the judge standeth before the door." (Jas. 5:9.) And someone has said: "One of the heaviest loads a man can carry is a grudge."

In the midst of discordant sounds of hate, bitterness and revenge expressed so often today, the soft note of forgiveness comes as a healing balm. Not least is its effect on the forgiver.

> One of the glorious aspects of the principles of forgiveness is the purifying and ennobling effects its application has upon the personality and character of the forgiver. Someone wisely said, "He who has not forgiven a wrong or an injury has not yet tasted one of the sublime enjoyments of life." The human soul seldom rises to such heights of strength and nobility as when it removes all resentments and forgives errors and malice.[1]

Retaliation certainly is not repentance, but the suffering of indignities, on the other hand, may be the way toward that goal. The Lord's matchless Sermon on the Mount provides for the better way, one without revenge or retaliation. And Paul said to the Romans:

> Recompense to no man evil for evil. . . Dearly beloved, avenge not yourselves, but rather give place unto wrath: for it is written, Vengeance is mine; I will repay, saith the Lord. (Rom. 12:17, 19.)

Spinoza expresses it this way:

---

[1]From the Visiting Teacher's Message, October, 1963.

He who wishes to revenge injuries by reciprocal hatred will live in misery. But, he who endeavors to drive away hatred by means of love, fights with pleasure and confidence; he resists equally one or many men, and scarcely needs at all the help of fortune. Those whom he conquers yield joyfully, not from want of force, but increase thereof.

Do Not Judge

One man came in with his erring wife, and when she had been disciplined by disfellowshipment he taunted her, saying, "Now, how do you like it? You can't take the sacrament. Now don't you wish you had listened to me?" As this despicable husband was judging, it reminded me of the corrupt men who brought the adulteress to the Lord, whose soft answer puts all such accusers to flight: "He that is without sin among you, let him first cast a stone at her." (John 8:7.) The scriptures are very strict upon the unauthorized judging. The Lord himself made it clear and emphatic:

> Judge not, that ye be not judged.
>
> For with what judgment ye judge, ye shall be judged: and with what measure ye mete, it shall be measured to you again. (Matt. 7:1-2.)

The Lord will judge with the same measurements meted out by us. If we are harsh, we should not expect other than harshness. If we are merciful with those who injure us, he will be merciful with us in our errors. If we are unforgiving, he will leave us weltering in our own sins.

While the scriptures are plain in their declaration that man shall have meted out to him the same measure that he gives his fellowmen, the meting out even of warranted judgment is not for the layman, but for proper authorities in Church and state. The Lord will do the judging in the final analysis.

The bishop in his ordination to that office is made a "judge in Israel" to those of his own ward, but to none who are not so placed under his jurisdiction. The stake president, by his setting apart, is made a judge over the people of the stake over which he is to preside. Likewise, a branch president and mission president have somewhat similar responsibilities. The General Authorities, of course, have general jurisdiction, and have the duty to make judgments in certain instances.

The Lord can judge men by their thoughts as well as by what they say and do, for he knows even the intents of their hearts; but this is not true of humans. We hear what people say, we see what they do, but being unable to discern what they think or intend, we often judge wrongfully if we try to fathom the meaning and motives behind their actions and place on them our own interpretation.

A person who judges anyone else is just as likely to judge his Church leaders, often thereby bringing disharmony and contention to our wards and branches. But the spirit of forgiveness and not of judgment is what is required — forgiveness and understanding. If those who seem so disturbed about the actions of their leaders would only pray to the Lord with full purpose of heart, saying constantly, "Thy will be done," and "Father, lead me aright and I will accept," their attitude would change and they would return to happiness and peace.

People who are inclined to sit in judgment on others should read and reread these words of Paul to the Romans:

> Therefore thou art inexcusable, O man, whosoever thou art that judgest: for wherein thou judgest another, thou condemnest thyself; for thou that judgest doest the same things.
>
> But we are sure that the judgment of God is according to truth against them which commit such things.
>
> And thinkest thou this, O man, that judgest them which do such things, and doest the same, that thou shalt escape the judgment of God? (Rom. 2:1-3.)

The Redeemer's principle of not judging is not a single-action program — it is a day-to-day requirement of life. He tells us to clean up our own errors first — to remove the beam-size faults. Then, and not till then, is one justi-

fied in turning his attention to the eccentricities or weaknesses of another.

> And why beholdest thou the mote that is in thy brother's
> eye, but considerest not the beam that is in thine own eye?
>
> Or how wilt thou say to thy brother, Let me pull out the
> mote out of thine eye; and, behold, a beam is in thine own eye?
> (Matt. 7:3-4.)

This should leave no doubt in any mind. The unequal-
ness of the beam and the mote is telling. A mote is a tiny
sliver like a small portion from a toothpick, while the beam
is usually a great, strong timber or metal which runs from
wall to wall to support the heavy roof of the building. When
one is loaded down with beam-size weaknesses and sins, it
is certainly wrong to forget his own difficult position while
he makes mountains of the molehill-size errors of his brother.

Our vision is completely obscured when we have no
mirror to hold up to our own faults and look only for the
foibles of others. When we follow the instructions of the
Lord, we are kept so busy perfecting ourselves that we come
to realize that the faults of others are small in comparison.
We should establish the delightful habit, then, of minimizing the weaknesses of others and thus increase our own
virtues.

He who will not forgive others breaks down the bridge
over which he himself must travel. This is a truth taught
by the Lord in the parable of the unmerciful servant who
demanded to be forgiven but was merciless to one who asked
forgiveness of him. (See Matt. 18:23-35.)

It is interesting to note the difference in the debts. The
wicked servant owed 10,000 talents and was owed only 100
pence. The Bible dictionary says that a talent is 750 ounces
while a Roman penny is the eighth part of an ounce. In
the parable, then, the wicked servant who owed 10,000
talents and who begged for time and mercy was condemn-
ing and imprisoning for debt the man who owed him a
relatively paltry sum, one 600,000th of his own debt. Did
not Paul say that we are usually guilty of the same trans-

gressions and errors of which we accuse and condemn our fellowmen?

Once I had a "talents-and-pence," "mote-and-beam" situation when an injured husband finally persuaded his adulterous wife to come with him to my office. She admitted her guilt but justified herself in her losing interest in her own home in the fact that her husband was so righteous and fair and honorable that it gave her an inferiority complex. I asked her what he did to disturb her and justify her leaving her home and her children and him. She could find little fault with him. He provided well, was a good father, was kind and thoughtful, a good member of the Church, but because she had bad tendencies and impure thoughts, she felt inferior. Hers was the beam; hers was the 10,000-talent error; his was the mote and the 100-pence error.

No Escape Without Forgiveness

If the faults of two people are more nearly equal, if both of them have a beam-impaired vision, that still gives no justification for a selfish, unforgiving attitude. With this in mind, I once wrote to a woman with whom I had had previous occasion to discuss at length her family problems. I had given counsel in my desire to prevent further misunderstandings and avoid a separation or divorce. After some weeks, she wrote that she would accept my decision. I responded in part as follows:

> It is not *my* decision—it is up to you to make the decisions. You have your free agency. If you are determined to get a divorce it is your responsibility and your suffering if you are not willing to make adjustments. When I talked with you, I understood that you had forgiven each other and would start from there to build a beautiful life. Apparently, I was mistaken. All my warnings and pleadings seem to have fallen on deaf ears. I want you to know that I do not justify in your husband anything that was wrong, but I recognized all the way through that his was not the whole fault. I have never been able to feel that you had wholly purged the selfishness from your own soul. I do know that two people as seemingly intelligent and apparently mature as you

two, could have a gloriously happy life, if both of you would begin to let your concerns run in favor of the other, instead of in favor of your selfish selves.

The escapist never escapes. If two people, selfish and self-centered, and without the spirit of forgiveness, escape from each other, they cannot escape from themselves. The disease is not cured by the separation or the divorce, and it will most assuredly follow along in the wake of future marriages. The cause must be removed. Being young, both of you are likely to marry again. Each of you is likely to carry into the next marriage all the weaknesses and sins and errors you have now, unless you repent and transform. And if you will change your life for a new spouse, why not for the present one?

Perhaps you have thought that your home was the one home that was frustrated with problems. You should know that most couples have misunderstandings but many solve their problems instead of permitting their problems to crush them. Many wives have shed bitter tears, and many husbands have lain sleepless hours, but thanks be to the Lord that great numbers of these folks have been smart enough to solve their difficulties.

In my letter, I continued as follows:

Partners stay in business together for years. They may be as different as fish and fowl, but because there is a compelling and compensating reason for their understanding of each other, they overlook weaknesses, strengthen themselves, and work together. They seldom break up a partnership where they would both lose seriously and financially by doing so.

A celestial marriage is far more to fight for and to live for, and to adjust for, than any financial or other gain or beneficial arrangements that two partners might have between them.

Now, my beloved friends . . . the matter is in your hands—you may do as you please, but I warn you that the trouble is deeper than you realize, and not easily resolved by divorce. And I warn you also that, either separated or living together, you will be damaged and cankered and poisoned and dwarfed by bitterness and hatreds and loathings. The first need is to master yourselves.

The Poison of Bitterness

In that letter I mentioned bitterness and hatred, which so often accompany the unforgiving spirit. Bitterness poisons mostly the one who harbors it in his heart. It generates hatred, and "whosoever hateth his brother is a murderer: and ye know that no murderer hath eternal life abiding in him." (1 John 3:15.)

Generally, the hated one does not even know how bitter is the animosity leveled against him. He may sleep at night and enjoy a reasonable peace, but the one who hates estranges himself from good folk, shrivels his heart, dwarfs his soul, makes of himself an unhappy pygmy.

Usually such a person broadcasts his troubles, his prejudices and his hates, and thus is even less appreciated by his fellowmen than the one who must always be speaking of his physical infirmities and explaining his operations. It becomes wearisome, and people are bored by the harangues. Only good manners keeps people from running when the complainer, the hater, the critic appears.

I knew a man who took every occasion to criticize one of his colleagues for passing up the weekly sacrament meeting. His denunciation and condemnation were vituperative and frequent. Later, I noted that the same critic was frequently absenting himself from his sacrament meeting and he seemed in every case to justify it, but he had made no allowances for his brother in similar situations. Is not the gossip hardest on his fellow gossip? Is not the critic most critical of other critics?

The Lord and his Church do not justify any wrongdoing on the part of any of us. But if each of us keeps his own heart pure and his own mind free from bitterness, and serves the Lord with all his might, mind, strength, and heart, he can be at peace. He can be sure that every other soul, like himself, will have to pay full price for his misdeeds, and will receive due rewards for his good deeds.

> I returned, and saw under the sun, that the race is not to the swift, nor the battle to the strong, neither yet bread to the wise, nor yet riches to men of understanding, nor yet favour to men of skill; but time and chance happeneth to them all. (Eccles. 9:11.)

Our mission is to save, not to injure nor destroy. It is indeed unfortunate that people are not always discreet and diplomatic in their dealings with others. Sometimes the best people, and even the best Church leaders, though having the finest intentions, give offense and injury without meaning to do so. In my work, I have run into this often.

But neither real nor fancied offenses from others, leaders or not, justify the spirit of selfishness, jealousy, recrimination and resentment that sparks and then rekindles feuds and hostility. It is this same spirit, nourished by hurt feelings and fancied slights, which causes rifts and feuds in wards and branches. Those in positions of authority sometimes have their actions and motives questioned and are resented by members of their wards and branches and stakes when instead these members should be understanding and forgiving and willing to support and accept counsel from the leaders.

I knew a man who had had a fight with his neighbor over water and the filling in of a ditch common to both farms. Hatred increased till they watched each other like hawks. If one went to church, the other stayed home. If one went to town, the other remained at the farm so he would not meet him. When they did meet unexpectedly, their handshake was an icy one. They impugned each other's motives; each interpreted every intended good act of the other as having an ulterior motive. When the one was made a Church leader, the other and his family absented themselves from Church activity. When a reorganization took place and the other family was honored with leadership, the formerly active family could not now be induced to attend to their duties.

I knew a stake president who was released before he was desirous of being replaced. He became very bitter and his venom expressed itself in staying away from the Church services, in criticizing the leaders who had released him and then, gradually, the leaders who replaced him, and eventually, the Church which he was now injuring. On and on he skidded toward apostasy. His spite and hatreds injured him only. The stake continued to prosper.

The damage to one who becomes the critic and sets himself up as a judge is severe, especially if he finds fault with the leaders of the Church whom the Lord has appointed. Since the crucifixion, there have been tens of thousands of men called by the Savior to fill positions of responsibility, not one of whom has been perfect, and yet all are called of the Lord and must be upheld and sustained by those who would be disciples of the Lord. That is the true spirit of the gospel.

It is most regrettable that individuals permit themselves to be so disturbed about the actions of their leaders. I am sure that if such people would pray to the Lord with all their hearts and minds and voices, saying constantly, "Thy will be done," and "Father, lead me aright and I will accept," they would have a change of attitude and would return to happiness and peace.

Not Understood

There are many reasons why we should not judge our fellows, apart even from the Lord's commandment. A significant one is that usually we do not have all the facts on which to base judgment. We do not understand. A song from the pen of Thomas Bracken, put to music by our own Evan Stephens, has such a powerful message in this context that I quote excerpts from it:

> Not understood. We gather false impressions
> And hug them closer as the years go by.
>
> Not understood. Poor souls with stunted vision
> Oft measure giants by their narrow gauge.
>
> Not understood. How trifles often change us.
> The thoughtless sentence or the fancied slight
> Destroys long years of friendship, and estrange us,
> And on our souls there falls a freezing blight:
> Not understood. Not understood.
>
> O God, that men would see a little clearer,
> Or judge less harshly where they cannot see!

The Lord can judge men by their thoughts as well as by what they say and do, for he even knows the intents of their hearts; but that is not true of us humans. We hear what others say, we see what they do, but we cannot always tell what they think nor what they intend. Therefore, we often judge wrongfully if we try to fathom their meaning and give our own interpretation to it.

Forgiveness is the miraculous ingredient that assures harmony and love in the home or the ward. Without it there is contention. Without understanding and forgiveness there is dissension, followed by lack of harmony, and this breeds disloyalty in homes, in branches and in wards. On the other hand, forgiveness is harmonious with the spirit of the gospel, with the Spirit of Christ. This is the spirit we must all possess if we would receive forgiveness of our own sins and be blameless before God.

Chapter Nineteen

...As We Forgive Our Debtors

O man, forgive thy mortal foe,
Nor ever strike him blow for blow;
For all the souls on earth that live,
To be forgiven must forgive.
Forgive him seventy times and seven;
For all the blessed souls in heaven
Are both forgivers and forgiven.

—Alfred Lord Tennyson

IN THE PREVIOUS CHAPTER I DWELT MOSTLY ON THE negative aspects of this subject — on people who have been unforgiving, and the spirit and attitude they carry. In the present chapter I shall highlight the positive side, indicating the joy which comes to those who truly forgive.

From a Ward Teaching message comes this:

It is safe to assume that nothing Jesus did brought him more joy than to forgive his fellowmen. He gave his very life that Adam's transgression may be forgiven, and that we be spared the consequences thereof.

Let us each look back over his own life, and recall the time when he has forgiven someone. Has any other joy been more gratifying? Has any other feeling been more uplifting? The destructive feelings of smallness, pettiness, and hate, or longing for revenge, are crowded out by the attitude to forgive. "Forgiveness is better than revenge; for forgiveness is the sign of a gentle nature, but revenge the sign of a savage nature."[1]

---

[1] Ward Teacher's Message, January, 1944.

The great Abraham Lincoln understood this principle better than most. He had an answer to many problems. His Secretary of War, Edwin Stanton, was one of his problems. Edwin Stanton wrote a hot letter to a general who had abused him and accused him of favoritism. He read the letter to Lincoln, who listened and then exclaimed: "First rate, Stanton, you've scored him well, just right!"

As Stanton folded the letter into its envelope, Lincoln quickly asked, "Why, what are you going to do with it now?"

"Mail it to him."

"No, no, that would spoil it," responded Lincoln. "File it away; that is the kind of filing that keeps it sharp and doesn't wound the other fellow."

Paul and Stephen Forgave Enemies

A mark of true greatness is the forgiving heart. Consider the life of Paul. Though he may not have been perfect, he was a most righteous man after his conversion. He gave us a beautiful example of forgiving others. He recalled:

> Alexander the coppersmith did me much evil: the Lord reward him according to his works. (2 Tim. 4:14.)

Paul was willing to leave the judgment and penalty to the Lord, who would be wise and just. In spite of all he suffered at the hands of oppressors, some of whom were his own false brethren, he was not consumed and scorched with hate or bitterness or rancor. Quite the reverse.

To the Corinthians he urged the very traits he had so fully developed in himself. (2 Cor. 11:23-28.) Here we have the noble Paul who had suffered much from his contemporaries — Paul, who had been tortured with beatings, who had suffered incarceration in many prisons; Paul, who had received two hundred stripes across his back, who had been beaten with rods; Paul, who had been stoned and left for dead, and who had three times been shipwrecked and had struggled many hours in the water; Paul, who had suffered from robbers and had been hidden from his pursuers and had escaped in a basket over the wall — this Paul who had suffered so much at the hands of others came near the end of his life with a forgiving heart and said: "At my first answer no man stood with me, but all men forsook me: *I pray God that it may not be laid to their charge.*" (2 Tim. 4:16. Italics added.)

Another who exemplified the divine nature in forgiving was Stephen. One of the seven men chosen for temporal work in the Church, Stephen was a man "full of faith and of the Holy Ghost." His life closely approached the perfection line, so much so that people "saw his face as it had been the face of an angel." (Acts 6:15.) Following his piercing sermon to his antagonists, the wicked of the place, he became the victim of a rash, vicious assassination by men who rushed at him

> And cast him out of the city, and stoned him: and the witnesses laid down their clothes at a young man's feet, whose name was Saul.
>
> And they stoned Stephen, calling upon God, and saying, Lord Jesus, receive my spirit.
>
> And he kneeled down, and cried with a loud voice, *Lord, lay not this sin to their charge.* And when he had said this, he fell asleep. (Acts 7:58-60. Italics added.)

Great Example of Jesus

We have the supreme example of fortitude, kindness, charity and forgiveness in him who set the perfect example, our Savior, Jesus Christ, who commands us all to follow. All his life he had been the victim of ugliness. As a newborn infant he had been spirited away to save his life at the instruction of an angel in a dream, and had been taken to Egypt. At the end of a hectic life he had stood in quiet, restrained, divine dignity, while evil men spat foul, disease-germ-ridden spittle in his face. How nauseating! But what composure he showed! What control!

They pushed him around and jostled him and buffeted him. Not an angry word escaped his lips. What mastery of self! They slapped him in his face and on his body. What humiliation! How painful! Yet he stood resolute, unintimidated. Literally did he follow his own admonition when he turned his other cheek so that it too could be slapped and smitten.

His own disciples had forsaken him and fled. In such a difficult position, he met the rabble and their leaders. He stood alone at the mercy of his brutal, criminal assailants and vilifiers.

Words, too, are hard to take. Incriminations and recriminations and their blasphemy of things, persons, places and situations sacred to him must have been hard to take. They called his own sweet innocent mother a fornicator, yet he stood his ground, never faltering. No cringing, no denials, no rebuttals. When false, mercenary witnesses were paid to lie about him, he seemed not to condemn them. They twisted his words and misinterpreted his meanings, yet he was calm and unflustered. Had he not been taught to pray for them "which despitefully use you"?

He was beaten, officially scourged. He wore a crown of thorns, a wicked torture. He was mocked and jeered. He suffered every indignity at the hands of his own people. "I came unto my own," he said, "and my own received me not." He was required to carry his own cross, taken to the mount of Calvary, nailed to a cross, and suffered excruciating pain. Finally, with the soldiers and his accusers down below him, he looked upon the Roman soldiers and said these immortal words: *"Father, forgive them; for they know not what they do."* (Luke 23:34.)

We Must Forgive Regardless

It would have been easy for Paul, Stephen and Jesus to be revengeful — that is, if they had not assiduously cultivated the forgiving spirit. Revenge is a response of the carnal man, not the spiritual one. It enters into one's life when he allows it to through misunderstandings and injuries.

In our own dispensation, the Lord spoke pointedly of
this matter and made a statement which is startling in its
implications. It is found in Doctrine & Covenants Section
64, previously quoted. I shall never forget this scripture,
for it came to me in what seemed a miraculous manner.

I was struggling with a community problem in a small
ward in the East where two prominent men, leaders of the
people, were deadlocked in a long and unrelenting feud.
Some misunderstanding between them had driven them far
apart with enmity. As the days, weeks, and months passed,
the breach became wider. The families of each conflicting
party began to take up the issue and finally nearly all the
people of the ward were involved. Rumors spread and
differences were aired and gossip became tongues of fire
until the little community was divided by a deep gulf. I
was sent to clear up the matter. After a long stake conference, lasting most of two days, I arrived at the frustrated
community about 6 p.m., Sunday night, and immediately
went into session with the principal combatants.

How we struggled! How I pleaded and warned and
begged and urged! Nothing seemed to be moving them.
Each antagonist was so sure that he was right and justified
that it was impossible to budge him.

The hours were passing — it was now long after midnight, and despair seemed to enshroud the place; the atmos-
phere was still one of ill temper and ugliness. Stubborn
resistance would not give way. Then it happened. I aim-
lessly opened my Doctrine and Covenants again and there
before me it was. I had read it many times in past years
and it had had no special meaning then. But tonight it
was the very answer. It was an appeal and an imploring
and a threat and seemed to be coming direct from the Lord.
I read from the seventh verse on, but the quarreling participants yielded not an inch until I came to the ninth verse.
Then I saw them flinch, startled, wondering. Could that
be right? The Lord was saying to us — to all of us —

"Wherefore, I say unto you, that ye ought to forgive one another."

This was an obligation. They had heard it before. They had said it in repeating the Lord's Prayer. But now: ". . . for he that forgiveth not his brother his trespasses standeth condemned before the Lord . . ."

In their hearts, they may have been saying: "Well, I might forgive if he repents and asks forgiveness, but he must make the first move." Then the full impact of the last line seemed to strike them: "For there remaineth in him the greater sin."

What? Does that mean I must forgive even if my antagonist remains cold and indifferent and mean? There is no mistaking it.

A common error is the idea that the offender must apologize and humble himself to the dust before forgiveness is required. Certainly, the one who does the injury should totally make his adjustment, but as for the offended one, he must forgive the offender regardless of the attitude of the other. Sometimes men get satisfactions from seeing the other party on his knees and grovelling in the dust, but that is not the gospel way.

Shocked, the two men sat up, listened, pondered a minute, then began to yield. This scripture added to all the others read brought them to their knees. Two a.m. and two bitter adversaries were shaking hands, smiling and forgiving and asking forgiveness. Two men were in a meaningful embrace. This hour was holy. Old grievances were forgiven and forgotten, and enemies became friends again. No reference was ever made again to the differences. The skeletons were buried, the closet of dry bones was locked and the key was thrown away, and peace was restored.

In this regard the admonition of President Joseph F. Smith in 1902 is as applicable now as then:

> We hope and pray that you will . . . forgive one another and never from this time forth . . . bear malice toward another fellow creature.

. . . It is extremely hurtful for any man holding the gift of the Holy Ghost to harbor a spirit of envy, or malice, or retaliations, or intolerance toward or against his fellow man. We ought to say in our hearts, "Let God judge between me and thee, but as for me, I will forgive." I want to say to you that Latter-day Saints who harbor a feeling of unforgiveness in their souls are more censurable than the one who has sinned against them. Go home and dismiss envy and hatred from your hearts: dismiss the feeling of unforgiveness; and cultivate in your souls that spirit of Christ which cried out upon the cross, "Father, forgive them; for they know not what they do." This is the spirit that Latter-day Saints ought to possess all the day long.

Yes, to be in the right we must forgive, and we must do so *without regard to whether or not our antagonist repents,* or how sincere is his transformation, or whether or not he asks our forgiveness. We must follow the example and the teaching of the Master, who said: ". . . Ye ought to say in your hearts — let God judge between me and thee, and reward thee according to thy deeds." (D&C 64:11.) But men often are unwilling to leave it to the Lord, fearing perhaps that the Lord might be too merciful, less severe than is proper in the case. In this we could all take a lesson from the great David.

When David was being pursued to the death by the jealous King Saul, and David came upon an easy opportunity to kill him, the young, pure-minded David refrained from ridding himself of his enemy. He cut off the skirt of Saul's robe to prove to the king that he had been in David's hand and at his mercy. Speaking later to Saul, he said:

. . . I have not sinned against thee; yet thou huntest my soul to take it.

The Lord judge between me and thee, and the Lord avenge me of thee: but mine hand shall not be upon thee . . . wickedness proceedeth from the wicked. (1 Sam. 24:11-13.)

And Saul, when he realized how helpless he had been when at the mercy of David, responded:

Thou art more righteous than I; for thou hast rewarded me good, whereas I have rewarded thee evil. (1 Sam. 24:17.)

One of the world's most beautiful mountains, located in Jasper National Park in Canada, was named for Edith Cavell. Edith Cavell was a nurse who was executed by her enemies for having hidden, nursed, and fed wounded soldiers. As she stood before the firing squad she uttered these deathless words which are now preserved in bronze and granite: "I realize that patriotism is not enough. I must have no hatred or bitterness toward anyone."

The Ultimate in Forgiveness

Sometimes the spirit of forgiveness is carried to the loftiest height — to rendering assistance to the offender. Not to be revengeful, not to seek what outraged justice might demand, to leave the offender in God's hands — this is admirable. But to return good for evil, this is the sublime expression of Christian love.

In this regard we have the stimulating example of President George Albert Smith. It was reported to him that someone had stolen from his buggy the buggy robe. Instead of being angry, he responded: "I wish we knew who it was, so that we could give him the blanket also, for he must have been cold; and some food also, for he must have been hungry."

This brings to mind the classic story of Jean Valjean in Victor Hugo's immortal book, *Les Miserables*. President Henry D. Moyle summarized this for us in his address printed in the November, 1957, *Improvement Era*:

> Victor Hugo's description of Jean Valjean after nineteen years as a prisoner in the galleys is unforgettable. His initial offense was the stealing of a loaf of bread to feed his mother's starving family. At that time he was only a boy. Upon his release from prison, after all others had rejected him as a despised ex-convict, he was finally befriended by a bishop, M. Beauvian.

> This bishop treated Jean Valjean with great kindness and generosity. He trusted him and gave him food and lodging. Jean Valjean, unable to overcome the evil impulses fostered during his prison years, repaid the bishop by robbing him of his silverware, consisting of many priceless heirlooms. He was shortly after ap-

prehended by the gendarmes and brought back, with the bishop's treasures in his bag. The bishop forgave Jean Valjean and, in place of accusing him of his dastardly deed of ingratitude, instantly said to him, "You forgot the candlesticks," and giving them to Jean Valjean, told him that they were silver, too. After the officers had left, the bishop said to the ex-convict: "Jean Valjean, my brother, you belong no longer to evil but to good . . . I will draw it [his soul] from dark thoughts and from the spirit of perdition. . . ."

This act of forgiveness on the part of a man whose property had been stolen aroused the latent virtues of Jean. They had lain dormant for nineteen years. Even his long term in the galleys could not destroy the inherent desire in man to do good. Almost his first act after the saintly deed of the bishop was to befriend a golden-haired girl in dire distress known as Cosette. The author's ultimate description of Jean Valjean is indicative of the tremendous transformation in the character of this unfortunate man. Cosette completed the reformation of this man's life which the bishop had initiated. Victor Hugo writes: "The Bishop had caused the dawn of virtue on his horizon; Cosette evoked the dawn of love."

After a life filled with charity, forgiveness and other good deeds, Jean Valjean sacrificed life itself for the happiness and wellbeing of Cosette and her husband. In his final letter to her, he wrote these words:

"I am writing just now to Cosette. She will find my letter. To her I bequeath the two candlesticks which are on the mantel. They are silver, but to me they are gold. They are diamonds . . . I do not know whether he who gave them to me is satisfied with me . . . I have done what I could."

One act of complete forgiveness entirely altered the life of this ex-convict. Throughout his life, he was hounded and suffered humiliation and degradation almost beyond human endurance. The gendarmes continually sought for trivial reasons to reincarcerate him. Nevertheless, he succeeded in keeping the second great commandment throughout the remaining years of his life. He had once again regained the attributes of virtue, love and forgiveness, which he conscientiously exercised thereafter toward those who pursued and persecuted him.

We also see in the life story of Jean Valjean how closely repentance on his part followed his forgiveness by the man he had wronged. Thereafter he brought forth fruits meet for repentance.

It Can Be Done

A certain man found that he had a suspicious growth which presaged serious trouble. When the doctor had taken a biopsy and found the growth to be malignant, the man made arrangements at the hospital for radical surgery. When he learned the truth — that his life was hanging in the balance — this good man recoiled at first, then resigned himself, relaxed and smiled as he told the doctor:

"Before I go to the hospital, doctor, I have four items of unfinished business. First, I will check my insurance policies and my titles and see that all are in order; second, I'm going to settle all my financial obligations; third, I'm going to have my will rechecked; and fourth, I'm going to see Bill and apologize for the unkind things I have said about him and ask his forgiveness for the grudge I have long carried against him. Then, I am ready to go to the hospital, and to my grave if necessary."

In the context of the spirit of forgiveness, one good brother asked me, "Yes, that is what ought to be done, but how do you do it? Doesn't that take a superman?"

"Yes," I said, "but we are commanded to be supermen. Said the Lord, 'Be ye therefore perfect, even as your Father which is in heaven is perfect.' (Matt. 5:48.) We are gods in embryo, and the Lord demands perfection of us."

"Yes, the Christ forgave those who injured him, but he was more than human," he rejoined.

And my answer was: "But there are many humans who have found it possible to do this divine thing."

Apparently there are many who, like this good brother, hold the comfortable theory that the forgiving spirit as exemplified in the examples I have quoted is more or less the monopoly of scriptural or fictional characters and can hardly be expected of practical people in today's world.

This is not the case. That the forgiving spirit can be developed today is demonstrated by the accounts which follow — in which, be it noted, the provocation was in most instances more extreme than most of us meet.

Hatred and Bitterness Can Be Overcome

These are accounts of some contemporaries who have risen to great heights in self-mastery — in contrast to the many people who carry bitterness in their hearts for wrongs or fancied ones. Sometimes the injured ones get courage and strength from others who have had great trials and have borne up under them. Such is the experience of Mrs. Ruby Spilsbury Brown of El Paso, Texas, and her late husband, George, who lost their son in the Second World War and became bitter at the incident and bitter at the Japanese race because of it. They received much courage in their trial from the Glenn Kempton story related later in this chapter, and it may be that many readers will find strength in knowing that other folks have great tribulations and emerge from them and rise above them.

The Robert Brown story follows, in the words of his mother:

> Our son, Bobby, was taken prisoner by the Japanese at the fall of Bataan in April, 1941, and thus escaped the infamous Death March. He arrived at the prison camp of Cabanatuan ahead of the rest of the troops and stood at the gate as they filed slowly in. So many of them were missing, others seriously wounded and all of them pitifully hungry and weakened. No wonder he sobbed his heart out at the sight of them.
>
> Bobby enlisted in the New Mexico National Guard in October, 1940, and was inducted into the U. S. Army in January, 1941. By the time his unit left the last of August for places unknown he had risen to master sergeant, and in January, 1942, he was given a field commission as first lieutenant and was placed in charge of the regimental supply.
>
> For nineteen months, we had no word from the War Department other than the terse "missing in action." In the two-and-a-half years he was in the prison camps, we received only five messages from him. Very brief they were, on post cards with

checked blanks for the sender to fill in. They were signed by our son but heavily censored. At least it was in his handwriting and oh, how we treasured these! The rest of the information came to us piecemeal from his buddies, making their way to our door as they returned after the surrender.

Bobby was sent to the southern island of Mindanoa, in the Philippines, where the boys were put to work in the rice fields and on chicken farms. We are told that here our boys, in order to keep their starved bodies alive, found it necessary to take food wherever they could find it. A sick hen must be killed to keep the flock from infection, and eggs replaced the water in their canteens. Such ruses supplied some additional food for their emaciated bodies. Bobby learned to outwit them at their own game and was able to use his cunning and ability to the good of his troubled men.

Major Bob Davey of Salt Lake City said he heard singing in the nearby jungle and he could hardly believe his ears, for the song was "An Angel From on High." Leaping from his bed he clawed his way through the jungle undergrowth to a little clearing where a half-starved, ragged handful of LDS POW's were gathered to worship the Lord, and our Bobby was leading the song. This Major Davey told us many things about Bobby and how he had learned to understand the Japanese language and was thus able to help many of his buddies who could not understand the guards' commands. This saved them many brutal beatings.

In September, 1944, about 750 of our boys were loaded into an unmarked ship to be sent to Japan. Just a short way out from the island the ship was torpedoed by our U. S. Navy, blowing a large hole in the ship.

The men who were down in the hold of the ship scrambled for safety but the Japanese turned their machine guns on them. Bobby and the company doctor interceded, begging that they be given a chance to escape without being shot at, for they were just a few miles out in Zamboaga Bay. The last time Bobby was seen alive was when he and the doctor leaped into the water to help some of the boys who had been badly wounded. They were trying to keep afloat holding to pieces of debris and trying to aid those who were wounded. When Bobby called for them all to duck to escape the machine gun fire they all dived under, but Bobby was not among those who came up.

For many years George, my husband now deceased, was U. S. Deputy Marshal and handled hundreds of federal prisoners. Included among these charges were many Japanese who were held as spies. Both he and I had let this hatred grow in our hearts, for we felt that every Japanese that we saw was somehow responsible for Bobby's suffering and death. Knowing this, our Federal Judge R. E. Thomason, in deference to our feelings, used other deputies to handle the prisoners of that nationality. Our bitter feelings began to affect our family, and sensing this, we prayed for help to overcome this. Then Brother Kempton, a member of our stake high council, told how he had overcome the bitterness of hatred in his heart for the men who were responsible for the death of his father. After hearing his story, which was much like our own sad one, George and I felt that if Glenn Kempton could master himself and control his feelings we could do it also. And we made greater effort in prayer and fasting for divine help and realized that the Lord can comfort hearts filled with bitterness and hate.

Then you, Brother Kimball, came also to El Paso and we listened carefully to your advice, and you made us understand that before the Lord could put comfort into our torn hearts, we must get hatred and bitterness out of our hearts. Through fasting and prayer and determination we were able to eradicate these feelings. The Lord came to our assistance.

Later, members of the family and a few close friends met in the office of the commander at Ft. Bliss. There was the posthumous presentation of Bobby's medals, among which were two purple hearts and the coveted Bronze Star, five in all.

Sister Brown then tells how a measure of comfort came to her and her husband in Bobby's death when they saw some of the wrecks of bodies and minds which did come home, and when they recognized that there are many things worse than death, and especially when that death comes to a worthy priesthood carrier who goes to eternity clean and free from the sins of the world.

The Kempton Story

My memory takes me back to 1918 and to another story of forgiveness seldom equalled in my experience. It concerns my good friend, Glenn Kempton, who rose to spiritual heights not often attained by mortal man.

In February, 1918, in the Southern Arizona country, there occurred one of the most sensational tragedies of Arizona history. Four officers of the law went into the fastnesses of the mountains to enforce the draft law upon the Powers boys, who had failed to register. Three of the four officers were killed. Well do I remember the funeral, with the three caskets draped with the United States flag, and the three young widows and their nineteen orphaned children sitting on the front rows. Knowing the families intimately, the entire community in the Gila Valley was stirred deeply.

We saw the sweet young widows plod through the years in their loneliness, rearing their nearly a score of children. We saw the youngsters grow to maturity and become prominent in the community, while the Powers boys and Sisson were serving their long and desolate years in the state penitentiary.

When the shooting at Kilburn Canyon was over, "The Powers boys and Sisson fled and for 26 days eluded a posse of more than 3,000 men, including about 200 U. S. Cavalrymen."[2]

The Arizona papers carried big headlines. Excitement was at an all-time high. The whole country was at fever pitch. The men surrendered March 8, 1918, 14 miles below the Mexican border. They were tried, found guilty, and sentenced to life imprisonment in the Arizona Penitentiary.

Forty-two merciless, unending years had passed. Sisson had died three years before. The Powers boys, old men now, were released in April, 1960, by the Arizona Governor and walked out on ". . . their legs still bowed in the parenthesis of horsemen, their receding hair turned grey. Each lost the sight of his left eye in the gunfight."[3]

Our concern now with the tragic story involves this great man, Glenn Kempton, one of the nineteen orphaned children of 1918, who was big enough to forgive. He grew up deprived of a father and was subject to the usual prejudices, hates and bitternesses which would naturally surround a young boy under such circumstances. He has been gracious enough to tell me the story in his own way:

---

[2]*El Paso Times,* May 31, 1960.
[3]*Ibid.*

It happened on the tenth of February, 1918, high in the fastnesses of the Galiuro Mountains in southern Arizona. It was a cold, grey dawn, sky overcast, snow gently falling, when Father was shot down from behind. Two other law officers also lost their lives in the withering blast that emitted forth from the little log-cabin fortress in which the draft evaders had taken refuge.

After a cautious ten or fifteen minutes waiting, they came outside to view the remains of their grisly work. Having satisfied themselves that they had killed the entire party, they bore their father, who had received a mortal wound, into a nearby tunnel, covered him with an old blanket, sent word to a nearby rancher to look after him, saddled their horses and headed south. Destination — Old Mexico!

There followed one of the greatest man-hunts in the southwest history. The draft evaders were finally run down and caught near the Mexican border. They were tried and found guilty of murder, for which they received sentences of life imprisonment.

As a young boy in my early teens, there grew in my heart a bitterness and a hatred toward the confessed slayer of my Father, for Tom Powers had admitted killing my Dad.

The years swept by, I grew up, but still that heavy feeling stayed inside me. High school ended, and then I received a call to go to the Eastern States Mission. There my knowledge and testimony of the gospel grew rapidly, as all of my time was spent studying and preaching it. One day while reading the New Testament, I came to Matthew, fifth chapter, verses 43 to 45, wherein Jesus said:

"Ye have heard that it hath been said, Thou shalt love thy neighbour and hate thine enemy. But I say unto you, Love your enemies, bless them that curse you, do good to them that hate you, and pray for them that despitefully use you and persecute you; that ye may be the children of your Father which is in heaven. . . ."

Here it was, the words of the Savior saying we should forgive. This applied to me. I read those verses again and again and it still meant forgiveness. Not very long after this, I found in the 64th section of the Doctrine and Covenants, verses 9 and 10, more of the Savior's words:

"Wherefore, I say unto you, that ye ought to forgive one another; for he that forgiveth not his brother his trespasses standeth condemned before the Lord; for there remaineth in him the greater sin. I, the Lord, will forgive whom I will forgive, but of you it is required to forgive all men."

And then there were these timely words of President John Taylor:

"Forgiveness is in advance of Justice where repentance is concerned."

I didn't know whether or not Tom Powers had repented but I did know now that I had an appointment to make after I returned home, and I resolved before I left the mission field to do just that.

After returning home, I met and married a fine Latter-day Saint girl, and the Lord blessed our home with five lovely children. The years were passing rapidly and the Lord had been good to us, yet guilt arose within me every time I thought of the appointment I had not kept.

A few years ago, just shortly before Christmas, a season when the love of Christ abounds and the spirit of giving and forgiving gets inside of us, my wife and I were in Phoenix on a short trip. Having concluded our business in the middle of the second afternoon, we started home. As we rode along, I expressed the desire to detour and return home via Florence, for that is where the state prison is located. My wife readily assented.

It was after visiting hours when we arrived but I went on inside and asked for the warden. I was directed to his office.

After I had introduced myself and expressed a desire to meet and talk to Tom Powers, a puzzled expression came over the warden's face, but after only a slight hesitation, he said, "I'm sure that can be arranged." Whereupon he dispatched a guard down into the compound who soon returned with Tom. We were introduced, and led into the parole room where we had a long talk. We went back to that cold, gray February morning thirty years before, re-enacting that whole terrible tragedy. We talked for perhaps an hour and a half. Finally, I said, "Tom, you made a mistake for which you owe a debt to society for which I feel you must continue to pay, just the same as I must continue to pay the price for having been reared without a father."

Then I stood and extended my hand. He stood and took it. I continued, "With all my heart, I forgive you for this awful thing that has come into our lives."

He bowed his head and I left him there. I don't know how he felt then, and I don't know how he feels now, but my witness to you is that it is a glorious thing when bitterness and hatred go out of your heart and forgiveness comes in.

I thanked the warden for his kindness, and as I walked out the door and down that long flight of steps I knew that forgiveness was better than revenge, for I had experienced it.

As we drove toward home in the gathering twilight, a sweet and peaceful calm came over me. Out of pure gratitude I placed my arm around my wife, who understood, for I know that we had now found a broader, richer and more abundant life.

Not only had Glenn Kempton found the joy of forgiving, but the example he set as a faithful Latter-day Saint has had far-reaching influence on many others who know his story and have heard his testimony.

"Blessed are the merciful: for they shall obtain mercy."

Other Modern Examples

There was the young mother who lost her husband. The family had been in poor circumstances, and the insurance policy was only $2,000. The company promptly delivered the check for that amount as soon as proof of death was furnished. The young widow concluded she should save this for emergencies, and accordingly deposited it in the bank. Others knew of her savings, and one kinsman convinced her that she should lend the $2,000 to him at a high rate of interest.

Years passed, and she had received neither principal nor interest and she noticed that the borrower avoided her and made evasive promises when she asked him about the money. Now she needed the money and it could not be had.

"How I hate him!" she told me, and her voice breathed venom and bitterness and her dark eyes flashed. To think that an able-bodied man would defraud a young widow with a family to support! "How I loathe him!" she repeated over and over. Then I told her the Kempton story. She listened intently. I saw she was impressed. At the conclusion there were tears in her eyes, and she whispered: "Thank you. Thank you, sincerely. Surely I, too, must forgive my enemy. I will now cleanse my heart of its bitterness. I do not expect ever to receive the money, but I leave my offender in the hands of the Lord."

Weeks later, she saw me again and confessed that those intervening weeks had been the happiest of her life. A new peace had overshadowed her and she was able to pray for the offender and forgive him, even though she never received back a single dollar.

I saw a woman once whose little girl had been violated. "I will never forgive the culprit so long as I live," she repeated every time it came into her mind. Vicious and ugly was the act. Anyone should be shocked and disturbed at such a crime, but to be unwilling to forgive is not Christlike. The foul deed was done and could *not* be undone. The culprit had been disciplined. In her bitterness the woman shriveled and shrank.

Contrast this woman with the Latter-day Saint girl who climbed the heights of self-control as she forgave the man who disfigured her lovely face. Let the United Press newsman, Neal Corbett, tell her story as it appeared in the pages of the newspapers of the land.

"I would think he must be suffering, anybody who's like that, we ought to feel sorry for him," said April Aaron of the man who had sent her to a hospital for three weeks, following a brutal San Francisco knife attack. April Aaron is a devout Mormon, 22 years of age. . . . She is a secretary who's as pretty as her name, but her face has just one blemish — the right eye is missing, . . . April lost it to the "wildly slashing knife of a purse snatcher," near San Francisco's Golden Gate Park while en route to an MIA dance last April 18. She also suffered deep slashes on her left arm and right leg during a struggle with her assailant, after she tripped and fell in her efforts to elude him just one block from the Mormon chapel. . . .

"I ran for a block and a half before he caught me. You can't run very fast on high heels," April said with a smile. Slashes on her leg were so severe doctors feared for a time it would need amputation. The sharp edge of the weapon could damage neither April's vivaciousness, nor her compassion. ". . . I wish that somebody could do something for him, to help him. He should have some treatment. Who knows what leads a person to do a thing like this? If they don't find him, he's likely to do it again."

. . . April Aaron has won the hearts of the people in San Francisco Bay area with her courage and good spirit in face of tragedy. Her room at St. Francis hospital was banked with flowers throughout her stay and attendants said they couldn't recall when anyone received more cards and expressions of good wishes.

The following is taken from a Los Angeles newspaper
account attesting to the strength of people who have risen
above the sordid revenge and ugly bitterness which so often
prevails in such circumstances:

> . . . The three men apprehended for the kidnap-murder of
> Marvin V. Merrill were Negroes. There are those who could
> fan this incident into an uncontrollable blaze of racial hatred, but
> just the opposite spirit was present at the funeral service last week
> at Matthews Ward. Angelo B. Rollins, a Negro postal employee,
> was selected by the mail-carriers at Wagner Station to represent
> them by reading a eulogy at the services. Elder Merrill had
> served the postal department for more than 20 years. Scattered
> throughout the chapel and overflow room were scores of post-
> men who came directly from their postal routes, still in their
> uniforms. Many of these men were Negroes. . . . Rollins said:
> "No man can condone the actions of the perpetrators who ended
> his life. These vicious and vile acts that make us bow our heads
> in shame, point an accusing finger at innocent millions as a nation
> of offenders. In my sinful weakness, I would have rent them
> limb from limb, but the still small voice of the Master said,
> 'Vengeance is Mine.' . . . This Mormon Elder, Norman Merrill,
> firm in the strength of his faith, and steeped in the teachings of
> Christ, would probably have said of them, as did our Savior at
> Calvary, 'Father, forgive them, for they know not what they do.' "

Reconciliation Through Church Channels

When Church members cannot resolve their mutual
problems alone, they sometimes reach a point where the
Church steps in to help. Such a situation was brought to
my attention several years ago in a case involving two
older Latter-day Saints in the East who had become bitter
enemies to the point where each carried a gun to protect
himself from the other. The cause of their feud was a pur-
chase of property; the contract had been loosely written and
many misunderstandings had arisen. The seller was wealthy;
the buyer was poor. Each was certain his own memory of
the transaction was right. Each made angry accusations,
and feelings steadily became more bitterly intense.

The men were asked to meet with their branch presidents, but they refused to do so because of fear of bodily

harm should they meet each other. The case was scheduled to go to court and lawyers were hired. Through passing months the fires of bitterness flared and antagonism seethed.

Instead of the bitter, revengeful attitude built up, what was the proper thing to do? Paul told the Roman saints:

> Dearly beloved, avenge not yourselves, but rather give place unto wrath: for it is written, Vengeance is mine; I will repay, saith the Lord.
>
> Therefore if thine enemy hunger, feed him; if he thirst, give him drink: for in so doing thou shalt heap coals of fire on his head.
>
> Be not overcome of evil, but overcome evil with good. (Rom. 12:19-21.)

We remember too the injunction of the Lord:

> Resist not evil: but whosoever shall smite thee on thy right cheek, turn to him the other also.
>
> And if any man will sue thee at the law, and take away thy coat, let him have thy cloke also.
>
> And whosoever shall compel thee to go a mile, go with him twain. (Matt. 5:39-41.)

But the two antagonists were far from such thoughts now. Efforts at mediation continued, however, and by persistent efforts of their wise mission president the men were finally brought together in the home of a branch president. All this time the wives of both of the men had been praying almost ceaselessly that an understanding would come and forgiveness would result.

When the matter was fully explained and each point of view had been aired, in the spirit of the gospel both men accepted the decision and offered their hands in forgiveness and fellowship. The seller had in his heart also a real spirit of helpfulness, for in a surprise action he voluntarily signed a check for the full amount that was in dispute and presented it to the buyer who had asked his forgiveness. Thus through the spirit of understanding and forgiveness, the two men and their grateful wives returned to their homes, secure in the thought that all was settled. Peace was established, and in shame the men hid away the two guns, and two men became brothers again. Gifts could now conscientiously be placed on the altar.

> Therefore if thou bring thy gift to the altar, and there rememberest that thy brother hath ought against thee;
>
> Leave there thy gift before the altar, and go thy way; first be reconciled to thy brother, and then come and offer thy gift. (Matt. 5:23-24.)

Litigation Between Church Members

Paul takes the principle of forgiveness one step further when he suggests that for one Church member even to accept an injustice from another member is preferable to a court action. Disputes ought rather to be settled through channels of Church authority. Does one love his neighbor if he hales him into the courts? Paul found this fault among his Corinthian converts, and admonished them:

> Dare any of you, having a matter against another, go to law before the unjust, and not before the saints?
>
> But brother goeth to law with brother, and that before the unbelievers.
>
> Now therefore there is utterly a fault among you, because ye go to law one with another. Why do ye not rather take wrong? Why do ye not rather suffer yourselves to be defrauded? (1 Cor. 6:1, 6-7.)

Pride or Peace?

Frequently, pride gets in our way and becomes our stumbling block. But each of us needs to ask himself the question: "Is your pride more important than your peace?"

All too frequently, one who has done many splendid things in life and made an excellent contribution will let pride cause him to lose the rich reward to which he would be entitled otherwise. We should always wear the sackcloth and ashes of a forgiving heart and a contrite spirit, being willing always to exercise genuine humility, as did the publican, and ask the Lord to help us to forgive.

In 1906, my father received a letter from his dear friend, Matthias F. Cowley, who had been greatly embarrassed by being dropped from the Council of the Twelve. His letter showed great courage and a sweet, unembittered spirit: "In relation to the trial which has come to me, I will say that I accept it in all humility and meekness, with no fault to find against my brethren, but a strong desire to continue faithful and to devote my life and all my energies in the service of the Lord."

In the Spirit of Love

Inspired by the Lord Jesus Christ, Paul has given to us the solution to the problems of life which require understanding and forgiveness. "And be ye kind one to another, tender-hearted, forgiving one another, even as God for Christ's sake hath forgiven you." (Eph. 4:32.) If this spirit of kindly, tender-hearted forgiveness of one another could be carried into every home, selfishness, distrust and bitterness which break so many homes and families would disappear and men would live in peace.

This forgiving spirit has a quantitative as well as a qualitative aspect. Forgiveness cannot be a one-time program. Undoubtedly, Peter had been annoyed by some who were repeaters and who even after they were forgiven returned to their sin. To clear this up, he asked the Redeemer:

> Lord, how oft shall my brother sin against me, and I forgive him? till seven times?

> Jesus saith unto him, I say not unto thee, Until seven times: but, Until seventy times seven. (Matt. 18:21-22.)

This is in accord, of course, with the Master's teaching and practice of the highest gospel law, the law of love:

> A new commandment I give unto you, That ye love one another; as I have loved you, that ye also love one another.

> By this shall all men know that ye are my disciples, if ye have love one to another. (John 13:34-35.)

Difficult but Possible

Hard to do? Of course. The Lord never promised an easy road, nor a simple gospel, nor low standards, nor a low norm. The price is high, but the goods attained are worth all they cost. The Lord himself turned the other cheek; he suffered himself to be buffeted and beaten without remonstrance; he suffered every indignity and yet spoke no word of condemnation. And his question to all of us is: "Therefore, what manner of men ought ye to be?" And his answer to us is: "Even as I am." (3 Ne. 27:27.)

In his *Prince of Peace*, William Jennings Bryan wrote:

> The most difficult of all the virtues to cultivate is the forgiving spirit. Revenge seems to be natural with man; it is human to want to get even with an enemy. It has even been popular to boast of vindictiveness; it was once inscribed on a man's monument that he had repaid both friends and enemies more than he had received. This was not the spirit of Christ.

If we have been wronged or injured, forgiveness means to blot it completely from our minds. To forgive and forget is an ageless counsel. "To be wronged or robbed," said the Chinese philosopher Confucius, "is nothing unless you continue to remember it."

The injuries inflicted by neighbors, by relatives, or by spouses are generally of a minor nature, at least at first. We must forgive them. Since the Lord is so merciful, must not we be? "Blessed are the merciful, for they shall obtain mercy" is another version of the golden rule. "All manner of sin and blasphemy shall be forgiven unto men" said the Lord, "but the blasphemy against the Holy Ghost shall not be forgiven unto men." If the Lord is so gracious and kind, we must be also.

Sometimes the poets in their expressive lines touch our hearts even better than prose could. John Greenleaf Whittier gave us these thought-provoking lines:

> My heart was heavy, for its trust had been
> Abused, its kindness answered with foul wrong;
> So turning gloomily from my fellow men,

> One summer Sabbath day I strolled among
> The green mounds of the village burial-place;
> Where, pondering how all human love and hate
> Find one sad level; and how, soon or late,
> Wronged and wrongdoer, each with meekened face,
> And cold hands folded over a still heart,
> Pass the threshold of our common grave,
> Whither all footsteps tend, whence none depart,
> Awed for myself, and pitying my race,
> Our common sorrow, like a mighty wave,
> Swept all my pride away, and, trembling, I forgave.

When such people as the widow, Bishop Kempton, the Browns, and others grievously wronged can forgive; when men like Stephen and Paul can forgive vicious attacks against themselves and set the example of forgiveness; then all men should be able to forgive in their reach for perfection.

Across the barren deserts of hate and greed and grudge is the beautiful valley of paradise. We read in the papers and hear on TV constantly that the world "is in an awful mess." Not true! The world is still most beautiful. It is man who is off center. The sun still illumines the day and gives light and life to all things; the moon still brightens the night; oceans still feed the world and provide transportation; rivers still drain the land, and provide irrigation water to nourish crops. Even the ravages of time have not sloughed off the majesty of the mountains. Flowers still bloom and birds still sing, and children still laugh and play. What is wrong with the world is man-made.

It can be done. Man can conquer self. Man can overcome. Man can forgive all who have trespassed against him and go on to receive *peace* in this life and eternal life in the world to come.

Chapter Twenty

A Time of Reckoning

*. . . Prepare the saints for the hour
of judgment which is to come;
That their souls may escape the
wrath of God, the desolation of
abomination which awaits the
wicked, both in this world and in
the world to come. . .*

—Doctrine & Covenants 88:84-85

OF TWO VERY IMPORTANT THINGS WE MAY BE ABSO-
lutely certain — that it is not vain to serve the Lord,
and that *the day of judgment will come to all,* the righteous
and the unrighteous.

The time of reckoning is as sure as is the passage of time
and the coming of eternity. All who live shall eventually
stand before the bar of God to be judged according to their
works. Their final assignments will constitute rewards and
punishments according to the kinds of lives they lived on
earth.

Prosperity of the Wicked Is Temporary

It is on this assurance that we must pin our faith and
build our lives; let the wicked do what they will. Some
time ago a sister said to me: "Why is it that those who do
the least in the building of the kingdom seem to prosper
most? We drive a Ford; our neighbors drive a Cadillac.

We observe the Sabbath and attend our meetings; they play golf, hunt, fish, and play. We abstain from the forbidden; they eat, drink and are merry and unrestrained. We pay much for tithing and for other Church donations; they have their entire large income to lavish upon themselves. We are tied to home with our large family of small children, who are often ill; they are totally free for social life — to dine and dance. We wear cottons and woolens, and I wear a three-season coat; they wear silks and costly apparel, and she wears a mink coat. Our meager income is always strained and never seems adequate for necessities, while their wealth seems inexhaustible and wholly adequate for every luxury obtainable. And yet the Lord promises blessings to the faithful! It seems to me that it does not pay to live the gospel — that the proud and the covenant-breakers are the ones who prosper."

In reply, I said to this sister: "As I remember, Job in his great distress made a statement which parallels yours."

> But Job answered [Zophar] and said,
>
> Wherefore do the wicked live, become old, yea, are mighty in power?
>
> Their seed is established in their sight with them, and their offspring before their eyes.
>
> Their houses are safe from fear, neither is the rod of God upon them.
>
> Their bull gendereth, and faileth not; their cow calveth, and casteth not her calf.
>
> They send forth their little ones like a flock, and their children dance.
>
> They spend their days in wealth, and in a moment go down to the grave.
>
> Therefore they say unto God, Depart from us; for we desire not the knowledge of thy ways.
>
> What is the Almighty, that we should serve him? and what profit should we have, if we pray unto him? (Job 21:1, 7-11, 13-15.)

The Prophet Jeremiah asked a similar question:

> Righteous art thou, O Lord, when I plead with thee: yet let me talk with thee of thy judgments: Wherefore doth the way of

the wicked prosper? wherefore are all they happy that deal very treacherously?

How long shall the land mourn, and the herbs of every field wither, for the wickedness of them that dwell therein. . . . (Jer. 12:1, 4.)

Again, Malachi quotes the Lord as saying:

Your words have been stout against me, saith the Lord. Yet ye say, What have we spoken so much against thee?

Ye have said, It is vain to serve God: and what profit is it that we have kept his ordinance, and that we have walked mournfully before the Lord of hosts?

And now we call the proud happy; yea, they that work wickedness are set up: yea, they that tempt God are even delivered. (Mal. 3:13-15.)

Judgment Will Inevitably Come

For those who are concerned with this problem — and there are many — the Lord has given his answer in the parable of the wheat and tares:

. . . The kingdom of heaven is likened unto a man which sowed good seed in his field:

But while men slept, his enemy came and sowed tares among the wheat, and went his way.

But when the blade was sprung up, and brought forth fruit, then appeared the tares also.

So the servants of the householder came and said unto him, Sir, didst not thou sow good seed in thy field? from whence then hath it tares?

He said unto them, An enemy hath done this. The servants said unto them, Wilt thou then that we go and gather them up?

But he said, Nay; lest while ye gather up the tares, ye root up also the wheat with them.

Let both grow together until the harvest: and in the time of harvest I will say to the reapers, Gather ye together first the tares, and bind them in bundles to burn them: but gather the wheat into my barn. (Matt. 13:24-30.)

The interpretation of the parable given by the Lord himself makes clear that the books are not balanced daily,

but rather at the harvest time — in the day of judgment.
Malachi records more on this subject:

> Then they that feared the Lord spake often one to another:
> and the Lord hearkened, and heard it, and a book of remem-
> brance was written before him for them that feared the Lord,
> and that thought upon his name.
>
> And they shall be mine, saith the Lord of hosts, *in that day
> when I make up my jewels;* and I will spare them, as a man
> spareth his own son that serveth him.
>
> Then shall ye return, and discern between the righteous and
> the wicked, between him that serveth God and him that serveth
> him not. (Mal. 3:16-18. Italics added.)

From the same prophet's writings comes this:

> For, behold, the day cometh, that shall burn as an oven; and
> all the proud, yea, and all that do wickedly, shall be stubble:
> and the day that cometh shall burn them up, saith the Lord of
> hosts, that it shall leave them neither root nor branch.
>
> But unto you that fear my name shall the Sun of righteous-
> ness arise with healing in his wings. . . . (Mal. 4:1-2.)

I said to the disconsolate sister, "You have many blessings *today*. For many rewards, you need not wait until the
judgment day. You have your family of lovely children.
What a rich reward for the so-called sacrifices! The great
boon of motherhood is yours. With your limitations, a great
peace can fill your soul. These and numerous other blessings which you enjoy cannot be purchased with all your
neighbor's wealth." Then I reminded her of the parable
of the net and fishes, which goes as follows:

> Again, the kingdom of heaven is like unto a net, that was
> cast into the sea, and gathered of every kind:
>
> Which, when it was full, they drew to shore, and sat down,
> and gathered the good into vessels, but cast the bad away.
>
> So shall it be at the end of the world: the angels shall come
> forth, and sever the wicked from among the just,
>
> And shall cast them into the furnace of fire: there shall be
> wailing and gnashing of teeth. (Matt. 13:47-50.)

People who are concerned about the prosperity of the
wicked are sometimes blinded to their own weaknesses yet

magnify greatly the errors of others. If other men make errors or deliberately break laws and commandments, we may be sure that they will pay the "uttermost farthing." They will not escape the wrath of God, and they will pay the full price for their folly. There will be a wise and just God to sit in judgment on all men. There could be a delay in judgment. The wicked may prosper for a time, the rebellious may seem to profit by their transgressions, but the time is coming when, at the bar of justice, all men will be judged, "every man according to their works." (Rev. 20:13.) No one will "get by" with anything. On that day no one will escape the penalty of his deeds, no one will fail to receive the blessings he has earned. Again, the parable of the sheep and the goats gives us assurance that there will be total justice. (See Matt. 25:31-46.)

Mortal Blessings for Obedience

At times when we are inclined to think it is vain to serve the Lord, we should stir our faith, believe in the rich promises of God, and obey — and patiently wait. The Lord will fulfill all his rich promises to us. Paul says:

> . . . Eye hath not seen, nor ear heard, neither have entered into the heart of man, the things which God hath prepared for them that love him. (1 Cor. 2:9.)

Even for the present life, great blessings are promised to the obedient. Take, for example, the promise to the tithe-payer:

> Bring ye all the tithes into the storehouse, that there may be meat in mine house, and prove me now herewith, saith the Lord of hosts, if I will not open you the windows of heaven, and pour you out a blessing, that there shall not be room enough to receive it.
>
> And I will rebuke the devourer for your sakes, and he shall not destroy the fruits of your ground; neither shall your vine cast her fruit before the time in the field, saith the Lord of hosts.
>
> And all nations shall call you blessed. . . . (Mal. 3:10-12.)

To the faithful, lavish rewards are offered. Blessings beyond one's understanding will come. The land will yield bounteously and peace will abound. Of course, the proud, the unfaithful, the greedy wealthy, can never enjoy the sweet savor of the rewards for fasting and dispensing to the poor:

> Then [if ye live these commandments] shall thy light break forth as the morning, and thine health shall spring forth speedily: and thy righteousness shall go before thee; the glory of the Lord shall be thy rereward.
>
> Then shalt thou call, and the Lord shall answer; thou shalt cry, and he shall say, Here I am. . . .
>
> . . . Then shall thy light rise in obscurity, and thy darkness be as the noon day:
>
> And the Lord shall guide thee continually, and satisfy thy soul in drought, and make fat thy bones: and thou shalt be like a watered garden, and like a spring of water, whose waters fail not. (Isa. 58:8-11.)

What more could one ask? The companionship of the Lord, light and knowledge, health and vigor, constant guidance by the Lord as an eternal, never-failing spring! What more could one desire? And in our modern scripture there are still other great promises for the faithful who seek to serve the Lord:

> And [they] shall find wisdom and great treasures of knowledge, even hidden treasures;
>
> And shall run and not be weary, and shall walk and not faint.
>
> And I, the Lord, give unto them a promise, that the destroying angel shall pass by them, as the children of Israel, and not slay them. Amen. (D&C 89:19-21.)

Rich Promises for Eternity

Great as are the blessings in mortality which follow righteousness, they are dwarfed beside those awaiting in the world to come. Naturally the faithful are required to renounce some of the things of this world as they reach after those of the eternal world. This is often thought of as a sacrifice, though those who eventually reach the heights will certainly not think so then. Listen to the words of the Savior on the results of genuine sacrifice for the kingdom:

And every one that hath forsaken houses, or brethren, or sisters, or father, or mother, or wife, or children, or lands, for my name's sake, shall receive an hundredfold, and shall inherit everlasting life. (Matt. 19:29.)

The one who delights in all of the worldly luxuries of today, at the expense of spirituality, is living but for the moment. His day is now. He will be barred from the rewards of the higher life he rejected.

In the impressive parable of the Prodigal Son the Lord taught us a remarkable lesson. This squanderer lived but for today. He spent his life in riotous living. He disregarded the commandments of God. His inheritance was expendable, and he spent it. He was never to enjoy it again, as it was irretrievably gone. No quantity of tears or regrets or remorse could bring it back. Even though his father forgave him and dined him and clothed him and kissed him, he could not give back to the profligate son that which had been dissipated. But the other brother, who had been faithful, loyal, righteous and constant, retained his inheritance, and the father reassured him: "All that I have is thine."

This parable of the Prodigal Son repays our closer analysis. It is contained in Luke 15:11-32.

> . . . A certain man had two sons:
>
> And the younger of them said to his father, Father, give me the portion of goods that falleth to me. And he divided unto them his living.
>
> And not many days after the younger son gathered all together, and took his journey into a far country, and there wasted his substance with riotous living.
>
> And when he had spent all, there arose a mighty famine in that land; and he began to be in want.
>
> And he went and joined himself to a citizen of that country; and he sent him into the fields to feed swine.
>
> And he would fain have filled his belly with the husks that the swine did eat: and no man gave unto him.
>
> And when he came to himself, he said, How many hired servants of my father's have bread enough and to spare, and I perish with hunger!

I will arise and go to my father, and will say unto him, Father, I have sinned against heaven, and before thee.

And am no more worthy to be called thy son: make me as one of thy hired servants.

Thus resolved, the son made his way homeward, and his father, seeing him coming home, went out to meet him, welcomed him back with a kiss, an embrace, and genuine compassion and forgiveness.

The son admitted his prodigality: "Father, I have sinned against heaven, and in thy sight, and am no more worthy to be called thy son." He did not ask for servant status as he had thought to do, perhaps because with such a warm welcome he may have had hopes of total reinstatement; for the happy father spread over him the best robe, put a ring on his hand and shoes on his feet, and killed the fatted calf to celebrate the great occasion as he expressed his joy in these words: "For this my son was dead, and is alive again; he was lost, and is found."

The elder son, on returning from his work in the field, was angered at the display of lavish festivities for the brother who had wasted his all with harlots, and he complained to his father, who entreated him to join the party:

. . . Lo, these many years do I serve thee, neither transgressed I at any time thy commandment: and yet thou never gavest me a kid, that I might make merry with my friends.

To this the father might have said something like this: "Son, this is your estate — all of it. Everything is yours. Your brother has squandered his part. You have everything. He has nothing but employment and our forgiveness and our love. We can well afford to receive him graciously. We will not give him your estate nor can we give him back all that he has foolishly squandered." He did say: "For this thy brother was dead, and is alive again; and was lost, and is found . . ." And he said also: "Son, thou art ever with me, and all that I have is thine."

Is there not significance in that statement of the father? Does not that signify eternal life?

When I was a child in Sunday School my teacher impressed upon me the contemptibility of the older son in his anger and complaining, while she immortalized the adulterous prodigal who was presumed to have expressed repentance. But let no reader compare grumbling and peevishness with the degrading sins of immorality and consorting with harlots in riotous living. John mentioned, "There is a sin unto death," and the younger son's transgressions might approach that terrifying condition if he did not repent and turn from his evil course. Elder Talmage comments as follows upon the sins of the two brothers:

> We are not justified in extolling the virtue of repentance on the part of the prodigal above the faithful, plodding service of his brother, who had remained at home, true to the duties required of him. The devoted son was the heir; the father did not disparage his worth, nor deny his desserts. His displeasure over the rejoicing incident to the return of his wayward brother was an exhibition of illiberality and narrowness; but of the two brothers the elder was the more faithful, whatever his minor defects may have been. . . .

> . . . Not a word appears in condonation or excuse for the prodigal's sin; upon that the Father could not look with the least degree of allowance; but over that sinner's repentance and contrition of soul, God and the household of heaven rejoiced.

> . . . There is no justification for the inference that a repentant sinner is to be given precedence over a righteous soul who has resisted sin; were such the way of God, then Christ, the one sinless Man, would be surpassed in the Father's esteem by regenerate offenders. Unqualifiedly offensive as is sin, the sinner is yet precious in the Father's eyes, because of the possibility of his repentance and return to righteousness. The loss of a soul is a very real and a very great loss to God. He is pained and grieved thereby, for it is his will that not one should perish.[1]

This superb parable contains many lessons which relate to the material in this book. It teaches the importance of remaining pure and undefiled and retaining virtue and righteousness; and it teaches the heavy penalties of transgression. It emphasizes the principle of repentance as a means of forgiveness and recovery of self. It teaches the

---

[1] Talmage, *Jesus the Christ,* pp. 460-461.

ugliness of pride, jealousy, peevishness, lack of understanding, and anger; and it stresses the glorious and ultimate blessings which are available to the worthy, even though they may exhibit some minor weaknesses.

The prodigal son certainly had every opportunity to enjoy permanently a full and valuable estate with resultant comforts, joys, harmony and peace. He had security. All was available to him until he left the path and dissipated his fortune, hating his birthright. He had demanded from his father, ". . . the portion of goods that falleth to me." He took it "all" into a far country, and there, pressed by the demands of a carnal world, wasted his substance with riotous living. He spent "all" of his estate and was relegated to penury and hunger.

He admitted rather than confessed his broken covenants. And what a difference between admission and confession! He acknowledged his unworthiness but said not a word about changing from unrighteousness to purity through a reformed life. "Coming to himself" seems to be more a realization of his physical plight, his hunger pangs and his unemployment, than a true repentance. Is there here any reference to new goals, a transformed life, escalating ideals and attitudes? He talked about bread of the oven rather than the "bread of life" — the water of the well rather than the "Living Water." He said nothing about filling a crown with jewels of righteous accomplishments, but made much of filling a stomach which was shriveled by near starvation.

The older son's being ever with his father is significant. If this parable is a reminder of life's journey, we remember that for the faithful who live the commandments there is a great promise of seeing the Lord and being with him always in exaltation. On the other hand, the younger son could hope for no more than salvation as a servant, since he "despised his birthright," and dissipated "all" of his inheritance, leaving nothing to develop and accumulate toward eternal heirship again. He had sold it for a mess of pottage as did Esau, another prodigal.

He had sold something he could not recover. He had exchanged the priceless inheritance of great lasting value for a temporary satisfaction of physical desire, the future for the present, eternity for time, spiritual blessings for physical meat. Though he was sorry for his rash trade, it was now so late, "everlastingly too late." Apparently neither his efforts nor his tears could retrieve his lost blessings. Thus God will forgive the repentant sinner who sins against divine law, but that forgiveness can never restore the losses he sustained during the period of his sinning.

But many wrongs can be repaired if repentance is sincere. President Joseph F. Smith amplified this thought as follows:

When we commit sin, it is necessary that we repent of it and make restitution as far as lies in our power. When we cannot make restitution for the wrong we have done, then we must apply for the grace and mercy of God to cleanse us from that iniquity.

Men cannot forgive their own sins; they cannot cleanse themselves from the consequences of their sins. Men can stop sinning and can do right in the future, and so far their acts are acceptable before the Lord and worthy of consideration. But who shall repair the wrongs they have done to themselves and to others, which it seems impossible for them to repair themselves? By the atonement of Jesus Christ the sins of the repentant shall be washed away; though they be crimson they shall be made white as wool. This is the promise given to you. We who have not paid our tithing in the past, and are therefore under obligations to the Lord, which we are not in position to discharge, the Lord requires that no longer at our hands, but will forgive us for the past if we will observe this law honestly in the future. That is generous and kind, and I feel grateful for it.[2]

When one realizes the vastness, the richness, the glory of that "all" which the Lord promises to bestow upon his faithful, it is worth all it costs in patience, faith, sacrifice, sweat and tears. The blessings of eternity contemplated in this "all" bring men immortality and everlasting life, eternal growth, divine leadership, eternal increase, perfection, and with it all, godhood.

---

[2]*Conference Report*, October, 1899, p. 42.

The Judgment Bar

That man must face the day of reckoning and stand before the bar of judgment to receive the rewards of righteousness or the penalties of sinfulness is amply attested in the scriptures. It will be a day when man cannot hide from his wickedness, for his deeds shall speak out against him accusingly, as Alma predicts:

> And now I ask of you, my brethren, how will any of you feel, if ye shall stand before the bar of God, having your garments stained with blood and all manner of filthiness? Behold, what will these things testify against you? (Al. 5:22.)

After describing the redemption of man by the Savior, Jesus Christ, a "redemption from an endless sleep, from which sleep all men shall be awakened by the power of God when the trump shall sound . . . ," Moroni told his hearers:

> And then cometh the judgment of the Holy One upon them; and then cometh the time that he that is filthy shall be filthy still; and he that is righteous shall be righteous still; he that is happy shall be happy still; and he that is unhappy shall be unhappy still. (Morm. 9:14.)

The judgment bar of God is spoken of in the very last verse in the Book of Mormon, where Moroni, ready to close up the record of his people, wrote:

> And now I bid unto all, farewell. I soon go to rest in the paradise of God, until my spirit and body shall again reunite, and I am brought forth triumphant through the air, to meet you before the pleasing bar of the Great Jehovah, the Eternal Judge of both quick and dead. Amen. (Moro. 10:34.)

Making a plea for repentance to avoid the awfulness of the punishment which is to be meted out to the wicked on the day of judgment, Jacob said:

> Know ye not that if ye will do these things, that the power of the redemption and the resurrection, which is in Christ, will bring you to stand with shame and awful guilt before the bar of God?

O then, my beloved brethren, repent ye, and enter in at the strait gate, and continue in the way which is narrow, until ye shall obtain eternal life.

O be wise; what can I say more?

Finally, I bid you farewell, until I shall meet you before the pleasing bar of God, which bar striketh the wicked with awful dread and fear. (Jac. 6:9, 11-13.)

And who will the judges be who will so justly hear our cases? Hundreds of years before Christ came to earth, in vision Nephi ". . . saw the heavens open, and the Lamb of God descending out of heaven . . . the Holy Ghost fell upon twelve others; and they were ordained of God, and chosen." (1 Ne. 12:6-7.) The angel then told Nephi:

Behold the twelve disciples of the Lamb, who are chosen to minister unto thy seed.

And these twelve ministers whom thou beholdest shall judge thy seed. . . . (1 Ne. 12:8, 10.]

The angel also said:

Thou rememberest the twelve apostles of the Lamb [i.e., those called in Palestine]? Behold they are they who shall judge the twelve tribes of Israel; wherefore, the twelve ministers of thy seed shall be judged of them; for ye are of the house of Israel. (1 Ne. 12:9.)

This ties in with the Savior's answer to Peter, who asked: "Behold, we have forsaken all, and followed thee; what shall we have therefore?" (Matt. 19:27.) The Redeemer's reply was to the point:

. . . Verily I say unto you, That ye which have followed me, in the regeneration when the Son of man shall sit in the throne of his glory, ye also shall sit upon twelve thrones, judging the twelve tribes of Israel. (Matt. 19:28.)

Repent in Mortality

I have referred previously to the significance of this life in the application of repentance but will emphasize it here in relation to the eventual judgment. One cannot delay repentance until the next life, the spirit world, and there prepare properly for the day of judgment while the ordinance work is done for him vicariously on earth. It must be remembered that vicarious work for the dead is for those who could not do the work for themselves. Men and women who live in mortality and who have heard the gospel here have had their day, their seventy years to put their lives in harmony, to perform the ordinances, to repent and to perfect their lives.

The people of Noah's day heard the message of the gospel from prophets of God. They lived worldly lives. They ate, drank and were merry. They also married and gave in marriage, which means broken homes, divorces and worldly living. They ignored the many testimonies of preachers of righteousness. Then they died by drowning. The harvest had come for them. The end of their "day" had come and the "night" was to be dark and long. They waited for what must have seemed to them an interminable period; and finally the Savior came and through his missionary program taught them again the gospel, giving them a chance to repent. But did they receive the blessings of earthly faithfulness? Read again this from the Doctrine and Covenants relative to inhabitants of the terrestrial world:

> And also they who are the spirits of men kept in prison, whom the Son visited, and preached the gospel unto them, that they might be judged according to men in the flesh;
>
> Who received not the testimony of Jesus in the flesh, but afterwards received it. (D&C 76:73-74.)

Were they ever to receive the celestial kingdom? They had had their opportunity; they had wasted the days of their probation; they had ignored the testimonies of the servants of God; they had followed the world and lived a worldly life. Perhaps many of them had taken the attitude, "I am not the religious kind." "I do not like to go to meetings." "I'm too busy; I can't be bothered." "I have other things of more interest."

Again, undoubtedly many of those people in that spirit prison, like their brothers of this generation, must have been good people in the sense of not being criminal. They must have been "honorable men of the earth." Perhaps many of them were honest, good neighbors, good citizens, and committed no heinous crime, but were not valiant. Are not the scriptures very clear that they have lost their opportunity for exaltation? Is it not clear that it was everlastingly too late for them when they had drowned, that they had wasted their days?

The terrestrial kingdom will not be enjoyed by the very wicked, for they shall obtain only the telestial. Neither will the terrestrial be given to the valiant, the faithful, the perfected, for they will go into the celestial kingdom prepared for those who live the celestial laws. But into the terrestrial will go those who do not measure up to the celestial. Speaking of one category of terrestrial people, the Lord says: "These are they who are not valiant in the testimony of Jesus; wherefore, they obtain not the crown over the kingdom of our God." (D&C 76:79.) The "unvaliant" Latter-day Saint will find himself there.

It is true that repentance is always worth while. But spirit world repentance cannot recompense for that which could and should have been done on earth.

Judgment Upon Nations

Just as blessings for the righteous are promised for this life, so are judgments for the wicked, and this is true of nations as well as individuals. Our world is in turmoil. Its ills have frequently been diagnosed, and complex diseases catalogued. But any remedies applied have been ineffective, infection has set in, and the patient's suffering intensifies.

In an ancient situation somewhat comparable to our own there was a great destruction, and when the quiet came, those who were spared were wailing:

> O that we had repented before this great and terrible day, and then would our brethren have been spared . . . [and] our mothers and our fair daughters, and our children . . . not have been buried. . . . (3 Ne. 8:24-25.)

Today is another day it is true, but history repeats itself. Men have "been destroyed from generation to generation according to their iniquities; and never hath any of them been destroyed save it were foretold them by the prophets of the Lord." (2 Ne. 25:9.) And modern prophets are warning frequently and constantly that people are being destroyed by their own acts.

The Plight of America

America is a great and glorious land. It is "choice above all other lands." It has a tragic and bloody past, but could have a glorious and peaceful future, if the inhabitants would really learn to serve their God. It was consecrated as a land of promise to the people of the Americas, to whom God gave these conditional promises:

It will be a land of liberty to its people.

They shall never be brought down into captivity.

There shall be none to molest them.

It is a land of promise.

It shall be free from bondage.

It shall be free from all nations under heaven.

There shall be no enemies come into this land.

There shall be no kings upon the land.

This land shall be fortified against all other nations.

He that fighteth against Zion shall perish.

The Lord made these promises. But generous though they may be, desirable as they are, they can come to pass only "if they [the inhabitants] will but serve the God of this land, who is Jesus Christ."

Jesus Christ our Lord is under no obligation to save us, except insofar as we repent. We have ignored him, disbelieved him, and failed to follow him. We have changed the laws and broken the everlasting covenant. We stand at his mercy, which will be extended only if we repent. But to what extent have we repented? Another prophet said,

"We call evil good and good evil." We have rationalized ourselves into thinking we are "not so bad." We see evil in our enemies, but none in ourselves. Are we fully ripe? Has the rot of age and flabbiness set in? Will we change?

Apparently we would rather do things the devil's way than the Lord's way. It seems, for instance, that we would rather tax ourselves into slavery than pay our tithing; rather build shelters and missiles and bombs than drop to our knees with our families in solemn prayer, night and morning, to our God who would give us protection.

It seems that, rather than fast and pray, we prefer to gorge ourselves at the banquet tables and drink cocktails. Instead of disciplining ourselves, we yield to physical urges and carnal desires. Instead of investing in building our bodies and beautifying our souls, we spend billions of dollars on liquor and tobacco, and other body-destroying, soul-stultifying concoctions.

Too many of our wives and mothers prefer the added luxuries of two incomes to the satisfactions of seeing children grow up in the fear and love of God. We golf and boat and hunt and fish and watch sports rather than solemnize the Sabbath. Total morality is found neither among the people nor among the leaders of the state and nation. Personal interests and ulterior motives block the way. Old Man "Rationalization" with his long beard is ever present to tell us that we are justified in these deviations, and because we are not vicious enough to be confined in penitentiaries we rationalize that we are not failing to measure up. The masses of the people are perhaps much like those who escaped destruction in the ancient days of this continent. The Lord said to them:

> O all ye that are spared because ye were more righteous than they [the slain ones], will ye not now return unto me, and repent of your sins, and be converted, that I may heal you? (3 Ne. 9:13.)

"Experience keeps a dear school," said Benjamin Franklin, "but fools will learn in no other." Thus, as a nation we continue in our godlessness. While the iron curtains fall and thicken we eat, drink, and make merry. While armies are marshalled and march and drill and officers teach men how to kill, we continue to drink and carouse as usual. While bombs are detonated and tested, and fallout settles on the already sick world, we continue in idolatry and adultery.

While corridors are threatened and concessions are made, we live riotously, and divorce and marry in cycles, like the seasons. While leaders quarrel and editors write and authorities analyze and prognosticate, we break all the laws in God's catalog. While enemies filter into our nation to subvert and intimidate and soften us, we continue on with our destructive thinking — "It can't happen here."

If we would but believe the prophets! For they have warned that if the inhabitants of this land are ever brought down into captivity and enslaved, *it shall be because of iniquity; for if iniquity shall abound cursed shall be the land . . ."* (2 Ne. 1:7.) This is a land which the Lord has preserved *". . . for a righteous people . . ."* (Eth. 2:7. Italics added.)

> And now, we can behold the decrees of God concerning this land, that it is a land of promise; and whatsoever nation shall possess it shall serve God, or they shall be swept off when the fullness of his wrath shall come upon them. And the fullness of his wrath shall come upon them when they are ripened in iniquity. (Eth. 2:9.)

God the True Protector

O that men would listen! Why should there be spiritual blindness in the day of brightest scientific and technological vision? Why must men rely on physical fortifications and armaments when the God of heaven yearns to bless them? One stroke of his omnipotent hand could make powerless all nations who oppose, and save a world even when in its death throes. Yet men shun God and put their trust in weapons of war, in the "arm of flesh."

All this continues despite the lessons of history. The great wall of China, with its 1,500 miles of impenetrable walls, its 25-foot-high impregnableness, its innumerable watchtowers, was breached by the treachery of man. The Maginot Line in France, those forts thought to be so strong and impassable, were bypassed as though they were not there.

The walls of Babylon were too high to be scaled, too thick to be broken, too strong to be crumbled, but not too deep to be undermined when the human element failed. When the protectors sleep and the leaders are incapacitated with banqueting and drunkenness and immorality, an invading enemy can turn a river out of its course and enter through a river bed.

The precipitous walls on the high hills of Jerusalem deflected for a time the arrows and spears of enemies, the catapults and firebrands of besieging armies. But even then the wickedness did not lessen; men did not learn lessons. Hunger scaled the walls; thirst broke down the gates; immorality, idolatry, godlessness, even cannibalism stalked about till destruction came.

Will we ever turn wholly to God? Fear envelops the world which could be at ease and peace. In God is protection, peace, safety. He has said, *"I will fight your battles."* But his commitment is on condition of our faithfulness. He promised to the children of Israel:

I will give you rain in due season.

The land shall yield her increase and trees their fruit.

Granaries and barns will bulge in seed-time and harvest.

Ye shall eat your bread in abundance.

Ye shall dwell in your land safely and none shall make you afraid.

Neither shall the sword go through your land.

And five of you shall chase an hundred and an hundred of you shall put ten thousand to flight.

In view of the promises God has given respecting America, who can doubt that he would be willing to do the same for us as for ancient Israel? Conversely, should we not expect the same punishments if we fail to serve him? To ancient Israel these were listed.

The land will be barren (perhaps radioactive or dry from drought).

The trees will be without fruit and the fields without verdure.

There will be rationing and a scarcity of food, and sore hunger.

No traffic will jam your desolate highways.

Famine will stalk rudely through your doors and the ogre of cannibalism will rob you of your children and your remaining virtues will disintegrate.

There will be pestilence uncontrollable.

Your dead bodies will be piled upon the materialistic things you sought so hard to accumulate and save.

I will give no protection against enemies.

They that hate you shall reign over you.

There will be faintness of heart, "and the sound of a shaken leaf" shall chase you into flight, and you will flee when none pursue.

Your power — your supremacy — your pride in superiority — will be broken.

Your heaven shall be as iron and your earth as brass. Heaven will not hear your pleadings nor earth bring forth its harvest.

Your strength will be spent in vain as you plow and plant and cultivate.

Your cities will be shambles; your churches in ruins.

Your enemies will be astonished at the barrenness, sterility, desolation of the land they had been told was

so choice, so beautiful, so fruitful. Then shall the land
enjoy her Sabbaths under compulsion.

You shall have no power to stand before your
enemies.

Your people will be scattered among the nations as
slaves and bondsmen.

You will pay tribute and bondage, and fetters shall
bind you.

What a bleak prediction! Yet "these are the statutes
and judgments and laws, which the Lord made between
him and the children of Israel in Mount Sinai by the hand
of Moses." (Lev. 26:46.) The Israelites failed to heed the
warning. They ignored the prophets. They suffered the
fulfillment of every dire prophecy.

Do we twentieth-century people have reason to think
that we can be immune from the same tragic consequences
of sin and debauchery if we ignore the same divine laws?

The outlook is bleak, but the impending tragedy can
be averted. Nations, like individuals, must "repent or suffer." There is only one cure for the earth's sick condition.
That infallible cure is simply *righteousness, obedience, god-
liness, honor, integrity*. Nothing else will suffice.

Time of Reckoning for All

To the unrighteous nation there comes a day of reckoning. To each individual, righteous or unrighteous, there is
similarly a time of judgment, a time of accounting for one's
mortal probation when that phase of eternal existence is
past. At that point the books will be finally balanced, all
accounts due will have to be paid, all debts satisfied.

Fortunately we have time to pay off our debts before
that awesome day of judgment arrives. By repenting now,
in this life, and living a life of righteousness thereafter, we
can appear before God clean and holy. If we do this, to us,

as to Moroni, the place of judgment will be "the pleasing bar of the great Jehovah." (Moro. 10:34.) It will not hold terrors for us, as it will for the unrepentant. And we shall then hear the gentle, loving words of commendation and welcome: "Come, ye blessed of my Father, inherit the kingdom prepared for you from the foundation of the world." (Matt. 25:34.)

The Church Will Forgive

> . . . *Whosoever transgresseth*
> *against me, him shall ye judge ac-*
> *cording to the sins which he has*
> *committed; and if he confess his*
> *sins before thee and me, and re-*
> *penteth in the sincerity of his*
> *heart, him shall ye forgive, and I*
> *will forgive him also.*
>
> —Mosiah 26:29

CONSCIENTIOUS MEMBERS OF THE TRUE CHURCH OF Jesus Christ cannot fail to be concerned about their sins and those of others in relation to Church fellowship. On this point let us remind ourselves of the effects of sin and the power of repentance, as expressed in an address by President Hugh B. Brown:

Sin creates inner conflict, causes loss of self-respect, saps moral strength, causes injury to and estranges others, makes men more susceptible to temptation, and in numerous other subtle ways retards, delays, and blocks our journey toward our goal. Its enticements tend to divert us from moral ideals and to obscure our vision of desirable objectives.

True repentance halts this disintegration and, when followed by baptism and the gift of the Holy Ghost, places one's feet on the highway of successful living. With the companionship of that Spirit, one may release the power which is in the human soul even as men have been able to release the power of the atom.

This power, when released and given divine direction and guidance, will lead to immortality and eternal life.[1]

Truly one has this power when he is a faithful member of the Church, the Church being the principal medium through which this power can be exercised and developed. Thus it is important that a member have full fellowship in the Church. Serious sin brings loss of this power, for the sinner then almost invariably cuts himself off from Church association and the influences that come from association with people who are striving for righteousness. The power then lies dormant and ineffective in the soul of the transgressor.

But the power can be set loose from its chains of bondage. Repentance and its promise of forgiveness will set this power free so that it is again effective in one's life. And to do this, where the sin is of major proportions, there are two forgivenesses which the unrepentant one should obtain — the forgiveness of the Lord, and the forgiveness of the Lord's Church through its proper authorities.

Forgiveness by the Church

Forgiveness by the Lord is dealt with in the next chapter. On the general subject of forgiveness by the Church I wrote in part as follows to a young man who had confessed to adulterous transgressions:

> The other forgiveness is obtained through your ecclesiastical leader, the bishop, stake president, mission president or General Authority who has the authority to waive penalties. You have offended the Church and its people as well as the Lord by having broken the law of chastity, which is the next most serious sin to murder. If you are arrogant, cocky, and unrepentant, you may be "cut off" or excommunicated from the Church. But if the ecclesiastical officer is convinced of total and sustained repentance, he may waive that penalty — which may be termed a forgiveness in that sense. Simultaneously, the transgressor should begin his petitions to the Lord for a final forgiveness. God may obliterate or absolve sins. Your bishop has no such power. Your Heavenly Father has promised forgiveness upon total repentance

[1]Taken from a radio address given December 7, 1947.

and meeting all the requirements, but that forgiveness is not granted merely for the asking. There must be works — many works — and an all-out, total surrender, with a great humility and "a broken heart and a contrite spirit."

It depends upon you whether or not you are forgiven, and when. It could be weeks, it could be years, it could be centuries before that happy day when you have the positive assurance that the Lord has forgiven you. That depends on your humility, your sincerity, your works, your attitudes.

Continue your work with increased zeal and your prayers with increased intensity. Read the book of Enos and "go and do thou likewise." Read the scriptures which are enclosed and memorize the shorter ones.

Function of Church Leaders

The affairs of the Church of Jesus Christ are administered by the Presidency of the Church and the Twelve Apostles, with numerous other General Authorities assisting, and also through the stake and mission presidents and the bishops. These men are the shepherds of the flock. The Lord has placed these men to lead his kingdom on earth, and upon them he has placed authority and responsibility, each in his particular sphere. He has given these men the Melchizedek Priesthood, which is his own power and authority delegated to men. He recognizes and ratifies the acts of these chosen and anointed servants.

The Lord will forgive the truly repentant. But before the Lord can forgive, the sinner must open his heart to him in full contrition and humility, unburdening himself, for the Lord sees into our very souls. Likewise, to have the forgiveness of the Church there must be an unburdening of the sin to those properly appointed within the Church.

The function of proper Church leaders in the matter of forgiveness is two-fold: (1) to exact proper penalty — for example, to initiate official action in regard to the sinner in cases which warrant either disfellowshipment or excommunication; (2) to waive penalties and extend the hand of fellowship to the one in transgression. Whichever of the two steps is taken, either forgiveness or Church disciplinary action, it must be done in the light of all the facts and the inspiration which can come to those making the decision. Hence the importance of the repentant transgressor making full confession to the appropriate authority.

Penalties Involve Deprivation

Every departure from the right way is serious. One who breaks one law is guilty of them all, says the scripture. (Jas. 2:10.) Yet there are the lesser offenses which, while neither the Lord, his leaders, nor the Church can wink at them, are not punished severely. Then there are serious sins which cannot be tolerated without judgment, which must be considered by the appropriate leader, and which place the sinner's Church standing in jeopardy.

Church penalties for sin involve deprivations — the withholding of temple privileges, priesthood advancements, Church positions and other opportunities for service and growth. Such deprivations result from errors which are not always punishable by serious measures but which render the perpetrator unworthy to give leadership and receive high honors and blessings in God's kingdom. These are all retardations in our eternal progress which a person brings on himself. Even without any official Church action, for example, a person breaking the Word of Wisdom excludes himself from Church office and often — by staying away from church — from Church fellowship.

When the bishop is ordained he becomes judge of his people. He holds the keys to the temples and none of his ward members may enter one without the turning of the key by the bishop. If he considers someone unworthy to receive these glorious temple privileges, he may punish by withholding the privilege. Many other blessings are withheld to give the individual some time to bring his life up to the standard required. Deprivation, then, is the usual method of disciplining in the Church. In extreme cases, as described below, the transgressor is deprived of Church activity and participation by disfellowshipment or is totally severed from the Church by excommunication.

Powers of Church Officers

Not every person nor every holder of the priesthood is authorized to receive the transgressor's sacred confessions of guilt. The Lord has organized an orderly and consistent program. Every member in the Church is answerable to an ecclesiastical authority. In the ward, it is the bishop; in the branch, a president; in the stake or in the mission, a president; and in the higher Church echelon of authority, the General Authorities with the First Presidency and the Twelve Apostles at the head.

The function of each is much the same as that of the bishop, so we shall mention him particularly as showing the pattern. The order of heaven provides that the members of the ward will counsel with the bishop. A bishop is, by the very nature of his calling and his ordination, a "judge in Israel." (See D&C 107:72.) The Lord has given to the bishop, in his ordination, certain powers and authority:

> And unto the bishop of the church, and unto such as God shall appoint and ordain to watch over the church and to be elders unto the church, are to have it given unto them to discern all those gifts lest there shall be any among you professing and yet be not of God. (D&C 46:27.)

> Thus, none shall be exempted from the justice and the laws of God, that all things may be done in order and in solemnity before him, according to truth and righteousness. (D&C 107:84.)

The bishop will determine the merits of the case. He it is who will determine by the facts, and through the power of discernment which is his, whether the nature of the sin and the degree of repentance manifested warrant forgiveness. He may deem the sin of sufficient gravity, the degree of repentance sufficiently questionable, and the publicity and harm done of such considerable proportions as to necessitate handling the case by a Church court under the procedure outlined by the Lord. All this responsibility rests on the bishop's shoulders. Seminary teachers, institute directors and auxiliary and other Church workers can wield a powerful influence on people in distress by imparting wise counsel and sympathetic understanding, but they are without ecclesiastical authority and jurisdiction and will not attempt to waive penalties but will send the sinner to his bishop who should determine the degree of public confession and discipline that is necessary.

If careful consideration indicates the necessity, action for disfellowshipment is taken and this denies the blessings of Church activity and participation, though it does not deprive the sinner of membership or priesthood. When such action is taken, it remains for the repentant one to continue in his efforts to be faithful and prove himself worthy to do all that he would normally be permitted to do. When this is done sufficiently, to the satisfaction of the Church court which imposed the penalty, generally the hand of fellowship may be restored and full activity and participation be permitted the erring one.

But if, after all factors are considered, the nature and seriousness of the transgression seem to the bishop to require excommunication, the transgressor is required to stand trial before a proper Church court to have his case considered. In the cases of male members of the Church holding the Aaronic Priesthood or no priesthood, and all female members of the Church, the action of a bishop's court only is required in judgment, even including excommunication, though the higher courts may take original jurisdiction. For holders of the Melchizedek Priesthood, a bishop's court may give first consideration and may disfellowship only; the court must remand the transgressor to the higher court if more drastic action is recommended.

After the stake presidency and high council have tried a case, if the defendant feels that justice has not been given, or that the hearing did not give him a fair trial, he may appeal his case to the First Presidency of the Church and the Council of the Twelve. (See Handbook of Instructions for more detail.)

Excommunication

The scriptures speak of Church members being "cast out" or "cut off," or having their names "blotted out." This means excommunication. This dread action means the total severance of the individual from the Church. The person who is excommunicated loses his membership in the Church and all attendant blessings. As an excommunicant, he is in a worse situation than he was before he joined the Church. He has lost the Holy Ghost, his priesthood, his endowments, his sealings, his privileges and his claim upon eternal life. This is about the saddest thing which could happen to an individual. Better that he suffer poverty, persecution, sickness, and even death. A true Latter-day Saint would far prefer to see a loved one in his bier than excommunicated from the Church. If the one cut off did not have this feeling of desolateness and barrenness and extreme loss, it would be evidence that he did not understand the meaning of excommunication.

An excommunicant has no Church privileges. He may not attend priesthood meetings (since he has no priesthood); he may not partake of the sacrament, serve in Church positions, offer public prayers, or speak in meetings; he may not pay tithing except under certain conditions as determined by the bishop. He is "cut off," "cast out," and turned over to his Lord for the final judgment. "It is a fearful thing to fall into the hands of the living God" (Heb. 10:31), and especially already branded as an apostate or transgressor.

> Inasmuch as ye are cut off for transgression, ye cannot escape the buffetings of Satan until the day of redemption.
>
> And I now give unto you power from this very hour, that if any man among you, of the order, is found a transgressor and repenteth not of the evil, that ye shall deliver him over unto the buffetings of Satan; and he shall not have power to bring evil upon you. (D&C 104:9-10.)

There is a possibility of an excommunicant returning to the blessings of the Church with full membership, and this can be done only through baptism following satisfactory repentance. The way is hard and rough and, without the help of the Holy Ghost to whisper and plead and warn and encourage, one's climb is infinitely harder than if he were to repent before he lost the Holy Ghost, his membership, and the fellowship of the saints. The time is usually long, very long, as those who have fought their way back will attest. Any who have been finally restored would give the same advice: Repent first — do not permit yourself to be excommunicated if there is a possible way to save yourself from that dire calamity.

Ample scriptures indicate the power of proper Church authorities to judge its members in sin. The prophet Alma judged those who had been in iniquity and who confessed and repented, and waived the usual penalties.

> And whosoever repented of their sins and did confess them, them he did number among the people of the church;
>
> And those that would not confess their sins and repent of their iniquity, the same were not numbered among the people of the church, and their names were blotted out.
>
> And it came to pass that Alma did regulate all the affairs of the church. (Mos. 26:35-37.)

The Lord had previously said to Alma:

> Therefore I say unto you, Go; and whosoever transgresseth against me, him shall ye judge according to the sins which he has committed; and if he confess his sins before thee and me, and repenteth in the sincerity of his heart, him shall ye forgive, and I will forgive him also. (Mos. 26:29.)

When the Lord told the Palestinians, "Judge not that ye be not judged," he evidently was giving general instructions to the mass of humanity through the assembly gathered. In the scripture above quoted, he is talking to ecclesiastical leaders whose responsibility it is to judge the people and regulate the affairs of the Church. As an individual, the bishop or other Church leader will not judge his fellowman, but in his official position as bishop and judge he must be the judge of their actions.

The Lord's promise to Alma is reassuring: "Yea, and as often as my people repent will I forgive them their trespasses against me." (Mos. 26:30.)

Power to Bind and Loose

There are cultists who claim that the Church might sever a person from the Church but could not affect his eternal status or take from him the Holy Ghost or his priesthood or temple blessings. This is but wishful thinking, for the Lord has pledged to acknowledge the acts of his servants, and his Church is his kingdom. And when the person is excommunicated by the bishopric, the high council, or the higher councils, it is as though the Lord had personally with his own voice pronounced the penalty.

That this kind of authority, reaching in its effects from this life into the future phases of eternity, was to be a feature of the Church of Jesus Christ is clearly shown by the Savior's words:

> And I say also unto thee, That thou art Peter, and upon this rock I will build my church; and the gates of hell shall not prevail against it.
>
> And I will give unto thee the keys of the kingdom of heaven: and whatsoever thou shalt bind on earth shall be bound in heaven: and whatsoever thou shalt loose on earth shall be loosed in heaven. (Matt. 16:18-19.)

The Lord was speaking to Peter, who was the chief apostle, and it is the first apostle who holds all the keys of the priesthood. At a later time Jesus said:

> Verily I say unto you, Whatsoever ye shall bind on earth shall be bound in heaven: and whatsoever ye shall loose on earth shall be loosed in heaven. (Matt. 18:18.)

The Prophet Joseph Smith explains:

> Now the great and grand secret of the whole matter . . . consists in obtaining the powers of the Holy Priesthood. For him to whom these keys are given there is no difficulty in obtaining a knowledge of facts in relation to the salvation of the children of men. . . .

Herein is glory and honor, and immortality and eternal life. . . .
(D&C 128:11-12.)

Bishops Remove Penalties, Not Sins

Although there are many ecclesiastical officers in the
Church whose positions entitle and require them to be
judges, the authority of those positions does not necessarily
qualify them to forgive or remit sins. Those who can do
that are extremely few in this world.

The bishop, and others in comparable positions, can
forgive in the sense of waiving the penalties. In our loose
connotation we sometimes call this forgiveness, but it is
not forgiveness in the sense of "wiping out" or absolution.
The waiver means, however, that the individual will not
need to be tried again for the same error, and that he may
become active and have fellowship with the people of the
Church. In receiving the confession and waiving the penalties the bishop is representing the Lord. He helps to carry
the burden, relieves the transgressor's strain and tension,
and assures to him a continuation of Church activity.

It is the Lord, however, who forgives sin. This point,
and the position of the bishop and comparable officers in
the matter, was brought out in the following instruction
given to bishops of the Church by President J. Reuben Clark
on April 5, 1946:

> I have been very much interested in what the bishop has said
> about forgiveness. There is a great principle involved there, as
> he indicated, and we must not, I think, conclude that forgiveness
> can be obtained merely for the asking. It has come to our atten-
> tion that in one of our foreign missions boys came to the presid-
> ing officer, admitted their sin, they confessed, they were sorry, I
> suppose they wept, and he forgave them. Then they went back
> into the ranks, came back a month or six weeks later, confessed
> again, and were again forgiven.
>
> I do not understand that that is the law of the Church. Sin
> is a terrible thing. The Lord does forgive, and he requires us to
> forgive, because he has said, "I will forgive whom I will, but of
> you it is required to forgive all men." We forgive them as mem-

bers of the Church and receive them back into membership and
fellowship.

There is in the Church . . . the power to remit sins, but I
do not believe it resides in the bishops. That is a power that
must be exercised under the proper authority of the priesthood
and by those who hold the keys that pertain to that function. Woo
back every sinner. Forgive them personally. The Lord has said
that. Do all you can, but short of that formal remission the
matter then rests between the transgressor and the Lord, who is
merciful, who knows all of the circumstances, who has no dispo-
sition but to aid his children, give them comfort, guide them, and
help them. But the Lord has said, "I cannot look upon sin with
the least degree of allowance." So we leave it with him, and
our prayers go with the prayers of the transgressor that God
will forgive him, but the path of the sinner was never smooth
and I believe never will be. We must pay the penalty, but God's
mercy tempers his justice. His love is boundless, his desire to
save us is infinite. . . . All of us have done something that would
be better left undone. All of us need the mercy of God and his
love, and we should look at all the others, our brothers and sisters, knowing that we, with them, have something for which to
be forgiven, but we must remember we must pay whatever the
price be that the Lord exacts.

Let it be said in emphasis that even the First Presidency
and the Apostles do not make a practice of absolving sins.
They waive penalties in the course of their ministrations.
Thus the forgiveness or waiver of penalty is not something
to be taken idly or thoughtlessly and is not to be given for
a mere token effort or trial, but only for a genuine, whole-
hearted repentance. Little reward can be expected for a
tiny effort to repent, for the Lord has said that it must be
a total repentance "with all his heart" and the error must
be forsaken fully and wholly, mentally as well as physically.
The "filthy dreamer" of the day or night, or an adulterer
who still has desires toward the object of his sin, who still
revels in the memories of his sin, has not forsaken it "with
all his heart" as required by holy scripture. But if the
repentance is total, the scriptural "thou shalt forgive" not
only is required of individuals but seems to unlock doors
even for leaders.

False Claims on Remitting Sins

All that has been said about waiver of penalties and absolution of sin makes nonsense of any idea that money, or suffering, or penance, or fasting, or confessing will of itself bring forgiveness. Moroni's prophetic foresight looked forward to the time of such a concept. He said that the eternal promises of the Lord should roll on, until all his promises should be fulfilled. And this would come in a day when it should be said that miracles were done away with; when the power of God should be denied; when there would be much backbiting in the churches; when there would be wars and rumors of wars, earthquakes, and much pollution on the earth, with murders, robberies and many sins.

> Yea, it shall come in a day when there shall be churches built up that shall say: Come unto me, and for your money you shall be forgiven of your sins. (Morm. 8:32.)

Since the power to remit sins is so carefully and strictly limited within the true Church of Jesus Christ, where so many men bear the true priesthood of God, it is monumental presumption for unauthorized men elsewhere to claim to absolve people from sin. ". . . Whosoever exalteth himself shall be abased . . ." (Luke 14:11.) We may be sure that there will be great condemnation on those who assume such authority. The word of the Lord is a solemn warning against impostors:

> Wherefore, let all men beware how they take my name in their lips —
>
> For behold, verily I say, that many there be who are under this condemnation, who use the name of the Lord, and use it in vain, having not authority. (D&C 63:61-62.)

Confession Confidential and Voluntary

The bishop is expected to keep confidential the confession of the transgressor, unless he considers the sins serious enough and the repentance slack enough to take the matter before the bishop's court or the high council court. The keeping of full confidence makes it possible for the repentant individual to retain the confidence and win the friendly support of all with whom he associates. If the bishop sees fit to forgive the transgression, that is, to waive penalties, he may wish to keep very close to the sinner for a substantial period to assist and encourage him while the person is overcoming his errors and transforming his life. And at the discretion of the bishop, those who have cleared their transgressions and shared their burdens with their bishop or proper authority, can then move forward in Church activity with freedom and assurance.

While most missionaries go into the mission field clean and worthy, there is an occasional one who has carried unadjusted guilt into his mission and has had a continual fight to keep the spirit of the mission. Some have even failed in the fight, for the conflict in the soul is near annihilating. But the missionary, guilty of transgression, who has truly repented, confessed his sin fully and cleared his burden totally, so far as possible, goes into the mission field with a light heart, with full freedom and assurance. He has acted voluntarily to free himself. His confession and the resultant forgiveness bring security and rich rewards.

The matter of his transgression is held in strict confidence between him and his bishop and stake president. It is their prerogative as bishop and stake president to decide in their hearts, with the help of their Heavenly Father, whether the young man in question is worthy to go, and if they feel he is sufficiently repentant, after having examined all facts in the case, and that he is worthy for missionary service, they may proceed with the recommendation. A General Authority is usually called also to pass on the more difficult morals cases.

Varied Treatment for Similar Sins

The question is often raised as to why the treatment of transgressors is varied, why a particular sin does not always bring the same penalty. Here it needs to be realized that errors are of different magnitudes, that the reasons and incentives are different. The degree and intensity of repentance are different also.

A member in an eastern city wrote to me asking why a certain man had not been excommunicated. He said the case was flagrant and was generally known. He also wanted to know why the bishop was not disciplined for having forgiven the offender and having granted him continued activity in the Church. The answer I gave might clear the matter in other's minds, and I quote in part here:

Dear Brother:

The sin of adultery is a most heinous one and deserves strict discipline. Our bishops and stake presidents are instructed to handle these matters with dispatch and with mercy and with understanding and with love.

Each individual case is the responsibility of each individual ecclesiastical leader. Sometimes the stake president too may wish to take original jurisdiction.

The rules concerning the handling of these matters are somewhat flexible. Recognizing that repentance is vital to the salvation of all of us since all men sin in a lesser or a greater degree, and since the intensity of repentance, which is an intangible thing, can be determined fully only by inspiration and discernment, it is left generally to the discretion of the ecclesiastical leader to decide on the treatment of the case, since all cases are different. Some are vicious, intentional, premeditated, repeated and unrepented of; others seem to have some extenuating circumstances or may have been done under a moment of passion or pressures of unusual situations, and are followed by sincere repentance. Accordingly the treatment of these cases is left largely to the bishop in the ward or the president in the stake or the president of the mission.

In my experience, I have found repentance is also an intangible. One must judge by the feel rather than by what is said or done, and in my experience, numerous times two people have committed the same sin and one might be eligible for forgiveness and the blessing of the Church in months where another would not be ready in years. In fact, I have seen this — one hard and cold and belligerent and unrepentant, and the other bowed in "sackcloth and ashes" with a "broken heart and a contrite spirit" and willing to do anything to make good. It must be obvious that no period of one year or ten years or one month or a lifetime should be the determining factor. Even the Lord will not forgive a person *in his sins*. If the bishop or stake president is careless and grants forgiveness when it is not justified, the responsibility is with him.

It is obvious that the public cannot know the degree nor intensity of repentance. A person having committed a serious sin may have shed bushels of tears and prayed numerous hours and fasted many days, and may have the most total and effective repentance, and yet the public would have no way of knowing it. It would be quite improper for the bishop or stake president who has been doing the interviewing, to announce this publicly. Hence, the people must leave this matter to the bishop or stake president and, as indicated above, they may do so with confidence. It is proper for us, when we feel that something is wrong and might have been overlooked by the presiding authority, to call it to his attention, and when we have done this the responsibility is passed to the ecclesiastical leader.

Repentance Is the Key

Church leaders called upon to judge members in transgression carry a heavy burden of responsibility. With their aid, and through sincere repentance, the sinner may make the adjustments which will restore him to full fellowship with the Church. The same kind of repentance will assure him the miracle of God's forgiveness — which is discussed in the remaining chapters.

Chapter Twenty-two

God Will Forgive

*Behold, he who has repented of
his sins, the same is forgiven, and
I, the Lord, remember them no
more.*

—Doctrine & Covenants 58:42

WHEN A TRUE CONSCIOUSNESS OF GUILT FINALLY settles down upon the one who has sinned and he feels the heaviness of it — its throttling force and crushing power — only then can the sinner begin to realize how powerless he is on his own to rid himself of his transgressions. Only then can he begin to understand how futile are his unaided efforts to wash away the stains so indelibly stamped on his life and character. In his anguish he must come to lean heavily upon the Lord and trust in him, acknowledging that "with God all things are possible."

Jesus Christ the Only Way

The purging out of sin would be impossible but for the total repentance of the individual and the kind mercy of the Lord Jesus Christ in his atoning sacrifice. Only by these means can man recover, be healed and washed and purged, and still be eligible for the glories of eternity. On the Savior's great role in this, Helaman reminded his sons of King Benjamin's comments:

. . . There is no other way nor means whereby man can be saved, only through the atoning blood of Jesus Christ, who shall come, yea, remember that he cometh to redeem the world. (Hel. 5:9.)

And, in recalling the words which Amulek spoke to Zeezrom, Helaman emphasized man's part in obtaining forgiveness — repenting from his sins:

. . . He said unto him that the Lord surely should come to redeem his people, but that he should not come to redeem them *in their sins,* but to redeem them *from their sins.*

And he hath power given unto him from the Father to redeem them from their sins *because of repentance.* . . . (Hel. 5:10-11. Italics added.)

Hope Motivates to Repentance

Such scriptures breathe hope into the soul of the convinced sinner. Hope is indeed the great incentive to repentance, for without it no one would make the difficult, extended effort required — especially when the sin is a major one.

An experience I had some years ago emphasized this. A young woman approached me in a city far from my home and came under some pressure from her husband. She admitted to me that she had committed adultery. She was a bit hard and unyielding, and finally said: "I know what I have done. I have read the scriptures, and I know the consequences. I know that I am damned and can never be forgiven, and therefore why should I try now to repent?"

My reply to her was: "My dear sister, you do not know the scriptures. You do not know the power of God nor his goodness. You *can* be forgiven for this heinous sin, but it will take much sincere repentance to accomplish it."

Then I quoted to her the cry of her Lord:

Can a woman forget her sucking child, that she should not have compassion on the son of her womb? yea, they may forget, yet I will not forget thee. (Isa. 49:15.)

I reminded her of the Lord's words in our own dispensation to the effect that whoever repents and obeys God's commandments will be forgiven. (D&C 1:32.) My visitor looked bewildered but seemed to be yearning as though she wanted to believe it. I continued: "Eventually forgiveness will come for all but the unpardonable sins to that transgressor who repents sorely enough, long enough, sincerely enough."

She remonstrated again, though she was beginning to yield. She wanted so much to believe it. She said she had known all her life that adultery was unforgivable. And I turned again to the scriptures and read to her the oft-repeated statement of Jesus:

> Wherefore I say unto you, All manner of sin and blasphemy shall be forgiven unto men: but the blasphemy against the Holy Ghost shall not be forgiven unto men.
>
> And whosoever speaketh a word against the Son of man, it shall be forgiven him: but whosoever speaketh against the Holy Ghost, it shall not be forgiven him, neither in this world, neither in the world to come. (Matt. 12:31-32.)

She had forgotten that scripture. Her eyes lighted up. She reacted joyously to it, and asked, "Is that really true? Can I really be forgiven?"

Realizing that hope is the first requirement, I continued by reading many scriptures to her, to build up the hope that was now awakened within her.

How great the joy to feel and know that God will forgive sinners! Jesus declared in his Sermon on the Mount: ". . . Your heavenly Father will also forgive you." (Matt. 6:14.) This is on certain conditions, of course.

As I have previously said, in modern revelation the Lord has said to his prophet: "Behold, he who has repented of his sins, the same is forgiven, and I, the Lord, remember them no more." (D&C 58:42.) Our Lord gave the same word through the prophet Jeremiah: ". . . For I will forgive their iniquity, and I will remember their sin no more." (Jer. 31:34.) How gracious is the Lord!

On the occasion I am recalling, this woman, who was basically good, straightened up and looked me in the eye, and in her voice was a new power and resoluteness as she said: "Thank you, thank you! I believe you. I shall really repent and wash my filthy garments in the blood of the Lamb and obtain that forgiveness."

Not long ago, she returned to my office a new person — bright of eye, light of step, full of hope as she declared to me that, since that memorable day when hope had seen a star and had clung to it, she had never reverted to adultery nor any approaches to it.

Recently, I had another experience related to this particular scripture. I had just finished performing the holy ordinance in the temple wherein a delightful young couple had been sealed for eternity. The large group of relatives and close friends were congratulating the bride and groom. Having other pressing appointments I slipped out of the room and started down the hall, and I was startled when someone grasped my left arm. As I turned about, I saw a woman of about forty-five, who had a pleading look in her eyes. She asked, rather abruptly, "Do you remember me?"

She was intently looking to see if I would recognize her. Numerous times this question has been asked me and, though I try to remember those whom I have met, sometimes I fail. This time I was disconcerted for, though there was the feeling that I had seen her before, I had to admit with some embarrassment: "I am sorry "

To my surprise, she whispered with deep feeling, "I am glad you do not remember me. I was afraid you would. If *you* can forget me and my transgressions, I have the hope that my Father in heaven may forget, as he said: '. . . I will forgive their iniquity, and I will remember their sin no more.' "

She then briefly reminded me of a long, sad, troubled night when I had sat through the hours with her and her husband at a time when their eternal marriage was in jeopardy, and when I had worked with them and pleaded with them and warned them and quoted scriptures to them to bring repentance and to save their disintegrating marriage. After reminding me of the incident, she continued:

"It has been fifteen years since that crucial night, and I have done everything in my power to prove my repentance to my Lord. Our marriage was saved and is cemented. It is glorious! Our family life is wonderful and our children are growing up in faith and peace. Thank you! Thank you!"

And she softly breathed, as she left me: "I've hoped and yearned and prayed for the assurance that the Lord had totally forgiven me and forgotten my transgressions; and now that you remember neither me nor my sins, my hope has soared. Do you think that my Savior may also have forgotten my errors?"

In my office one day sat a sober couple who had a large family of little children. Early in their married life they had both committed adultery, and for many years had been suffering untold agonies of remorse. They had forgiven each other but were still suffering tortures.

The couple came to get some questions answered. They could stand it no longer. The husband broke the silence. "I told my wife that because of our adultery years ago we could never hope for salvation in the celestial kingdom, much less exaltation and eternal life, but that we could receive great satisfactions as we bore children and reared them to be so righteous that we could be sure they would all receive all the blessings of the gospel and the Church and eventually reach their exaltation."

When I quoted a long list of scriptures showing that forgiveness was possible eventually, when the heavy price had been paid, I could see hope stir within them and a peace settle over them. They left my office radiant with a new-found ecstasy.

Promises to the Repentant Sinner

Certainly the Lord loves the sinner, and especially the one who is trying to repent, even though the sin is abhorrent to him. (D&C 1:31.) Those who have transgressed can find many scriptures which will comfort them and impel them to move forward into total and continuing repentance. For instance, continuing his revelation to all men dated November 1, 1831, and referred to above, the Lord stated:

> Nevertheless, he that repents and does the commandments of the Lord shall be forgiven;
>
> And he that repents not, from him shall be taken even the light which he has received; for my Spirit shall not always strive with man, saith the Lord of Hosts. (D&C 1:32-33.)

It should be remembered that these commandments from the Standard Works of the Church are to "all men, and there is none to escape." This means that the call to repentance from sin is to all men and not to the members of the Church only, and not to those only whose sins are considered major ones. And the call promises forgiveness of sin to those who respond. What a farce it would be to call people to repentance if there were no forgiveness, and what a waste of the life of Christ if it failed to bring the opportunity for salvation and exaltation!

Sometimes a guilt consciousness overpowers a person with such a heaviness that when a repentant one looks back and sees the ugliness, the loathsomeness of the transgression, he is almost overwhelmed and wonders, "Can the Lord ever forgive me? Can I ever forgive myself?" But when one reaches the depths of despondency and feels the hopelessness of his position, and when he cries out to God for mercy in helplessness but in faith, there comes a still, small, but penetrating voice whispering to his soul, "Thy sins are forgiven thee."

The image of a loving, forgiving God comes through clearly to those who read and understand the scriptures. Since he is our Father, he naturally desires to raise us up, not to push us down, to help us live, not to bring about our spiritual death. "For I have no pleasure in the death of him that dieth," he has said, "wherefore turn yourselves, and live ye." (Ezek. 18:32.)

From Ezekiel too come these words of solace and hope:

> Again, when I say unto the wicked, Thou shalt surely die; if he turn from his sin, and do that which is lawful and right;
>
> If the wicked restore the pledge, give again that he had robbed, walk in the statutes of life, without committing iniquity; he shall surely live, he shall not die.
>
> None of his sins that he hath committed shall be mentioned unto him: he hath done that which is lawful and right; he shall surely live. (Ezek. 33:14-16.)

The same prophet wrote also, in the name of the Lord:

> Then will I sprinkle clean water upon you, and ye shall be clean: from all your filthiness, and from all your idols, will I cleanse you.
>
> A new heart also will I give you, and a new spirit will I put within you: and I will take away the stony heart out of your flesh, and I will give you an heart of flesh. (Ezek. 36:25-26.)

We are indebted to John for the encouraging and beautiful expression: "If we confess our sins, he is faithful and just to forgive us our sins, and to cleanse us from all unrighteousness." (1 John 1:9.)

As he fervently prayed at the dedication of the Kirtland Temple in 1836, the Prophet Joseph Smith expressed his assurance that sins could be blotted out: "O Jehovah, have mercy upon this people, and as all men sin forgive the transgressions of thy people, and let them be blotted out forever." (D&C 109:34.) The thought of blotting out of sins during the process of forgiveness was also expressed by the Lord when he said: "I, even I, am he that blotteth out thy transgressions for mine own sake, and will not remember thy sins." (Isa. 43:25.)

"Great are the words of Isaiah," said the Savior (3 Ne. 23:1), and that prophet's words rise to the sublime in the well-known passage wherein he made a promise of forgiveness to all who will repent:

> Seek ye the Lord while he may be found, call ye upon him while he is near:
>
> Let the wicked forsake his way, and the unrighteous man his thoughts: and let him return unto the Lord, and *he will have*

mercy upon him; and to our God, for *he will abundantly pardon.* (Isa. 55:6-7. Italics added.)

What a glorious promise of forgiveness the Lord made through the great Isaiah! Mercy and pardon! What more could men want or hope for!

Come now, and let us reason together, saith the Lord: though your sins be as scarlet, they shall be as white as snow; though they be red like crimson, they shall be as wool. (Isa. 1:18.)

Specific assurances of forgiveness are several times recorded in the Doctrine and Covenants. For instance, on the bank of the Missouri River, down which the Prophet and ten elders were traveling in canoes, the Lord gave the group these words of comfort:

Behold, verily thus saith the Lord unto you, O ye elders of my church, who are assembled upon this spot, whose sins are now forgiven you, for I, the Lord, forgive sins, and am merciful unto those who confess their sins with humble hearts. (D&C 61:2.)

And speaking of his elect who subscribe to his requirements, the Lord says:

For they will hear my voice, and shall see me, and shall not be asleep, and shall abide the day of my coming; for they shall be purified, even as I am pure. (D&C 35:21.)

The promise is again given "that by keeping the commandments they might be washed and cleansed from all their sins." Here the reader is urged to read the whole of the 76th Section of the Doctrine and Covenants, but particularly from the 51st verse on. Those who have overcome their sins and been perfected are ". . . the church of the Firstborn. They are they into whose hands the Father has given all things." (D&C 76:54-55.)

Forgiveness for Adultery

When Paul preached to the Galatian people, he listed the sins which leave people wretched. He cautioned:

. . . Walk in the Spirit, and ye shall not fulfill the lust of the flesh.

For the flesh lusteth against the Spirit, and the Spirit against the flesh: and these are contrary the one to the other: so that ye cannot do the things that ye would. (Gal. 5:16-17.)

Paul then recounted the numerous sins and added: ". . . they which do such things shall not inherit the kingdom of God." (Gal. 5:21.)

Many people who have sinned grievously have been terrified at this statement of Paul's. In the matter of sexual sin many have likewise been deeply worried by their interpretation of a statement by the Prophet Joseph Smith, which perhaps makes a greater impact on people of our dispensation. In a High Council meeting, the case of Harrison Sagers was tried. He was charged with seduction and had said that Joseph Smith taught that such was right. The Prophet records further:

I was present with several of the Twelve, and gave an address tending to do away with every evil, and exhorting them to practice virtue and holiness before the Lord; told them that the Church had not received any permission from me to commit fornication, adultery, or any corrupt action; but my every word and action has been to the contrary. *If a man commit adultery, he cannot receive the celestial kingdom of God. Even if he is saved in any kingdom, it cannot be the celestial kingdom.* I did think that the many examples that have been made manifest, such as John C. Bennett's and others, were sufficient to show the fallacy of such a course of conduct.[1]

It might seem presumptuous for us to try to clarify the statement of the Prophet or indicate what were his total concepts, but because so many who have fallen into sexual sin and have done all in their power to repent have been devastated with the above statement, there is a constant appeal for clarification. May I offer some suggestions for the thoughtful reader?

A letter came to me from a woman who many years before had been involved in adultery. Having come to realize her plight, she had confessed her sins to her husband and the Church, penalties had been waived, and she had

---

[1] *Documentary History of the Church*, Vol. 6, p. 81. Italics added.

been permitted to go forward with her life in the Church. Now many years had passed — years of faithfulness, activity and worthiness. She had felt she was forgiven — she had been breathing again freely. Recently she had been asked to teach Relief Society theology lessons, and in one of her first lessons she had come to the statement of the Prophet Joseph Smith as above quoted. This devastated her, and she wondered if all she had suffered and all her years of repentance meant nothing for her, and if she was still condemned. She asked: "Can I never get it straightened out? Will I be deprived of the celestial kingdom no matter what I do? Will I lose my beloved husband? Will my children be taken from me? What can I do? Am I lost? What have I to look forward to? Is there no hope?"

If the above quotation were taken literally, it would seem difficult to reconcile it with other scriptures and with the practices and policies of the Church. Is it possible that the Prophet just did not take time to elaborate on the matter at that time, or that in recording it he did not double check the implications? Or was it properly recorded when he gave it?

The same Joseph Smith who gave us that quotation also gave us many scriptures which state that there is forgiveness; and other holy scriptures attest that repentance can bring forgiveness if that repentance is sufficiently "all-out" and total. Here are some of the words from the pens of Joseph Smith and other prophets. For brevity, I give here in summary only the key phrases. Some of them I have quoted previously.

> Nevertheless, he that repents and does the commandments of the Lord shall be forgiven. (D&C 1:32.)

> But he that has committed adultery and repents with all his heart, and forsaketh it, and doeth it no more, thou shalt forgive. (D&C 42:25.)

> Behold, he who has repented of his sins, the same is forgiven, and I, the Lord, remember them no more. (D&C 58:42.)

> . . . I am able to make you holy, and your sins are forgiven you. (D&C 60:7.)

... I, the Lord, forgive sins, and am merciful unto those who confess their sins with humble hearts. (D&C 61:2.)

... I, the Lord, forgive sins unto those who confess their sins before me and ask forgiveness, who have not sinned unto death. (D&C 64:7.)

... When ... they repent of the evil, they shall be forgiven. (D&C 64:17.)

... They shall be purified, even as I am pure. (D&C 35:21.)

... I will forgive their iniquity, and I will remember their sin no more. (Jer. 31:34.)

I have blotted out, as a thick cloud, thy transgressions. ... (Isa. 44:22.)

... If he ... repenteth in the sincerity of his heart, him shall ye forgive, and I will forgive him also. (Mos. 26:29.)

... Their sins and iniquities will I remember no more. (Heb. 10:17.)

... And the Lord said unto him: I will forgive thee and thy brethren of their sins. (Eth. 2:15.)

... Be converted, that I may heal you. (3 Ne. 9:13.)

... And I shall heal them; and ye shall be the means of bringing salvation unto them. (3 Ne. 18:32.)

Less than a year after the restoration of the Church of Jesus Christ, the Redeemer spoke concerning the ugly sin of infidelity and lustfulness and the conditions for receiving forgiveness:

And he that looketh upon a woman to lust after her shall deny the faith, and shall not have the Spirit; and if he repents not he shall be cast out.

Thou shalt not commit adultery; and he that committeth adultery, and repenteth not, shall be cast out.

But he that has committed adultery and repents with all his heart, and forsaketh it, and doeth it no more, thou shalt forgive. (D&C 42:23-25.)

And Section 132 of the Doctrine and Covenants indicates that, though he may be subjected to the buffetings of Satan, a person may eventually be forgiven of adultery even after marriage for time and eternity in the temple:

And again, verily I say unto you, if a man marry a wife by my word, which is my law, and by the new and everlasting covenant, and it is sealed unto them by the Holy Spirit of promise, by him who is anointed, unto whom I have appointed this power and the keys of this priesthood . . . and if ye abide in my covenant, and commit no murder whereby to shed innocent blood, it shall be done unto them in all things whatsoever my servant hath put upon them, in time, and through all eternity: and shall be of full force when they are out of the world; and they shall pass by the angels, and the gods, which are set there, to their exaltation and glory in all things, as hath been sealed upon their heads, which glory shall be a fullness and a continuation of the seeds forever and ever. (D&C 132:19.)

I have already referred to the statement of the Savior that all manner of sin except blasphemy against the Holy Ghost can be forgiven. (See Matt. 12:31.) It is of interest that in preparing his inspired revision of this passage Joseph Smith added the significant words "who receive me and repent," which are italicized in the following passage:

. . . All manner of sin and blasphemy shall be forgiven unto men *who receive me and repent;* but the blasphemy against the Holy Ghost, it shall not be forgiven unto men. (Matt. 12:26, Inspired Version.)

Going back to the Prophet's original statement, had he inserted in it the three words I believe it implies — "and remains unrepentant" — this statement would fit perfectly in the program as given in the numerous scriptures, many of which came through the Prophet himself. If such words were inserted, the statement would read as follows:

If a man commit adultery (*and remain unrepentant*) he cannot receive the celestial kingdom of God. Even if he is saved in any kingdom, it cannot be the celestial kingdom.

This restriction on the unrepentant adulterer is in line with that on all who remain in sin. President Joseph Fielding Smith, writing in the *Improvement Era,* made this comment: "No unrepentant person who remains in his sins will ever enter into the glories of the celestial kingdom."[2] This statement is consistent with all we read in the scriptures on

---

[2]*Improvement Era,* July, 1955, p. 542.

the subject, which is perhaps summed up in Alma's words: ". . . for there can no man be saved except his garments are washed white; yea, his garments must be purified until they are cleansed from all stain . . ." (Al. 5:21.)

In offering these suggestions let it be understood that I have no intent to minimize the seriousness of the sexual sins or other transgressions but merely to hold out hope to the transgressor, so that men and women of sin may strive with all their power to overcome their errors, wash themselves "in the blood of the Lamb" and be purged and purified, and thus be able to return to their Maker. Those involved must not relax because of the possibility of forgiveness. Let me repeat that it is a serious and solemn matter when people permit themselves to get into sexual sins, of which adultery is only one of the more serious ones.

In view of all these scriptures I have quoted, and many others which could be added, is it not reasonable to believe that the Prophet's statement of 1843 which so deeply concerns so many people is really in harmony with all the other scriptures?

Perhaps Paul's comment to the Corinthians shows a like situation.

> . . . Be not deceived: neither fornicators, nor idolaters, nor adulterers, nor effeminate, nor abusers of themselves with mankind,
>
> Nor thieves, nor covetous, nor drunkards, nor revilers, nor extortioners, shall inherit the kingdom of God. (1 Cor. 6:9-10.)

Here is an extremely limiting statement which seems to coincide in import with that of Joseph Smith mentioned above. And it is true! Certainly, the kingdom cannot be populated with such men as Paul had found in the Church branches where he worked. It could hardly be glory and honor and power and joy if the eternal kingdom were made up of fornicators, adulterers, idolaters, sexual perverts, thieves, covetous persons, drunkards, liars, rebels, reprobates, extortioners and such people. But Paul's next thought is comforting as well as clarifying:

> And such were some of you: but ye are washed, but ye are
> sanctified, but ye are justified in the name of the Lord Jesus,
> and by the Spirit of our God. (1 Cor. 6:11.)

This is the great secret. Some of those who inherit the
kingdom may have committed such grievous sins but are
no longer in those categories. They are *no longer unclean,*
having been washed, sanctified and justified. Paul's hearers
had been in those despicable categories, but having now received the gospel with its purifying, transforming powers
they were changed. The cleansing process had been applied
and they were washed clean and had become eligible for
the first resurrection and for exaltation in God's kingdom.

The Cleansing Process

When a physical body is filthy, the process of cleansing
is a thorough bath, the brushing of teeth, the shampooing
of hair, the cleaning of fingernails, and the donning of fresh,
clean clothing. When a home is renovated, roofs are mended
or replaced, walls washed or painted, floors swept and
scrubbed, furniture repaired and dusted, curtains laundered
and metals polished. When a defiled man is born again,
his habits are changed, his thoughts cleansed, his attitudes
regenerated and elevated, his activities put in total order,
and everything about him that was dirty, degenerate or reprobate is washed and made clean.

The analogy holds also in other areas of life. When
soiled clothes have been through the laundry and washed,
starched and pressed, they are no longer filthy. When the
smallpox victim has been healed and cleansed, he is no
longer contaminated. In the moral area also there is im-
munization. Are not the social and physical diseases much
the same? They come through exposure and low resistance,
and unless there is early and adequate treatment they are
likely to run their courses and even take life. The one is
physical and temporary while the other has eternal consequences. When one is washed and purged and cleansed,
he is no longer an adulterer. The washing, purging, cleans-

ing process is mentioned many times, many places, by many prophets.

The effect of the cleansing is beautiful. These troubled souls have found peace. These soiled robes have been cleansed to spotlessness. These people formerly defiled, having been cleansed through their repentance — their washing, their purging, their whitening — are made worthy for constant temple service and to be found before the throne of God associating with divine royalty.

Difficult but Attainable

Those who, having committed grievous sexual sin, assume this sin to be unforgivable under any and all conditions are perhaps confusing difficulty with impossibility. Certainly the road of repentance from such sin is not easy, which is one good reason for abstaining in the first place. And as I have stressed throughout this book, even though forgiveness is so abundantly promised there is no promise nor indication of forgiveness to any soul who does not totally repent.

To every forgiveness there is a condition. The plaster must be as wide as the sore. The fasting, the prayers, the humility must be equal to or greater than the sin. There must be a broken heart and a contrite spirit. There must be "sackcloth and ashes." There must be tears and genuine change of heart. There must be conviction of the sin, abandonment of the evil, confession of the error to properly constituted authorities of the Lord. There must be restitution and a confirmed, determined change of pace, direction and destination. Conditions must be controlled and companionship corrected or changed. There must be a washing of robes to get them white and there must be a new consecration and devotion to the living of all of the laws of God. In short, there must be an overcoming of self, of sin, and of the world.

Sanctification Through Overcoming

In the Book of Revelation it is written that *he that overcometh* shall "eat of the tree of life," receive "a crown of life," not be hurt of the second death. He shall receive of the "hidden manna," a "white stone," and a "new name," shall have "power over the nations." He shall be clothed in "white raiments," and his name will "not be blotted out." *"To him that overcometh* will I grant to sit with me in my throne, even as I also overcame, and am set down with my Father in his throne." (Rev. 3:21. Italics added.) How glorious and rich are the promises to those who overcome!

"What are these which are arrayed in white robes?" asked one of the elders in John's vision, and the answer was: ". . . These are they which came out of great tribulation, and have washed their robes, and made them white in the blood of the Lamb. Therefore are they before the throne of God, and serve him day and night in his temple . . ." (Rev. 7:14-15.)

It would seem that these people had not always been perfect. They had had soiled robes and many weaknesses, but had now overcome and had washed the soiled raiment in the blood of the Lamb. They were now clean and purified, as is indicated in the blessings promised.

The Prophet Alma discourses on the mercies of the Lord through the cleansing power wherein repentance has purged sin, and joy leads toward "rest" or exaltation:

> Therefore they were called after this holy order [of the high priesthood], and were sanctified, and their garments were washed white through the blood of the Lamb.
>
> Now they, after being sanctified by the Holy Ghost, having their garments made white, being pure and spotless before God, could not look upon sin save it were with abhorrence; and there were many, exceeding great many, who were made pure and entered into the rest of the Lord their God. (Al. 13:11-12.)

This passage indicates an attitude which is basic to the sanctification we should all be seeking, and thus to the repentance which merits forgiveness. It is that the former transgressor must have reached a "point of no return" to sin wherein there is not merely a renunciation but also a deep abhorrence of the sin — where the sin becomes most distasteful to him and where the desire or urge to sin is cleared out of his life.

Surely this is what is meant, in part at least, by being pure in heart! And when we read in the Sermon on the Mount that the "pure in heart" shall see God, it gives meaning to the Lord's statement, made through the Prophet Joseph Smith in 1832, that presently impure people can perfect themselves and become pure:

> Therefore, sanctify yourselves that your minds become single to God, and the days will come that you shall see him; for he will unveil his face unto you, and it shall be in his own time, and in his own way, and according to his own will. (D&C 88:68.)

Again, in 1833, the Prophet gave assurance that the totally repentant one will see the Lord; and this means forgiveness, for only the pure in heart will see God.

> Verily, thus saith the Lord: It shall come to pass that every soul who forsaketh his sins and cometh unto me, and calleth on my name, and obeyeth my voice, and keepeth my commandments, shall see my face and know that I am. (D&C 93:1.)

With such a magnanimous promise, why would anyone hesitate to throw off the evils of his life and come to his Lord?

The Buffetings of Satan

A phrase that occurs several times in modern revelation should certainly be an incentive to prompt, unreserved repentance. This term talks of sinners being delivered to the "buffetings of Satan." For instance, the Lord consigns to the buffetings of Satan those who, having organized themselves "by a bond or everlasting covenant that cannot be broken," subsequently broke that covenant. "And he who breaketh it shall lose his office and standing in the church, and shall be delivered over to the buffetings of Satan until the day of redemption." (D&C 78:12.)

Again the Lord speaks:

> And the soul that sins against this covenant, and hardeneth his heart against it, shall be dealt with according to the laws of my church, and shall be delivered over to the buffetings of Satan until the day of redemption. (D&C 82:21.)

To some of the Church members earlier in our dispensation who had broken their covenants and thereby come under condemnation, the Lord stated:

> Therefore, inasmuch as you are found transgressors, you cannot escape my wrath in your lives.
>
> Inasmuch as ye are cut off for transgression, ye cannot escape the buffetings of Satan until the day of redemption.
>
> And I now give unto you power from this very hour, that if any man among you, of the order, is found a transgressor and repenteth not of the evil, that ye shall deliver him over unto the buffetings of Satan; and he shall not have power to bring evil upon you. (D&C 104:8-10.)

Similarly in the revelation relating to the new and everlasting covenant, the Lord emphasizes the seriousness of certain transgressions by saying that even though the offenders may be redeemed and finally be exalted, ". . . they shall be . . . delivered unto the buffetings of Satan unto the day of redemption, saith the Lord God." (D&C 132:26.)

Just what constitutes the "buffetings of Satan" no one knows except those who experience them, but I have seen many people who have been buffeted in life after they have come to themselves and realized to some degree the horror of their acts. If their sufferings were not the "buffetings of Satan," they must be a near approach to them. Certainly they reflect great sorrow, anguish of soul, shame, remorse, and physical and mental suffering. Perhaps this condition approaches the sufferings of which the Lord spoke when he said:

> But if they would not repent they must suffer even as I;
>
> Which suffering caused myself, even God, the greatest of all, to tremble because of pain, and to bleed at every pore, and to suffer both body and spirit. . . . (D&C 19:17-18.)

Always Better Not to Sin

In all our expressions of wonder and gratitude at our Father's loving and forgiving attitude we must not be misled into supposing either that forgiveness may be considered lightly or that sin may be repeated with impunity after protestations of repentance. The Lord will indeed forgive, but he will not tolerate repetitions of the sin:

> . . . And the Lord said unto him: I will forgive thee and thy brethren of their sins; but thou shalt not sin any more, for ye shall remember that my Spirit will not always strive with man; wherefore, if ye will sin until ye are fully ripe ye shall be cut off from the presence of the Lord. . . . (Eth. 2:15.)

Another error into which some transgressors fall, because of the availability of God's forgiveness, is the illusion that they are somehow stronger for having committed sin and then lived through the period of repentance. This simply is not true. That man who resists temptation and lives without sin is far better off than the man who has fallen, no matter how repentant the latter may be. The reformed transgressor, it is true, may be more understanding of one who falls into the same sin, and to that extent perhaps more helpful in the latter's regeneration. But his sin and repentance have certainly not made him stronger than the consistently righteous person.

God will forgive — of that, we are sure. How satisfying it is to be cleansed from filthiness, but how much better it is never to have committed the sin! Even though one may have the assurance that God and all others have forgiven him, will a man ever totally forgive himself for gross sin? How splendid for one to be able to stand tall and look straight and honestly to affirm that, though he may have committed some follies and lesser errors, he has never broken the major laws! Ezekiel gives comfort to that soul who has never lost his footing when, speaking for the Lord, the prophet emphasizes that he that "hath walked in my statutes, and hath kept my judgments, to deal truly; he is just, he shall surely live, saith the Lord God." (Ezek. 18:9.)

There are prodigals like the murderer who commits crime no more because he is in the death cell, or the gambler who abandons the roulette wheel because he has no more to gamble. Forgiven? Yes, if repentance is adequate. Exalted? That is the question, and perhaps only the Lord can answer it. But in any event the situation is not hopeless. The prodigal may still have a good life with many blessings. And the Lord in his mercy can indeed work miracles of forgiveness.

A man may have served a prison term for a felony and through good behavior have been pardoned, but will he be able to vote, hold public office, become the president of the country? A Church member may have been involved in certain gross crimes and finally be forgiven, but will he be appointed bishop or stake president? Consideration of questions like these dispels the illusion that it is somehow better to have trod the rugged path of sin and repentance than to have been consistently faithful.

Mercy Does Not Rob Justice

There are many people who seem to rely solely on the Lord's mercy rather than on accomplishing their own repentance. One woman rather flippantly said, "The Lord knows my intents and that I'd like to give up my bad habits. He will understand and forgive me." But the scriptures will not bear this out. The Lord may temper justice with mercy, but he will never supplant it. Mercy can never replace justice. God is *merciful,* but he is also *just.* The Savior's atonement represents the mercy extended. Because of this atonement, all men can be saved. Most men can be exalted.

Many have greatly misunderstood the place of mercy in the forgiveness program. Its role is not to give great blessings without effort. Were it not for the atonement of Christ, the shedding of his blood, the assumption by proxy of our sins, man could never be forgiven and cleansed. Justice and mercy work hand in hand. Having offered mercy to us in the overall redemption, the Lord must now let justice rule, for he cannot save us in our sins, as Amulek explained. (Al. 11:37.)

Perhaps the greatest scriptural exposition on the respective roles of mercy and justice, and God's position in it all, is that of Alma to his son Corianton. It is important for all of us to understand this concept.

> But there is a law given, and a punishment affixed, and a repentance granted; which repentance mercy claimeth; otherwise, justice claimeth the creature and executeth the law, and the law inflicteth the punishment; if not so, the works of justice would be destroyed, and God would cease to be God.
>
> But God ceaseth not to be God, and mercy claimeth the penitent, and mercy cometh because of the atonement; and the atonement bringeth to pass the resurrection of the dead; and the resurrection of the dead bringeth back men into the presence of God; and thus they are restored into his presence, to be judged according to their works, according to the law and justice.
>
> For behold, justice exerciseth all his demands, and also mercy claimeth all which is her own; and thus, none but the truly penitent are saved.
>
> What, do ye suppose that mercy can rob justice? I say unto you, Nay; not one whit. If so, God would cease to be God. (Al. 42:22-25.)

"There should be no license for sin," said the Prophet, "but mercy should go hand in hand with reproof." And again, "God does not look on sin with allowance, but when men have sinned, there must be allowance made for them."[3]

Forgiveness — The Divine Invitation

From what has been said in this chapter I hope it is clear that forgiveness is available to all who have not committed the unpardonable sins. Fortunately for some, when repentance is adequate God will forgive even one who has been excommunicated — which, like surgery, unfortunately is sometimes necessary.

---

[3]*Documentary History of the Church*, Vol. 5, p. 24.

But if he repent not he shall not be numbered among my people, that he may not destroy my people, for behold I know my sheep, and they are numbered.

Nevertheless, ye shall not cast him out of your synagogues, or your places of worship, for unto such shall ye continue to minister; for ye know not but what they will return and repent, and come unto me with full purpose of heart, and I shall heal them; and ye shall be the means of bringing salvation unto them. (3 Ne. 18:31-32.)

We can hardly be too forceful in reminding people that they cannot sin and be forgiven and then sin again and again and expect repeated forgiveness. The Lord anticipated the weakness of man which would return him to his transgression, and he gave this revelation in warning:

And now, verily I say unto you, I, the Lord, will not lay any sin to your charge; go your ways and sin no more; but unto that soul who sinneth shall the former sins return, saith the Lord your God." (D&C 82:7.)

Forgiveness of sins is one of the most glorious principles God ever gave to man. Just as repentance is a divine principle, so also is forgiveness. Were it not for this principle, there would be no point in crying repentance. But because of this principle the divine invitation is held out to all — Come, repent of your sins and be forgiven!

Chapter Twenty-Three

The Miracle of Forgiveness

> *Wherefore, my beloved brethren, have miracles ceased because Christ hath ascended into heaven, and hath sat down on the right hand of God, to claim of the Father his rights of mercy which he hath upon the children of men?*
>
> *And [Christ] hath said: Repent all ye ends of the earth, and come unto me, and be baptized in my name, and have faith in me, that ye may be saved.*
>
> —Moroni 7:27, 34

MAKING A STIRRING APPEAL FOLLOWING THE BLOODY extinction of his people, the lonely Moroni, last survivor of a great civilization, looked down the stream of time to our own day when the Book of Mormon should come forth. Among other erroneous concepts then held, he predicted, would be the idea that "miracles are done away." (Morm. 8:26.)

Modern Miracles

We who live now recognize the fulfillment of this prophecy. Fortunately, active Church members are aware of modern miracles — angelic visitations, gospel restoration, the Book of Mormon, for example. When we think of miracles, most of us think of healings under the power of the priesthood. But there is another, even greater miracle — the miracle of forgiveness.

Importance of Spiritual Sight

Indeed the day of miracles has not passed except for those who will not heed the call of the Lord and of his servants, who night and day warn and plead and implore. There is a glorious miracle awaiting every soul who is prepared to change. Repentance and forgiveness make a brilliant day of the darkest night. When souls are reborn, when lives are changed — then comes the great miracle to beautify and warm and lift. When spiritual death has threatened and now instead there is resuscitation, when life pushes out death — when this happens it is the miracle of miracles. And such great miracles will never cease so long as there is one person who applies the redeeming power of the Savior and his own good works to bring about his rebirth.

There are two kinds of miracles, as there are two parts to life in every area. There is the body and the spirit. Thus there are two kinds of healings.

As the Lord passed down the path, two blind men begged for light. "So Jesus had compassion on them, and touched their eyes: and immediately their eyes received sight, and they followed him." (Matt. 20:34.) These were their mortal eyes which were opened.

The scripture says, ". . . and they followed him." This last phrase might mean that they would receive their spiritual sight. If they followed him really, lived his commandments, were totally obedient, their souls would receive sight unto eternal life.

Of the two, spiritual sight is by far the more important. Only those whose physical eyes do not see can know of the deprivation this entails, and it is a serious one. But even this cannot be compared to the blindness of those who have eyes and will not see the glories of that spiritual life which has no end.

The Blessing of Peace

The essence of the miracle of forgiveness is that it brings peace to the previously anxious, restless, frustrated, perhaps tormented soul. In a world of turmoil and contention this is indeed a priceless gift.

The Nephite civilization did not learn this in time. As it began to funnel to a rough and tragic conclusion, the prophet Mormon thought he glimpsed a possibility of the people's repenting and receiving forgiveness for their great sins. But he was mistaken. All his life, since his boyhood, he had decried the hardness of his people and watched with sadness and tears the approaching darkness. Finally his hope vanished. He wrote:

> But behold this my joy was vain, for their sorrowing was not unto repentance, because of the goodness of God; but it was rather the sorrowing of the damned, because the Lord would not always suffer them to take happiness in sin.

> And it came to pass that my sorrow did return unto me again, and I saw that the day of grace was passed with them, both temporally and spiritually; for I saw thousands of them hewn down in open rebellion against their God, and heaped up as dung upon the face of the land. (Morm. 2:13, 15.)

Alma said it well. He had tasted the bitterness of a sinful life and of spiritual rebellion, so he knew well what he was saying — "Wickedness never was happiness." (Al. 41:10.) And since happiness brings peace, wickedness brings its antithesis — strife and turmoil.

"The greatest need of this world today is peace," said President David O. McKay. "The turbulent storms of hate, of enmity, of distrust, and of sin are threatening to wreck humanity. It is time for men — true men — to dedicate their lives to God, and to cry with the spirit and power of the Christ, 'Peace, be still!' . . ."

Peace is the fruit of righteousness. It cannot be bought with money, and cannot be traded nor bartered. It must be earned. The wealthy often spend much of their gains in a bid for peace, only to find that it is not for sale. But the poorest as well as the richest may have it in abundance if the total price is paid. Those who abide the laws and live the Christ-like life may have peace and other kindred blessings, principal among which are exaltation and eternal life. They include also blessings for this life.

> And may the Lord bless you, and keep your garments spotless, that ye may at last be brought to sit down with Abraham, Isaac, and Jacob, and the holy prophets who have been ever since the world began, having your garments spotless even as their garments are spotless, in the kingdom of heaven to go no more out.

> And now, may the peace of God rest upon you, and upon your houses and lands, and upon your flocks and herds, and all that you possess, your women and your children, according to your faith and good works, from this time forth and forever. . . . (Al. 7:25, 27.)

Transforming Power of God

The effect of the Lord's transforming power is seen in many personal lives. When Saul had been selected, called and appointed to be the King of Israel, when he had been anointed and blessed and set apart, ". . . God gave him another heart . . ." and he ". . . turned into another man . . ." (1 Sam. 10:6, 9.) Miracles had enveloped Saul.

The Apostle Paul is often mentioned in this connection. Although his former persecution against the Church of God had been done with sincere motives, he recognized the sin and, through the redeeming grace of Christ, found peace through forgiveness despite a life in which he was now the persecuted. His testimony is impressive:

> . . . Christ Jesus came into the world to save sinners; of whom I am chief.

> Howbeit for this cause I obtained mercy, that in me first Jesus Christ might shew forth all longsuffering, for a pattern to them which should hereafter believe on him to life everlasting. (1 Tim. 1:15-16.)

But perhaps the best documented scriptural life showing the dramatic regeneration and the peace obtained through the miracle of forgiveness is that of the Prophet Alma. (See Mos. 27.) His earlier life had been one of open rebellion against God, of systematic attempts to destroy the Church, despite the training in the truth which his father had undoubtedly given him. His had indeed been a life of great sin, to which he had added the evil of idolatry.

Then came the visit from the angel, the terrible rebuke which rendered him dumb and paralyzed for three days and nights. During this period he suffered anguish of remorse, an agony of soul which he describes as being "racked with eternal torment." His description is a classic in scripture. I have referred to it before, but do so at some length again because of its great relevance to this concluding chapter.

> But I was racked with eternal torment, for my soul was harrowed up to the greatest degree and racked with all my sins.
>
> Yea, I did remember all my sins and iniquities, for which I was tormented with the pains of hell; yea, I saw that I had rebelled against my God, and that I had not kept his holy commandments.
>
> Yea, and I had murdered many of his children, or rather led them away unto destruction; yea, and in fine so great had been my iniquities, that the very thought of coming into the presence of my God did rack my soul with inexpressible horror.
>
> Oh, thought I, that I could be banished and become extinct both soul and body, that I might not be brought to stand in the presence of my God, to be judged of my deeds.
>
> And now, for three days and for three nights was I racked, even with the pains of a damned soul. (Al. 36:12-16.)

In Alma's account the sensitive reader can in a measure identify with him, feel his pains, experience his great sense of horror at the recognition of the depth of his sin. The reader can then share also in the great relief which Alma was to find. How did he gain this relief? In the same way every transgressor does — by partaking of the miracle of forgiveness through genuine repentance and by casting himself wholly on the mercies of Jesus Christ.

> And it came to pass that as I was thus racked with torment, while I was harrowed up by the memory of my many sins, be-

hold, I remembered also to have heard my father prophesy unto the people concerning the coming of one Jesus Christ, a Son of God, to atone for the sins of the world.

Now, as my mind caught hold upon this thought, I cried within my heart: O Jesus, thou Son of God, have mercy on me, who am in the gall of bitterness, and am encircled about by the everlasting chains of death.

And now, behold, when I thought this, I could remember my pains no more; yea, I was harrowed up by the memory of my sins no more.

And oh, what joy, and what marvelous light I did behold; yea, my soul was filled with joy as exceeding as was my pain!

Yea, I say unto you, my son, that there could be nothing so exquisite and so bitter as were my pains. Yea, and again I say unto you, my son, that on the other hand, there can be nothing so exquisite and sweet as was my joy. (Al. 36:17-21.)

Now anguish was turned to joy, pain to calm, darkness to light. Only now could Alma have peace. He emphasized to his son Shiblon the sole source of that peace.

. . . And never, until I did cry out unto the Lord Jesus Christ for mercy, did I receive a remission of my sins. But behold, I did cry unto him and I did find peace to my soul. (Al. 38:8.)

Peace Through Preparing for Christ's Coming

It is not easy to be at peace in today's troubled world. Necessarily peace is a personal acquisition. As is implied throughout this book, it can be attained only through maintaining constantly a repentant attitude, seeking forgiveness of sins both large and small, and thus coming ever closer to God. For Church members this is the essence of their preparation, their readiness to meet the Savior when he comes. Any other course will align them with the five foolish virgins in the Master's parable.

Then shall the kingdom of heaven be likened unto ten virgins, which took their lamps, and went forth to meet the bridegroom.

And five of them were wise and five were foolish.

They that were foolish took their lamps, and took no oil with them:

But the wise took oil in their vessels with their lamps.

While the bridegroom tarried, they all slumbered and slept.

And at midnight there was a cry made, Behold, the bridegroom cometh; go ye out to meet him.

Then all those virgins arose, and trimmed their lamps.

And the foolish said unto the wise, Give us of your oil; for our lamps are gone out.

But the wise answered, saying, Not so; lest there be not enough for us and you:· but go ye rather to them that sell, and buy for yourselves.

And while they went to buy, the bridegroom came; and they that were ready went in with him to the marriage: and the door was shut.

Afterward came also the other virgins, saying, Lord, Lord, open to us.

But he answered and said, Verily I say unto you, I know you not.

Watch therefore, for ye know neither the day nor the hour wherein the Son of man cometh. (Matt. 25:1-13.)

Luke's Gospel expresses the same idea in another way:

Let your loins be girded about, and your lights burning;

And ye yourselves like unto men that wait for their Lord, when he will return from the wedding; that when he cometh and knocketh, they may open unto him immediately.

Blessed are those servants, whom the lord when he cometh shall find watching: verily I say unto you, that he shall gird himself, and make them to sit down to meat, and will come forth and serve them. (Luke 12:35-37.)

Those who are ready will be at peace in their hearts. They will be partakers of the blessing the Savior promised to his apostles:

Peace I leave with you, my peace I give unto you: not as the world giveth, give I unto you. Let not your heart be troubled, neither let it be afraid. (John 14:27.)

The Miracle of Forgiveness

The mission of The Church of Jesus Christ of Latter-day Saints is to call people everywhere to repentance. Those who heed the call, whether members or nonmembers of the Church, can be partakers of the miracle of forgiveness. God will wipe away from their eyes the tears of anguish, and remorse, and consternation, and fear, and guilt. Dry eyes will replace the wet ones, and smiles of satisfaction will replace the worried, anxious look.

What relief! What comfort! What joy! Those laden with transgressions and sorrows and sin may be forgiven and cleansed and purified if they will return to their Lord, learn of him, and keep his commandments. And all of us needing to repent of day-to-day follies and weaknesses can likewise share in this miracle.

Can we not understand why the Lord has been pleading with man for these thousands of years to come unto him? Surely the Lord was speaking about forgiveness through repentance, and the relief that could come from the tenseness of guilt, when he followed his glorious prayer to his Father with this sublime entreaty and promise:

> Come unto me, all ye that labour and are heavy laden, and I will give you rest.
>
> Take my yoke upon you, and learn of me; for I am meek and lowly in heart: and ye shall find rest unto your souls.
>
> For my yoke is easy, and my burden is light. (Matt. 11:28-30.)

It is my hope and prayer that men and women everywhere will respond to this gentle invitation and thus let the Master work in their individual lives the great miracle of forgiveness.

Index